FULL CIRCLE

Memories and Magic from a Family Table

FORREST HEDDEN

Full Circle, Memories and Magic from a Family Table © Copyright Forrest Hedden

Photographs by Ben Hider
Cover and Layout by www.formatting4U.com

This book includes a collection of the author's family recipes. Any resemblance to another recipe is purely coincidental. These recipes are to be followed at the reader's own risk. It is the reader's responsibility to ensure that none of the ingredients are personally harmful to one's health. The author will not be held liable for any damage, medical or otherwise, resulting from the reader making these recipes.

All rights reserved. This book is licensed for your personal use only. No part of this work may be used, reproduced, stored in an information retrieval system, or transmitted in any form or by any means (electronic, mechanical, photocopying, recording, or otherwise) without prior written consent by the author. Any usage of the text, except for brief quotations embodied in critical articles or reviews, without the author's permission, is a violation of copyright.

Published by On The Plate Press
New York, NY

*Not to know what happened before you were born
is to be forever a child.*
—Cicero

Table of Contents

Acknowledgments	i
Foreword by David Beahm	iii
Introduction	1
Section One: On Mothers and Fathers	11
Section Two: On Being a Grandson	99
Section Three: On Being a Southerner	171
Section Four: On Growing Up Navy and Gen X	207
Section Five: On Returning to the South Carolina Low Country	273
Section Six: On Finding the Flavors of Friendship	321
Index of Recipes	381

ACKNOWLEDGMENTS:

There are too many people to thank for helping in the creation of this book. First, thanks to all of my family, who came before. To my brother Christopher, thanks for his encouragement and inspiration. To my cousin Martha, thanks for the support, recipes and stories. To Sharon Rainey for her literary guidance. Joelle Stallone for her wordsmith magic as my editor and creative coach, and her sister, Christina Matteucci, who introduced us. My dear close friends John, Mike, Karen, Melissa, Fred, and many others who have shared stories that travel daily with me in my heart. Lauren Ross as my amazing food stylist. Ben Hider for the fabulous photos. Ronnie Davis for inspiring me to write about something personally meaningful. And of course, David Beahm, experience and dream creator extraordinaire, for believing enough in the message behind this book to write kind words at its start. Finally, thanks to my mother and father, who gave me the very human understanding of what it means to be loved. May this volume speak that lesson and more.

Foreword by David Beahm

My grandmother Eva's potato salad and my granddaddy Lyle's homegrown tomatoes… If I had to pinpoint items of food that helped me define my "food heritage," these would both be at the top of my list. They weren't only comfort food for me, they were teaching moments. They were touch points of my heritage.

I was born in the beautiful Shenandoah Valley of Virginia. In earlier times, communities there were so poor that no places kept formal birth records. Thus, my lineage on both my mother and father's sides is very cloudy. Any clues to the origins of my clan were only communicated by word of mouth. That is, until one day, I realized that a lot of clues about my family's story could come from one simple thing—the way my dad's mother had cooked!

It certainly wasn't my mom's mother, Loring's food. Her cooking had been shaped by the processed food fads of the 1950s and 60s, like her meatloaf, which left me with memories of an unidentified, shockingly orange halo in the baking dish. Yet I have fond memories of her very informal meals accented with the background noise of television shows such as *Wheel of Fortune*. However, those were not the meals that gave me clues as to where our families came from.

Clues to my cultural heritage clearly came from my dad's mom. She had been cooking three meals a day from the time she was able. Because she was too busy with chores around the family home and gardens, cooking fads had never significantly influenced her. She had learned to cook the way her family had been cooking forever. As a result, she only cooked what she knew. And am I ever glad she did. Her food was incredibly delicious. Friends would vie for a spot at her table, and we would never even think of missing a meal that "Grandmaw" cooked.

More importantly, her cooking was also really informative as to where our family and the families in our valley had come from. Copious portions of cooked potato salad, boiled meats, baked vegetable puddings, heavy dumplings, and the ever-present gravies spoke loud and clearly, verifying our family's heritage.

Forrest Hedden's book, *Full Circle: Memories and Magic from a Family Table* beautifully chronicles one family's food heritage and the wonderful stories that food creates in the muscle memory of nearly everyone's lives.

I think it is important that, in the title, he chose the word "a" instead of "the" because every family is unique. Every family is a complex mix of various people with personalities, cooking talents, financial situations, and time availability for others. All of these factors combine to create a library of memories and influences that make us what we are.

I am amazed that even coming from disparate backgrounds, Forrest and I share similar life paths and food heritage. I, like him, will most likely not be passing on my food heritage to progeny. His book shows us how important it is to preserve and share these stories, recipes, and moments in time for future generations before they fade from memory.

I believe that this book will serve as an inspiration for others to seek out how food's influence on their own past is actually an important part of the formula of what made them *them*. Remind them that their own family stories about the chemistry and magic of groups of people in their own past coming together over food, sharing information, caring, and nourishing each other's minds, bodies, and souls is a part of their own identity. That the things that happened around food are part of what can make a family unit whole and sound.

Not only is this book a refreshing trip down a memory lane that many of us had forgotten, it is an inspiration to start sharing and experimenting in the kitchen. You can bet that I will be trying the California Patio Salad and Mexican Crack Cornbread. And that Baked Brown Sugar Bacon Crackers are going to make an appearance at my next gathering—as well as, maybe, just maybe, the Chatham Artillery Punch. Reading about that, wow! I really wanted to be at THAT party!

Enjoy these delightful travels and tastes with this American family. And let this book inspire you to explore your own personal food heritage and cement memories for future generations.

INTRODUCTION

CHAPTER ONE: PERSONAL FOOD HERITAGE

A Journey Home

They say you are what you eat. And, generally speaking, we know what this old adage means: healthy eating promotes healthy living. However, this maxim is more than just simple folk wisdom, and has far-reaching consequences on our lives and communities. A recent holiday experience revealed this truism's deeper meaning to me.

Rushing to the airport from my house in New York City the day before Christmas Eve, I fought my way through the TSA gauntlet, pushed to make my gate, trundled down the long boarding ramp, then found my seat in the very front row of the aircraft—the one I paid extra money for 'cause I'm tall and need humane leg-room. Settling in, I was ready to relax and unwind from the hectic start of my journey when, suddenly, from the row right behind me and over my right shoulder, it came.

It was the piercing shrill of a small child obviously in distress over the cabin pressure and the rumbling motions of the plane propelling itself along the runway into the dark night. Waves of cries came from the toddler as his desperate mother and father attempted, in vain, to stifle his shrieks.

Suddenly, that panic of the "trapped traveler" pulsed through my veins. "Oh my God!" I muttered under my breath. I turned inward, thought about what was happening around me, and breathed in and out deeply. "Someone, please hush that child up," I pleaded telepathically.

Then, as if by a miracle, a woman sitting behind the young family offered some words of advice to the mother. I could not make out what she said, but the mother quickly asked the stewardess for something. The stewardess returned with what looked like a glass of ginger ale (or maybe it was bourbon). The mother dipped a pacifier into the beverage and gave it to her child. She then began stroking the baby's hands and cooing to the infant softly. Satisfied with the tasty binky, the baby slowed its caterwauling.

Despite the baby quieting, the family drama behind me continued, as their other lad was busy throwing a stuffed animal and a ball about the cabin. It seemed like the young father's attempts to get the boy to settle down would be unsuccessful, that is, until the resourceful dad reached into his carry-on and handed the boy a snack container. It was filled with some sort of trail mix. He proceeded to tell his son about the treat he had just given him. "This special trail mix was made with Grandma's recipe by Mommy. Grandma's gonna make us all sorts of yummy things over the holiday that you'll really like." The boy dug into the trail mix with gusto, declaring it was really good.

And that was that.

I was surprised and somehow moved by this exchange. My panic lifted and a sense of humanity and, yes, silent shame about my anger took hold of me.

I thought to myself, "It's just normal kids' stuff. Relax, Asshole."

As I sat there, I thought about these children for a moment—the lives they would lead, and all the things they would learn, see, do, experience, and even taste with their parents and grandmother as they grow up.

It made me think about my own childhood, my grandmothers, and the foods they made that I enjoyed so much when I was young. And even some foods, like stewed okra, that I didn't.

That's when it struck me. We each possess pieces of our past brought to life by food. There are events and situations that we experience with others in connection to meals and particular dishes. These foods that we associate with people, places, and things create a taste and memory mosaic, and like the tiles in a mosaic, these memories form a picture through which we can reconnect to, and honor, our past.

A Meal and a Memory

There are births we celebrate, deaths we mourn, and occasions in which we revel. These events could be as grand as a wedding, as reoccurring as a birthday, or as simple as making an ordinary day special. Acknowledging these events can be done in a variety of ways, but breaking bread together is one of the simplest. And nothing brings people together like a meal. Food and its preparation are an obvious and natural way we communicate our love for those around us. It is through food we can celebrate momentous times, as well as bring relief in the darkest moments.

Expressing our love and concern through food has given rise to what our culture understands as comfort food—foods which, by their very being, bring us some sense of peace, wrapping us up in their unique aroma, texture, smell, appearance, and taste. They take us back to that place where we feel safe and warm. Isn't that one of the things we as humans most crave—a sense of peace and safety?

Food memories are mighty and meaningful; they hold a special place of prominence in our minds. Maybe it's a trait remaining from when our ancestors gathered in caves to feast and celebrate after arduous and successful hunts; the memory of the feast provided our ancestors hope that food, when scarce, would become available once again. Regardless of where this trait comes from, a memory related to food is a powerful thing.

I characterize memories involving food as an individual's "personal food heritage." It is the story of our lives told through recipes, their preparation, and the enjoyment of sharing those prepared dishes with others. Personal food heritage is one way that we pass along to our children, spouses, and friends moments and memories that have enriched and colored our time here. We are, indeed, what we eat.

Comfort foods are the basis of personal food heritage. They return you right back to the place where and when you remember that taste, being connected to people in a time you will never get back. When I summon up the spirits of yesterday by cooking the food that made me feel good in a faraway time, I pass that comfort along to others. And while the comfort manifests itself in the form of food, it's really the connection the food has with particular memories—people, places, and times—that make our connection to a dish meaningful.

Sharing memorable dishes and recipes with others is a way we can share stories about ourselves. It can also be a way to share the stories of prior generations, preserving our ancestral history and traditions. Personal food heritage is a great chain of memories—a chain that allows us to tell our personal and family's stories through food.

A great example of a dish that truly exemplifies personal food heritage—a dish that almost everyone who grew up in this country can identify with—is Thanksgiving stuffing.

Think about it.

If you grew up in a family that celebrated Thanksgiving, you probably have a very specific taste memory you associate with stuffing. Whenever you celebrate the holiday, it is that flavor you crave and hold sacred. The stuffing's flavor profile was firmly cemented in childhood and becomes the standard by which all other attempts are judged: "Now *this* is what Thanksgiving tastes like!" you say to yourself silently, enjoying the meal at the family table. And if you are a guest at someone else's table, the meal just isn't the same because the stuffing doesn't taste quite right because it's not *your family's* recipe. You know, everybody considers their own family stuffing recipe "The Best."

Maybe now *you* are the one making the stuffing, following the same recipe previously used by cherished family members. And, one day, your children will have the exact same experience as you when celebrating Thanksgiving at home and with others. This is what I mean when I talk about the chains of flavors that tie us to each other through food. Our past, present, and what we leave to the future are all contained in the foods we cook and share. Perhaps it is not stuffing but another dish you hold dear. For example, for my friend Deb, who is English, the dish is baked potatoes. As a child on November 5th, her family celebrated with that food on a national holiday, Bonfire Night.

A Little Taste of History

Your personal food heritage is much like a scrapbook. It's about when you experienced different foods during your life, gathering fragments of your life into a collection of recipes that hearken back to memorable times, people, and places. However, your personal food heritage is not only about the past; it is about cooking and sharing—living and eating together in the here and now.

Coming back to the Thanksgiving stuffing, your grandparents, parents, aunts, or uncles may no longer be with you at the table, but when you make *that* stuffing recipe on Thanksgiving and taste that first bite, all your Thanksgivings before are there in that one mouthful. And, in that instant, all those people of your past are again present at the table.

There is an old spiritual which talks about the passing down of faith, knowledge, and love from one generation to the next. Its main refrain asks:

> "Will the circle be unbroken?
> By and by Lord
> By and by…"

Sharing foods that hold special meaning to us is one way to keep the circle intact.

Our most powerful experiences with food are those that are communal. These experiences are savored more sweetly because we are sharing with others. And relationships between a particular dish and other people often begin at home. We've heard it said that the kitchen is the heart of the home. I believe it. It is the central hub of life in a house. We begin our day there. We spend some time there during the day as well, returning to it throughout the day to remain nourished. And we find our way back in the evening, often to dine together.

Holidays and special celebrations typically hinge on what takes place in the kitchen and is offered at the kitchen table. Cooking, food, and community are the hallmarks of the kitchen. Indeed, a home without a kitchen would be just a place to sleep and shower, not a place to find nourishment for body and soul. And it is in the kitchens of our memory that the stories about people and the foods we love still live.

When I am cooking and sharing meals with others, the person I most think about who is no longer with us is my father. I lost him when I was twenty-seven. He was a great father, teacher, and provider; he was my mother's best friend. I count myself fortunate to be able to say my dad was a good guy. These days, I sometimes take pause when I do something or say something because, upon reflection, I realize that it mirrors something I believe my father would have done or said. And I think it's funny how I am my father's son, like it or not. He loved food and cooking for his loved ones and so do I—another trait we have in common.

While thinking about my own food heritage, I saw that neither my brother Christopher nor I were probably going to have children. And unlike that little boy's father on the plane, we would have no one to share the stories my parents, grandparents, aunts, and uncles passed down to us, nor would I have any family to share their legacy with. This seemed sad—not because these people from my past were unique or extraordinary, but because they were simple, honest, good people. Their stories should be told and not forgotten. Writing this book is my way of passing their memory along to the future.

In looking for my own food heritage, I found stories about people I knew growing up, as well as stories about those I never met. I came to recognize how these individuals influenced not only my understanding and enjoyment of food, but also influenced my understanding of myself, my world, and my place in it. Making and sharing these connections is what is wonderful about discovering and finding your personal food heritage—feeling connected to family, friends, and life.

So here are some stories and some lessons from a life in the food, the people, places, meals, and laughs that have enriched my journey thus far.

As you travel back in time with me, I hope you will be drawn to explore your own personal food heritage. Reflect on the people, places, and foods that have shaped your own journey. Cook the comfort foods you cherish. Most importantly, find inspiration to pass the recipes and the stories along to those you love because the stories of every family should be told.

Our journey starts with a young boy and his family around the dinner table, but it continues with extended family and friends gathering together, savoring the offerings at life's great table.

My Heritage Thanksgiving Stuffing

James Beard, the anointed dean of American cookery, said famously, "American cooking is what Americans cook at home."

For holidays in my childhood home, we always had a rich cornbread-and-pecan stuffing. Traditionally, one would refer to this type of dish as a dressing (because it is baked in a casserole), but, in our family, we always called it stuffing. So that's what I call it. I actually found the recipe in my Grandma Irene's personal cookbook. I have been making this stuffing for years here in New York, and people can never get enough of it. It's so rich and decadent that friends actually remember it and ask to make sure it's present on our Thanksgiving table. They tell me that if they can't have the stuffing from their own childhoods, this is the next best thing!

Ingredients

- 3 1/2 cups of celery, finely chopped, including the leaves
- 1 very large white or yellow onion, finely chopped
- 4 ounces pecan halves and pieces, chopped
- 6 ounces slivered almonds
- 8 cups of Italian or white Peasant Bread cut up into cubes
- 4 cups of cornbread, cubed
- 4 cups of whole wheat bread cubes
- 2 1/2 cups good chicken stock mixed with 2 envelopes of liquid chicken base or 2 bouillon cubes
- 1 1/2 teaspoons salt
- 1/2 teaspoon black pepper
- 3 teaspoons garlic powder
- 1/2 teaspoon dried thyme
- 1/2 teaspoon celery salt
- 1/4 teaspoon dried dill
- 1 Tablespoon sage, dried

2 1/2 Tablespoons poultry seasoning
2 teaspoons turmeric powder
1 cup fresh parsley, finely chopped
1 1/2 cups butter, melted
2 eggs beaten

Method

- *In a large bowl, combine and mix the breads.*
- *Sauté the onions and celery in butter until soft, season with salt and pepper, then add the crushed pecan pieces. Sauté until the flavors bloom. Add spices and seasonings until also they bloom.*
- *Add stock and remaining ingredients, then pour over the bread, mixing gently until combined. Taste and season with salt and pepper. Add eggs and mix to combine. Mix should be fairly wet but not soupy.*
- *If too dry, add more stock or water.*
- *Place in a buttered large casserole dish or dishes. Add stuffed bird with the leftovers. Bake dish at 300 degrees for 45 mins.*

SECTION ONE

ON MOTHERS & FATHERS

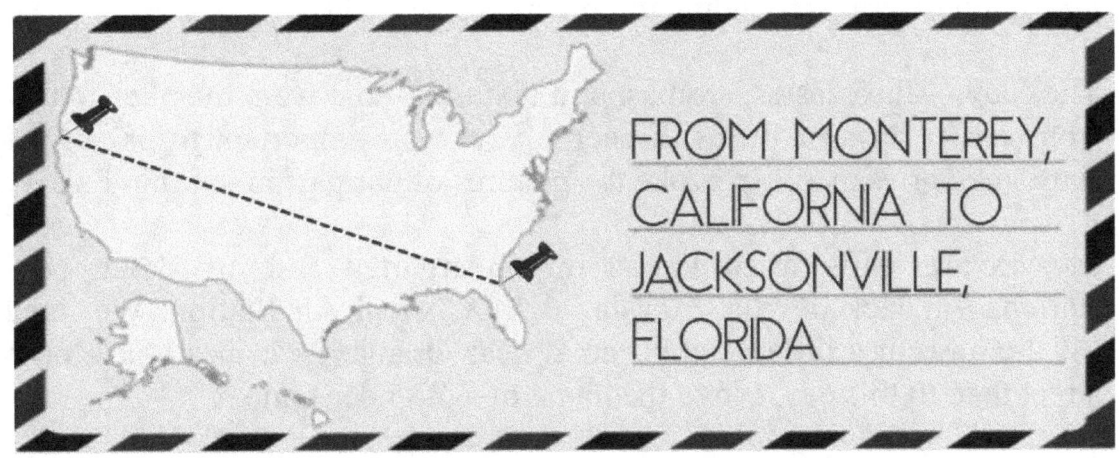

CHAPTER TWO: WONDER LANE, THE DINNER TABLE, AND A MEXICAN SALAD

Personal food heritage… where does it start? It starts when we are very small. I think, for most, it starts at home. For many, it starts with a mom and a dad.

Now that I'm an adult looking back on life, I feel like understanding who we are and where we came from is like looking at a faraway collage of impressions. Flashes of memories form pictures of these grown-up people we knew then, and the memories we have of them emerge and fade as we try to hold them up to the light.

These are the memories of our parents, grandparents, other relatives, best friends' moms, girlfriends, boyfriends, teachers, wives, husbands, and mentors. The memories can be of anyone who has ever influenced us, inspired us, or cared for us body and soul, but not in the sense of precisely chronicling occurrences or exhaustively cataloguing people or places. The recollections, instead, are more like a watercolor of soft memory. Feelings and thoughts and, yes, even tastes—diluted by time—somehow blend together to create a picture. This is nostalgia in its purest form: the innate human ability to color all remembered moments with good, cheery, and buoyant postscripts, rounding out reality's sharp edges.

The foods—their tastes, aromas, and textures—that we remember fondly from earlier days of life with people who were important to us are the sense memories that help evoke the pictures of our past in our mind's eye.

My picture starts when I was in kindergarten and my daddy was stationed in Jacksonville, Florida, at JAX Naval Air Station. We lived off the base in a little neighborhood near Orange Park in a house on a street that, to this day, I love the name of—Wonder Lane.

Wonder Lane was the perfect street name for a perfect time. It was the early-1960s, and I was so young. To me, life was new; the world was yet unknown and unexplored. My exploration took the form of Winnie-the-Pooh books, playing outside in the backyard or neighborhood with my brother, helping my mama in the kitchen, following my daddy as he did chores, or just watching the shadows on the ceiling of my bedroom late at night. I would lie in bed and listen to the sound of the music from the phonograph, voices from the television, or my parents talking—all familiar noises that gently filled the quiet corners of the house.

My first concrete childhood memory takes place in our home on Wonder Lane: I recall my father being gone, deployed on naval aircraft carriers. He would send us postcards from afar. Mama hung up a big map of the world on the kitchen wall and we would mark with thumbtacks or small paper flags where Daddy was.

No adult problems were yet to be had; no raging teenage angst was yet on the horizon. It was the time when being a kid was really all there was. Everything was new and different all the time because nothing had ever been seen or done before—a time when expectations were almost akin to imagination. The world was fresh, new, vibrant, and alive with all its possibilities. This was life as a boy in the house on Wonder Lane.

I can recall my parents going out to parties. My mama, so beautiful all done up in a floor-length, chiffon green gown, her hair piled up on her head like the hairdos from the early 1960s, looking like Julianne Moore in *A Single Man*, that Tom Ford movie. My daddy, looking dapper all dressed up in his blue dress uniform. In my mind, they were off to some grand event or ball, though it was probably just some command occasion at the base.

Later in my childhood, after leaving Wonder Lane, I recognized that we were a military family, and I also realized what that meant. We lived on or near bases in military neighborhoods for my entire childhood—places surrounded by barbed wire fences and gated entrances, where my mama got a salute from the MPs as an officer's wife.

Driving past planes and missiles and wharfs filled with a collection of various naval vessels, the world seemed very dramatic and powerful indeed, and our place in it was purposeful and understandable. My daddy was in the Navy, protecting our country. We were a family bound to each other like members of a small nomadic tribe, carrying our memories and possessions with us from billet to billet.

In moving from place to place, the strange familiarity of the bases brought a sort of calm to an otherwise total upheaval. To this day, whenever I go onto a military base, I experience a sense of peace and nostalgia as well as melancholy for what went before. Or maybe what I am feeling is a longing for that simple and satisfying time of life from my childhood so long gone.

Growing up in a military family such as ours meant that we lived in a house of order, where chores and playtime shared the billing. Homework always came before television or play. And the marching orders of the day always included dinner together. Yes, dinner was a family affair. When I became a teenager and my friends were running around, away from their families during dinnertime, my father informed my brother and me in his slight Southern drawl, "I don't run a hotel. Be home for supper." And we were.

When it came to creating a sense of family, my parents did not place an emphasis on material matters, but rather, on matters of the mind and heart. They were grounded individuals, and they found ways to keep us feeling like our family had a rhythm that was a constant—regardless of where we were living. Food actually played a big role in that.

Food and the meals we shared united our family. Therefore, dinnertime was sacred. Every evening, my father, mother, Grandma Irene (who lived with us from the time I was in second grade), my brother, and I partook in the Hedden nightly ritual of gastronomic celebration. Having two cooks in the house (my mom and grandmother), we were never bored by the menus. Our dinner meals came to be one of our favorite things to share, along with life's stories, school tales, work anecdotes, and plenty of parental advice—the last of which was passed around the table by my father as freely as the mashed potatoes.

Especially as teenagers and young adults, dinnertime was the one time in the day where we all could just enjoy being together without any of the pressures from our individual worlds. Whatever drama we had going on, we could leave it behind or, for a rise, parade it across the dining room table for some interesting and theatrical exchanges. Although, to my recollection, the latter choice never ended very well for my brother or me so we quickly learned to talk about those kinds of things in more private forums.

When I was a teenager, I could tell that being a grown-up wasn't always easy and that being at home always seemed better than being anywhere else if that home was a good place to be. And, lucky for me, mine was just that. Not perfect, mind you. There was plenty of drama, stress, tears, sickness, hardship, and pain. But from the lessons learned around our dining table—even the hard ones—I learned the value of belonging to and pulling together as a family.

One of my earliest memories of a particular meal from the house on Wonder Lane and eating together as a family, is sharing a Mexican salad my mother would sometimes make for dinner. Yep, a Mexican salad, one made with, of all things, canned tuna fish. In fact, I never knew Mexican salad was normally considered a "taco salad" until much later in life. This was no taco salad.

This Mexican salad became part of my family's food heritage in 1963. That year, still newlyweds, my mother and father had just been stationed in California and were invited to an outdoor dinner party in a beautiful manicured backyard in Carmel, California. It was one of those lovely warm California evenings. When it was time for dinner, my mom said the hostess sailed out the sliding glass doors and onto the patio, bringing dinner to the backyard table. My mom was surprised to see that the single, yet oversized, bowl that the caftan-clad hostess carried contained nothing more than a beautiful salad. Being from the East Coast, my mom was not familiar with California's salad-as-a-meal concept. Her state of confusion was quick and brief, though. As the story goes, the salad was apparently a hit, as the guests dug in and devoured it! After dinner, my mother asked the hostess for the recipe, and the dish soon after became a regular fixture in my mom's dinner recipe rotation. Later on as an adult, I asked my mama for the recipe. She neatly wrote it up on an index card and handed it to me with a smile.

When I was beginning this book, I asked her why that salad was so special to her. I knew it reminded *me* of being small and my first taste of the "exotic," but I wondered what she would say. Her answer was beautiful. She said that she loved that salad because every time she made it, the salad reminded her of when she was pregnant with me in Carmel and that exciting and happy time in her and my father's lives. Foods can certainly connect generations in the simplest of ways and for the loveliest of reasons.

My father, channeling Robert Frost, once defined home to me as the place they have to take you in. Wonder Lane was that, as were all the houses that came after. Home is wherever you are and those you love happen to find themselves—that much I have learned over the years from the meals around my dinner table.

California-Patio Mexican Salad with Creamy Avocado Dressing

Mama tells me that this salad had come from a magazine recipe first printed in the 1960s. The hostess who gave her the recipe said that every time she made this salad, people asked for the recipe. It had been a big favorite of home entertaining at the time but has somehow fallen out of the mainstream as generations passed. I have made tweaks to it along the way, but the originators deserve kudos.

Ingredients
For the Salad: (makes 6 portions)
- 4 cans of tuna (5 ounce cans)
- 4 cups chopped kale and green cabbage or a mix of both is best
- 6 cups iceberg or romaine lettuce, core removed and chopped into thin shreds
- 8 Campari-style tomatoes, cut into wedges
- 1 cup scallions, chopped (white parts and green parts)
- 1 8 ounce can black California olives, sliced
- 1 cup grated sharp cheddar cheese
- 1 cup grated Mexican Cotija cheese (reserve half for garnish)
- 1 bag FRITOS® Brand Corn chips (you MUST use FRITOS®)
- 2 cups of FRITOS® crushed into peanut-sized pieces for salad, the rest held in reserve for garnish
- Chopped cilantro (for garnish) or use more green onion if you don't like cilantro

For the Dressing
(Made with a hand mixer or beaten by hand— do not use a blender)
- 1 cup ripe avocados, mashed
- 2 Tablespoons lemon juice
- 1 cup sour cream
- 1 teaspoon sugar

2/3 cup salad oil—not olive
2 garlic cloves, minced
2 teaspoons cumin
2 teaspoons chili powder
1/2 teaspoon salt
1/2 teaspoon Tabasco or other hot sauce

Method

- *Beat with a hand blender in a bowl. If it's too thick, add water until smooth and creamy.*
- *To assemble salad, place all ingredients in a very large mixing bowl except the ones held in reserve for garnish.*
- *Add 1 cup dressing and toss. Add more dressing to your liking until salad is dressed well, but not soaked with the dressing.*
- *Place in a large, wide serving bowl, piling up as tall in a pointed mound as possible.*
- *Then sprinkle some chips on the top.*
- *Sprinkle each festively with Cotija cheese.*
- *Garnish with cilantro or green onions.*
- *Have extra dressing on the side for people if they want it.*

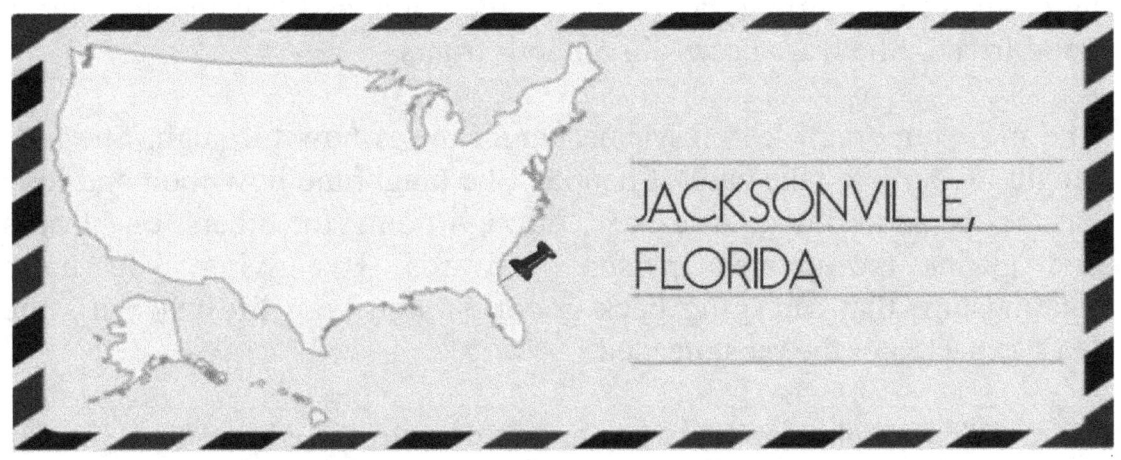

CHAPTER THREE: LESSONS FROM A MOTHER'S KITCHEN AND MEATLOAF

At birth, we first experience our mother. She is—if we are lucky like I was—the primary person who shapes and guides our journey to independent adulthood. Often, she is the first face we can remember, the first hand we hold, and the first person to teach us the rudimentary principles of being human. She is the first person to give us an understanding of what it means to be loved.

Mothers bring us into the world in more ways than just giving birth to us. They cradle us in their own knowledge and share with us truths they have discovered on their own journeys. They are the lamplighters, sending us out into the world with a brief, yet hopefully instructive, tutorial on life and welcoming us home with sympathetic and loving arms whenever we return.

Gloria, my mother—or Mama as we call her—is the toughest and the softest person I know. Bound by her own incredible will, she can move mountains. Guided by her deep faith, she moves them with sureness and placid power. And she also taught me that life could be daily celebrated with Manhattans and cocktail snacks if the occasion calls for it. She tried hard when I was little to be a good mother, and, as I became an adult, a good friend. She was successful on both fronts.

The most important lesson Mama taught me is how to laugh. She also taught me how to take care of people. She taught me how food and love can be the same thing. And how, through doing for others, one learns and gleans the greatest personal rewards. By giving, you build relationships that can bring back goodness into your life when it's the least expected or the most needed.

Mama also taught me how to cook. She introduced me to how one moves around a kitchen, and she bought me my first cookbook, *The How I Learned to Cook Book*, which I still have to this day; it's at Mama's house on her cookbook shelf. The first thing I ever cooked out of that book with her was meatloaf. I can recall standing in the kitchen under the warm glow of the amber-colored ceiling lamps. Mama put me up on a stepstool to reach the counter like an adult. I learned to cut the various vegetables which she then cooked and let cool. I mixed them with the meat in a bowl, the cold meat chilling my hands almost to the point of pain. We poured the mixture into a well-greased loaf pan and she placed it into the hot oven. I stared through the oven door's thick pane of glass, slightly tinged and bleary with a residue of heat and grease, to monitor by the glow of the oven bulb the progress of the baking. When the meatloaf came out of the oven bubbling and hot, it smelled amazing. The scent of meat, *jus*, and singed edges filled the kitchen—and the whole house—like a warm blanket of deliciousness. It was a simple, comforting dish. To this day, one of my favorite things to eat is meatloaf, and no matter where I have it, it always reminds me of home, and my first cooking lessons with my mother.

Everything I learned about working hard I learned from my father; everything I ever learned about working smart I learned from my mother. Industry and organization were hallmarks of her kitchen and her life. She was a master planner, and she needed to be: in addition to being a full-time wife and mother, she also taught high school math full-time. She excelled at all her responsibilities. Her homemaking skills set the standard for me on how a home should look and function. Her spirit taught me how a home should feel.

Mama was a great (and smart) cook as well. While I was growing up, she created dinners on a naval officer's income that always made us feel we were feasting like kings. My brother and I never had the feeling that we were rather poor, which, on a Navy salary in the '70s, we actually were.

There were other mothers in my life—grandmothers, great-grandmothers, aunts, and even longtime family lady friends—these were the mothers who also impacted the early trajectory of my life and my relationship with food. From the cookies they made for school groups and fundraisers, to the casseroles they prepared for church covered-dish suppers, to the food they delivered to family or mutual friends who needed a hand during times of crisis and sadness, these women taught me that giving to others, especially through food, is a powerful gift. And that food is, indeed, a form of love.

I have come to understand and appreciate that what I know and feel about food and comfort—and myself—all began with the lessons learned, literally, at a mother's apron strings.

Family Meatloaf:

I always thought this meatloaf had a little Spanish flair. Maybe it's because Mama started making meatloaf during her time in Tampa.

Ingredients
- 1 pound ground beef chuck (you could use all beef if you wanted)
- 1 pound ground pork
- 1 pound mushrooms (use a variety)
- 1 Tablespoon oil
- 1 Tablespoon butter
- 1 small onion
- 4 cloves garlic, minced
- 1 teaspoon salt
- 1/2 teaspoon pepper
- 1/4 teaspoon poultry seasoning
- 1/4 teaspoon dried thyme
- 6 Tablespoons good quality balsamic vinegar
- 4 slices of bread (white or sourdough), torn into fine pieces
- 2 Tablespoons milk or cream
- 2 eggs
- 2 teaspoons Worcestershire sauce
- 1/2 cup of grated Romano cheese
- 1/4 cup sliced green stuffed cocktail olives
- 1 1/2 cups ketchup

Method
- In a food processor, chop the mushrooms chunky, then the onion fine but not mush.
- Add the onion to a pan and sauté in the oil and butter. Add the garlic and cook until soft. Mix with the 4 Tablespoons of the balsamic. Add the mushrooms. Cook about 15 minutes, then cool.

- *In a large mixing bowl, combine the torn bread and milk or cream and let sit to get mushy. Then add in the meats, salt, pepper, seasonings, beaten egg, Worcestershire. Then add the cooled veggie mix. Add cheese. Mix well with your hands.*
- *Form meat mixture into 2 loaves about 5 inches wide on a lined baking sheet. Stud top with the olives, pressing them into the loaf's top.*
- *Combine the ketchup and last 2 Tablespoons of the balsamic. Spread over the meatloaf.*
- *Bake in a 375-degree F oven for about 55 minutes to one hour.*
- *When finished, remove from the oven and wait 15 minutes before slicing.*
- *When ready to serve, carefully slice meatloaf and serve 2 slices shingled, garnished with parsley, and serve with mashed potatoes.*

CHAPTER FOUR: PASSING ON A MOTHER'S HERITAGE

Now, Mama was raised in Logan Square in northwest Chicago in the 1930s. At that time, it was a Scandinavian neighborhood, home to a large Norwegian and Danish population.

My mama learned cooking and homemaking from her mother, Irene. Mama went on to college and became a successful educator before becoming a wife and mother. She is, as her mother called her, a "smart cookie."

Mama has, over the years, passed on her food heritage to my brother and me in a variety of ways. For example, there are numerous family recipes (especially those for smoked fish and holiday sweets and cakes) she shared from the Norwegian side of our family, as well as the stories connecting those recipes to her life. Passing down these memories as she would serve us certain foods connected my brother and me to those dishes. Sometimes, she even told us about foods she loved when she was young that were not homemade. From one such story comes a particularly strong food memory she has from those years growing up in Depression-era Chicago. It is a tradition she passed on to my brother and me.

Her powerful food memory is, of all things, going to a Chinese restaurant. This would happen twice a year, once when Grandma Irene took my mom window-shopping to buy her something nice on her birthday, and once when they would go back-to-school clothes shopping. They had a tradition that, after shopping, they would have lunch and then go see a movie.

The really interesting thing to me about these outings was her recollections of the old picture palaces, such as the Uptown Theater, which is still famous in Chicago with its gilded walls and embossed balconies. The theater featured orchestral or big band music to entertain the audience before the featured film. Mama had the chance to see such greats as Tommy Dorsey, Duke Ellington, and other famous bandleaders as well as hear singers like Jo Stafford perform on the large stage. All this musical magic before the lights dimmed and the newsreels played preceding the main feature. It sounds fantastic!

To my mother, however, the real special event was the lunch at a nearby Chinese restaurant. Strange as it sounds, it was there that she always had the best open-faced hot turkey sandwich and gravy, ever. Imagine getting that at your local Chinese place today!

Mama still loves a hot turkey sandwich and has tried on many an occasion to recreate it. That sandwich reminds her of being a little girl, recalling those relaxed and, what seemed at the time to be, pampered afternoons spent in the happy company of her mother. It's been eighty-plus years, and she is still trying to make that sandwich. Now that's a strong food memory! I always joke with her that that must have been some sandwich. She assures me it was.

So how did my mama pass this food memory along to her boys? Well, Mama would take my brother and me shopping before school started, just as her mother had done with her, and we also had lunch out as a tradition. The malls always had a plethora of chain restaurants from which to choose. My mother once asked if we would like to get burgers at "FuddF$#kers"?

"Mama!" I exclaimed.

It was only then she realized her alliterative mistake. Oh, how she laughed 'til she cried!

So our special, late-1970s' suburban tradition, as befitted a middle-class family, was going to Red Lobster for clam chowder and all-you-could-eat salad. We would also share some type of seafood, like a fried shrimp or fish platter. But it was that big, creamy, delicious bowl of clam chowder and sharp blue cheese salad dressing that kept me looking forward to our shopping trip year after year.

After a long day of climbing through the crowded mall, its stores awash in back-to-school clothing and gear, looking for bargains, we would roll into the parking lot of the Red Lobster. Upon entering the nautical-themed lobby, I would find myself gazing at the huge tank filled with live lobsters waiting to be plucked out and carried into the kitchen. The dark barn-red walls of the restaurant covered with buoys, ship's wheels, knotted ropes, fishing nets, lifesaver rings, and gold-rimmed pictures of ships and the sea captured my imagination.

The hostess would guide us to our table with its brass lantern candleholder and crisply rolled white napkins and silverware. After ordering our meal, my brother and I would nosh on hush puppies (the restaurant's famous Cheddar Bay Biscuits were not yet offerings on its menu) and wait patiently for the first course to arrive.

When that bowl of creamy white, salty goodness hit the table, we were ready to eat. The deliciously unforgettable and crisp iceberg salad with red onions, cucumbers, crunchy garlic croutons, and sliced hothouse tomatoes followed close on the heels of the soup. Oh, and let's not leave out that blue cheese dressing! Creamy white, the slightly sharp dressing blanketed the salad like a snowdrift, covering the salad's festive colors.

My mother, brother, and I would sit there reflecting on our great purchases and discovered bargains, discussing the upcoming school year, and recounting some of our best moments from the slowly waning summer. We would laugh or bicker as we debated the summer's best memories, enjoying the food and the time together at the restaurant. Regardless of what we were eating and drinking, it was the time spent together before everyone got busy in the fall that was special.

This was one simple way my mother passed her food heritage on to us. I'm sure that my memory of that soup and salad dressing far exceeds the reality, but my memory of our time spent together is as real as real could be.

The Best Hot Turkey Sandwich Ever!

Ingredients

    8 slices of thick cut brioche or Texas toast
    3 or 4 turkey legs or 3 turkey thighs, skin on
    1 cup white wine
    2 cups of chicken stock
    2 cups of whole milk
    1 cup heavy cream
    4 pieces of bacon
    10 ounces of white mushrooms
    4 large white onions, sliced
    2 Tablespoons corn starch
    Fresh sage leaves
    Fresh thyme leaves
    Fresh rosemary leaves
    2 cloves minced garlic
    2 Tablespoons soy sauce
    2 teaspoons cornstarch
    1 cup shredded Swiss or Gruyère cheese
    Chopped parsley

Method

- *Place all ingredients except bread, butter, cornstarch, and cheese into a large roasting pan and roast in a 350-degree oven for about 2 and 1/2 hours.*
- *Remove from the oven and take the meat out of the liquid. Let cool. Shred with a fork and reserve.*
- *Place the contents of the cooking pot in a food processor and pulse until smooth. Return to a pot, bring to boil, and reduce by about a third or until thick. Stir in cornstarch mixed with 1 cup of the liquid. Stir in cheese until melted. Check for seasoning.*

- *Butter bread on both sides and grill until golden and crisp.*
- *Place on a plate and top with the shredded turkey and then gravy.*
- *Mashed potatoes make this a meal. Garnish with parsley.*

Back-to-School Clam Chowder

Ingredients
6 strips of bacon, diced
6 medium potatoes, peeled and diced into medium cubes
1 large onions, finely diced
2 stalks celery, finely diced
1 teaspoon finely chopped thyme
For the roux: 1/2 cup flour and 1/2 cup butter
2 cups whole milk
2 bottles 8 ounces of clam juice
1 1/2 cups heavy cream
1/4 teaspoon Worcestershire sauce
1 teaspoon finely chopped thyme
1 pound diced canned clams
Several dashed hot sauce

Method
- In a pan, sauté the bacon until done. Remove and drain. Discard the grease.
- Boil potatoes in a pot until cooked. Drain them and hold.
- Sauté onions and celery with thyme in the butter until soft and translucent but not brown. Add flour and cook until slightly browned and the flour taste is cooked out. Slowly add the milk until the sauce thickens.
- Add clam juice and pepper.
- Add the bacon, potatoes, cream, hot sauce, and the Worcestershire.
- Slowly simmer until thick and all combined and heated through. (20 minutes)
- Add clams just before serving. Simmer and serve.

Maytag Blue Cheese Dressing (serve with your favorite tossed salad)

Ingredients
    6 ounces of Maytag Blue Cheese at room temp
    1 Tablespoon warm water
    2 or 3 drops of Worcestershire sauce
    1/4 teaspoon garlic powder
    1 cup mayonnaise
    1/2 cup sour cream
    1 Tablespoon white vinegar
    1/4 teaspoon salt
    1/4 teaspoon white pepper
    Dash of hot sauce

Method
- Combine cheese and warm water to soften.
- Place all ingredients in a bowl and stir well to combine.
- Serve cold.

CHAPTER FIVE: SOUTHERN GENTLEMEN AND THE ART OF BEING A MAN

What fathers teach their sons and daughters, good or bad, stays forever with them. While we are raised by our mothers and are weaned on their love, often we look to our fathers for direction and guidance. To a child, a father provides an example of what being a man is.

My father was, in many ways, a very Southern person. He was one of those people who could best be described as a "Southern gentleman." People who did not grow up in the South may have the wrong idea of what that term means to those of us who did. When they hear the term, it usually brings to mind a man with good manners and a deep Southern drawl—think Colonel Sanders. Well, Daddy definitely had good manners and a slight Southern accent (he tried to lose it in the Navy, but no such luck), however, being a Southern gentleman is so much more. Daddy was a smart fellow, highly educated, well read, well traveled domestically and abroad, opinionated, and deeply rooted in family, community, faith, and work. He was a proud member of his Southern society. These things and others made him a Southern gentleman.

He was a Renaissance man—with many talents and interests. He started off as a medical student, but due to illness, he was unable to complete his studies. He ended up in naval intelligence. After a twenty-year career in the Navy, he went on to become a successful consultant in defense contracting. Later on, he founded and ran his own firm manufacturing replacement parts for military ships. And, in addition to handily meeting the demands of his career, he pursued many other interests and hobbies.

I remember when I was young, my father had model homes made of balsa wood all over the house which I was not allowed to play with. I can remember staring over the edges of tables, edges I could barely see above, wondering what magic those model buildings might hold. I had entire scenarios in my imaginings as to what the people who would work and live in them might be doing. The temptation to touch and play with the houses and buildings was strong, but my brother and I remained respectful—mostly out of fear of what fate would befall our behinds should we tamper with them. Later on, I learned that Daddy was working on a concept for a planned community—a new type of town with coordinated architecture and multi-use living and working spaces. His ideas, while now common, were ahead of their time.

My father was also constantly improving our home. My brother and I were often pulled into these projects, such as helping refinish every basement in every house we ever lived in. When we were called for dinner on the weekends, we would emerge from the basement (the soon-to-be rumpus room) smelling of sawdust and varnish. Other times, we were called to the table covered in dirt from tilling the ground for our annual vegetable garden. Even though yard work was not one of my favorite things to do, I am glad my father put me to the task because he did teach me a lot about landscaping and gardening. Most importantly, Daddy taught us honor and pride in living and in working, for which I am grateful.

My father was very modern, cosmopolitan, and current, but he was also deeply rooted in his heritage. He never forgot where he came from; he once confided in me that he felt that, for a hillbilly kid, he had done rather well.

My father loved all things outdoors and would not let himself be confined by the city. When we moved back to Charleston, South Carolina (and when he wasn't working or executing some project on the weekends), he would most likely be found with his business partner and companions out hunting in the nearby woodlands or fishing in the creek. And many a Saturday started out with his friends on the boat which was amply supplied with bait, rods, and a whole lot of cold beer, just off shore in the creek or the harbor, telling stories and catching fish, or maybe just telling fish tales!

My father taught my brother and me to value the South, this nation, and our life in it. Not just cultural things, but natural things—the land, the water, the air. He taught us to value ocean life, land animals, and flora, and to understand the great responsibility we have in being the stewards of these gifts.

He dispensed wisdom judiciously. In fact, he had a manner of steering my brother and me through youthful follies by using a trademark phrase. When listening to our passionately argued points with youthful vigor, my father would never interrupt or directly oppose our opinions. Instead, when it was his time to talk, he would start his comments with his signature expression: "Now, that might well be true, but have you considered...?" We hated that phrase and the impending avalanche of logic that was sure to follow. And while I often resisted lessons taught by my father (and by my mother, too) at various times in my youth, the older I become, I laugh thinking how much smarter their lessons seem to be today.

My father had eternal patience and he instilled wisdom gently in my brother and me. Likewise, he always demanded that we pay attention to details and consider all options. To this day, I never make a decision about anything without thinking things through fully as my father would have wanted. At least, I try to.

I think because my dad did not have a father growing up (my grandfather died when my father was eight months old) my dad actually put a lot of thought into being a parent. I believe he thought hard about what it meant to be a father and was mindful about what would be best to raise two boys, raising them to have a sense of self and of the world around them.

I think that, growing into middle adulthood, I felt compassion and empathy for my father losing his father so young. Losing my dad in my 20s, I understood how, as a young man making big life choices, I wished, as he probably had, that I could have had the benefit of a father's living wisdom. I think losing your father at a formative age makes you wish that you could have asked his opinion or even argued with him to hear what might be wrong with yours. And growing older and facing life challenges with health crises and the very normal human journey into the world of aging, you might wish you could have watched him lead the way. Showed you how it was done. Because, truthfully, as all of us will come to know, when confronted with the harsh realities of life and growing older, you feel sometimes like a little child again, lost in the woods and unsure how to get home.

Shall that circle of family wisdom be unbroken? Well, for me, and others like me, losing a parent young makes it feel like it might be. You would give anything for one more word, one more day, one more sign that you are loved and on the right path. And yet, things you learned and remember from that parent guide your steps along the way. They become part of you just like you are part of them.

I am working hard to keep the circle of my father's example to me of what it means to be a man intact by giving to others as my father gave to me. In various ways—as a mentor at work and as a teacher in my social and spiritual community—I get to pass his lessons along to others.

My father passed on to my brother and me what he learned growing up and what he had come to believe as an adult: living involves understanding where you come from, respecting others, being engaged in your community, having faith in what's beyond, working hard, and giving of one's time and attention to those you love. Not in a monetary way, but in a get-up-and-do-for-yourself-and-others sort of way. I honor his memory daily. He was a good guy. And he was indeed a Southern gentleman.

Daddy's Northern California-Style Scallops

On chilly winter evenings on the weekends, my father would sometimes cook dinner. Having lived in northern California, my parents came to love this simple style of shellfish cooking. One of the dishes that he would make was a dish that he called Football Scallops; it was so quick it could be whipped up during a televised game's half-time show. It was based on a 1960s' magazine recipe. Whenever I make it, I think of him.

Ingredients
- 1 pound large sea scallops, about four to five per person, patted dry on paper towels. Season with salt and pepper.
- 3 Tablespoons olive oil
- 2 Tablespoons minced garlic
- 2 Tablespoons tarragon vinegar
- 1/2 teaspoons dried oregano
- 1/2 teaspoons dried basil
- 1/4 cup finely chopped fresh Italian parsley
- 1 cup California sauterne wine (or you can use Sauvignon Blanc)
- 2 Tablespoons butter
- 1 Tablespoon fresh lemon juice
- Salt and pepper to taste

Method
- *Heat a pan you can move to the table as a serving dish on high heat.*
- *Add olive oil and butter.*
- *Add garlic and scallops to pan and let cook for 3-4 minutes. Turn when browned. Remove pan from heat and reduce to medium low.*
- *Add wine, vinegar, dried seasonings, and 1/2 of the parsley. Place pan on heat and cook for 5 minutes. Do not overcook the scallops.*

- *Remove from the heat. Spoon lemon juice over the scallops and sprinkle with the remaining parsley.*
- *Serve immediately with toasted garlic bread for sopping up the juice and a salad, along with your favorite white wine.*

CHAPTER SIX: MAMA MAKES CORNBREAD AND ADVICE IS BEST SERVED COLD FROM SISTERS-IN-LAW

Mark Twain famously said, "The North thinks it knows how to make cornbread, but this is gross superstition."

My Northern mama makes a cornbread that my daddy loved growing up. It is a recipe from Big Mama, my Southern father's mother. (We'll talk more about her later.) It was nicknamed "Depression Cornbread" because back in the 1930s (when my father was small) and then during World War II, eggs, milk and even sometimes flour were unavailable. So, people made cornbread and many other dishes without them. Using only the simplest and cheapest ingredients—cornmeal, baking powder, baking soda, salt, water, and bacon grease—the cornbread came out of the oven deliciously thin, crispy, and savory. After the Depression and the war, buttermilk and flour returned to the recipe, making the cornbread all the more delectable.

As a new bride, Mama tried (unsuccessfully) for several years to replicate Big Mama's recipe. She wrote it down a number of times and even bought a cast iron pan like Big Mama used. But Mama never quite got it right. Finally, one day in frustration, while she and my daddy were visiting Big in Walhalla, South Carolina, Mama asked Big if they could make it together.

Standing in Big's sun-washed yellow, lovingly-used kitchen, with a large, ceramic, white mixing bowl (which my mother still has to this day) in hand, my mom was ready for her baking lesson.

So the first thing Big said was, "All right, Gloria, I'm going to watch you make it. What's the first thing you do?"

My mother replied, "You start with cornmeal."

Big nodded. "Okay. What kind of cornmeal are you using?"

My mother paused and then answered, "Well, why regular yellow cornmeal, of course."

Big stopped for a moment as if she were struck, taking in my mother's words. Big's expression slowly changed, her lips pursed and then broadened into a slight smile. With her eyes twinkling, she looked at my mother and in her soft Southern brogue said, "Well, Gloria, I think we have found the problem!"

"*Really?*" my mother questioned. "What's the problem?"

Big looked at her across the kitchen and exclaimed in a droll, matter-of-fact kind of way, "Why, Gloria, everyone knows yellow corn is for pigs!"

And just like that my mother got the secret to making great Southern cornbread—white cornmeal. You see, in the Old South, white cornmeal was the specific varietals eaten; yellow cornmeal is generally not for human consumption. And in the minds of many Southern cooks, they cook up very differently (which is debatable).

Who knew a food's color could be so powerful in changing the taste of something so profoundly? It was a lesson about how the right ingredients make everything better. Just like in life.

Now, the one thing Big Mama rarely did was give advice to any of her daughters-in-law. Big Mama had had to figure life out on her own; she felt her daughters-in-law should as well.

There was one person in the family, though, who gave my mama loads of advice, and, thankfully, also a recipe that Mama used to great success over the years. That person was my father's oldest sister, Leoah.

My Aunt Leoah was a very colorful woman. She was a tall, regal, and elegant lady. She favored Big with her dark hair and aristocratic features. She was very beautiful when she was young. She had perhaps the most beautiful rolling and lilting Southern brogue I've ever heard.

Lo, as she was called, was a very nineteenth-century person. She was a romantic in every way and would have been easily recognized in any Victorian-era novel. For example, picnics are typically a casual occasion, but not for Lo. No, she would bring her picnic basket filled with china and silver and a lovely blanket with matching cloth napkins.

My father said Leoah always had a tough time dealing with things just as they were in the twentieth century. She'd rather add a little lace to the truth to make it a bit better; not that she meant to mislead, she just wanted to improve things in her mind.

Lo was the person who introduced my parents. She was the secretary at the school where my mama was teaching. She decided that her brother should meet my mama. And, as they say, that was that.

Over the years Leoah gave my mother a lot of "advice." You know, the kind of advice an older sister-in-law might give to her younger brother's wife. This was, of course, amplified by the fact that Leoah thought that, because my mother was a Yankee, Mama had "things" to learn about being a good wife and a potential mother to the children of a Son of the South. This unintended condescension was a bit of a bone of contention between my father and mother—a bone that my mother would mostly accept with quiet grace as she would just silently listen and nod as Leoah bestowed nuggets of truth and wisdom upon her. Every now and then, though, my mama would get a little chuckle out of one of their exchanges.

One of my favorite stories is from a time after my parents were just married and were visiting Aunt Leoah, Uncle Bob, and my ten-year-old cousin Priscilla. Seems Leoah was not one for rising early, but Mama was. So when Mama got up her first morning there, she headed out of the guest bedroom and found Priscilla waiting in the kitchen.

Mama asked, "Prissy, would you like some breakfast?"

Priscilla nodded.

My mama continued, "Well, what does your mother normally make for you?"

"Toast," Priscilla declared.

"Is that all?" my mother asked.

"Yes," came the answer.

My mother opened the icebox door and looked inside. "Well, how about if I make you some scrambled eggs and bacon to go with your toast?"

"Oh, Daddy makes those," Priscilla replied. "Mama only makes toast."

So, my mother got out the eggs, bacon, and bread, and proceeded to fry up the bacon and make the eggs. She popped the toast under the broiler for a minute, until it was lovely, crisp and golden brown. She set the jam and butter out on the table along with some silverware and orange juice, and placed a plate of food down in front of Priscilla.

Just then, Leoah rounded the corner into the kitchen, wearing a gorgeous silk dressing gown and matching slippers.

Leoah greeted them with a grand gesture, calling out, "Good morning, everybody!" She made her way to the coffee percolator, which was happily chirping on the counter, and poured herself a cup.

"Gloria, would you like a cup of coffee?" she asked my mama.

"Yes, thank you."

It was then my mother noticed Priscilla just staring at the plate of food in front of her.

"Is there something wrong, Priscilla?" my mama asked.

"Aunt Gloria, that's not how you make toast."

"Really? How does your mother make it?"

"Well, first you put it under the broiler. Then you catch it on fire. Then you scrape off the black stuff into the sink. That's how you make toast."

Leoah just sipped her coffee calmly and remarked, "Prissy, eat what your Aunt Gloria made you. People make toast all sorts of ways; there's not one that's holy."

My mother continued, "That's true, Prissy. All sorts of things in life are like that. Things can be done *many* different ways. Right, Leoah?"

My aunt, pouring my mother a cup of coffee, just looked over her spectacles at her. "Milk, Gloria?"

Big's Depression Cornbread (comes out thin and crisp)

Ingredients
    1 cup white cornmeal
    1/2 cup flour
    2 teaspoons baking powder
    1/4 teaspoon baking soda
    1/4 teaspoon salt
    1/2 cup buttermilk
    Water

Method
- Heat oven to 450.
- Oil pan with bacon grease or oil very generously.
- Combine all ingredients, adding enough water to make a batter.
- Pour into pan.
- Bake for 15 to 20 minutes. Serve with lots of butter.

Aunt Leoah's Asparagus Appetizers

Leoah loved pedigrees so why shouldn't the food have one, too? According to Aunt Leoah's recipe card for this appetizer, handed down to my mother, this recipe came from a Mrs. James Petty of Columbia, South Carolina. It was given then to a Mrs. Camille Weems of Gainesville, Florida, then was passed to Mrs. Leoah West, also of Gainesville, and then, finally, sent to my mother, Mrs. Gloria Hedden. With a pedigree like that, it better be good! And it is! The note from Lo on the recipe card reads: "Make plenty of these for a party; people come back."

Ingredients

- *20 pieces of white bread, crusts removed*
- *3 ounces of Maytag Blue Cheese*
- *8 ounces of room-temperature cream cheese*
- *1 beaten egg*
- *14 1/2 ounces of canned asparagus (yes, canned)*
- *1 cup melted butter or margarine*

Method

- *Use a rolling pin to flatten each slice of bread.*
- *Combine the blue cheese, cream cheese, and egg in a small mixing bowl. Mix well.*
- *Spread the cheese mixture onto the bread slices, covering to the edges.*
- *Place one asparagus spear on each slice and roll up tightly. Secure with three toothpicks.*
- *Dip each into the melted butter and place onto a baking sheet and freeze. Store on a plastic bag.*
- *When ready to serve, partially thaw the asparagus rolls and slice into three equal sections*
- *Bake at 375 for about 15 minutes. Yields 60 pieces.*

Mexican Cheddar-Jalapeño Crack Cornbread

I had to include this recipe because it is the cornbread I make most regularly. I mean, I love my Big Mama's cornbread, but this recipe is so good that my friends request it all the time for dinners at my place. My friend Fred made it once for me, and, after tasting it, I had to have the recipe.

Ingredients
    1 1/4 cups cornmeal
    1 cup all-purpose flour
    2/3 cup sugar
    1 1/2 teaspoons salt
    1 Tablespoon baking powder
    1/4 teaspoon baking soda
    1/2 cup freshly shredded white extra sharp cheddar cheese
    1/2 cup freshly shredded Jack cheese
    4 eggs
    1 can canned cream corn
    1 small can mild green chilies, drained
    1 1/2 sticks of butter, softened
    Bacon grease or cooking spray for the pan

Method
- *Preheat oven to 400 degrees.*
- *Mix all dry ingredients except sugar together.*
- *Mix butter and sugar together well, then add eggs, chilies, corn, cheese. Mix dry into wet until just combined. Don't over-mix.*
- *Pour into a greased pre-heated medium 9 inch cast-iron pan or a 9x9 cake pan.*
- *Bake 35 to 45 until golden brown. Do not over-bake.*
- *Serve warm. Slice and enjoy. This tastes best right out of the oven.*

CHAPTER SEVEN: THE ART OF HOSTING PARTIES: COMPANY FOOD AND PUNCH

Mama was quite the party-giver. Often, because of my daddy's work, she was called upon to entertain. Early on, she did this as a naval officer's wife and then, later, as a wife to an executive in the defense industry outside of Washington, DC.

She hosted parties with ease. Armed with a few solid, sure-fire recipes, she could offer up some fine hospitality wherever it was needed. I can remember helping her and my grandmother prepare for days before the really big shindigs. My brother and I were often set up in the kitchen to clean mountains of shrimp for shrimp cocktail or shrimp mousse, or to hand roll scores of Norwegian meatballs that were to be served warm in a silver chafing dish on the overloaded buffet table.

One of my favorite stories about my parents' parties comes from the time when we were first stationed in Charleston, South Carolina. My daddy was asked by his commanding officer to throw a holiday party for his entire command. What this really meant was my mother had to throw a party for the entire command, about fifty people. So Mama pulled out all the stops. Casseroles and canapés, meatballs and vegetables, rolls with shaved ham and sliced cheese, and assorted dips and deviled eggs were prepped and displayed for the occasion. She put out a great groaning board of food.

For beverages, my daddy decided it would be both hospitable and economical to serve a very old, Low Country beverage from South Carolina called Chatham Artillery Punch, known as such because it had vague military origins from Chatham County in nearby coastal Georgia. One thing was for sure: the beverage packed a lethal punch.

I remember being a very young boy staring out with wonder at this party through the wooden, louvered door slats that separated me from the adults and the rest of the house. I saw all these smartly uniformed gentlemen and tall, beautiful ladies swirling around the living room, dining room, and kitchen. The ladies with knee-length dresses and chic high-heeled shoes, their lips thick with red lipstick, holding cigarettes in one hand and balancing a buffet plate or cocktail glass in the other. The whole house smelled of food, punch, drifting cigarette smoke, and heavy perfume. Rising above the happy noise of laughter and chatter, the music of Doris Day, Julie London, and Frank Sinatra played on the phonograph as each record dropped onto the automatic turntable in the living room (the origin of the play-list). People were having such a grand time, and the party lasted well into the night.

The party's longevity could be attributed, in part, to the punch. But, of course, my parents didn't realize the full impact of the punch right away. It wasn't until the next day when our neighbor John Shells, who had been a guest, came knocking mid-afternoon on our back door that my parents even began to suspect how drunk people had been the night before. Mister Shells was a marine officer who, by all accounts, was a rather good-natured fellow and knew his way around a cocktail or two. When he appeared at our back door, however, he looked somewhat of a sight. He entered the house without removing his sunglasses, very unusual for such a chivalrous fellow.

I remember he asked my daddy, "Forrest, what in God's name was in that punch?" Officer Shells went on to explain that, in his day, he had seen his fair share of hangovers, but never in his life had he felt so totally destroyed as this morning after. This feeling apparently was a common thread that ran through the entire command's experience with Daddy's punch. Mama was not happy that my daddy had picked such a lethal concoction! Despite the immediate aftermath, that party, and many others like it, have been fondly remembered throughout the years by my family and our guests. In fact, my mama still throws a large holiday party for up to fifty guests to this day, which is quite the Christmas do, and invitations are much sought after among her circle of friends. It's a wine-tasting event with a different wine and appetizer in every major room of the house, culminating with a bountiful dinner buffet in the kitchen. Of course, these days, she has help putting it all together, but, like a conductor, she orchestrates every detail. Sharing our memories about these parties is almost as fun as the parties themselves!

All American Deviled Eggs

At potluck parties, Gloria's deviled eggs are always high on everyone's request list. They are always a favorite.

Ingredients
8 large eggs, hard boiled and peeled
2 Tablespoons quality mayonnaise
1 heaping Tablespoon whipped cream cheese
3 Tablespoons celery, diced very fine
2 teaspoons yellow mustard
1 Tablespoon drained dill pickle relish
1 Tablespoon drained sweet pickle relish
1/4 teaspoon garlic powder
1/4 teaspoon curry powder
2 teaspoon fresh parsley, chopped
2 Tablespoons scallion, chopped finely, green and white parts
Salt and pepper to taste
Hot sauce—about 2 dashes, more if you like heat
Chopped parsley and chives for garnish

Method
- *Cut the eggs in half. Scoop out the yolks into a bowl.*
- *Mix in the other ingredients.*
- *Mash mixture into eggs until a smooth paste forms.*
- *Fill the whites using a fork to make heaping filling.*
- *Chill, covered, for 1 hour.*
- *To serve, garnish with chopped chives and parsley.*

Mama's Shrimp Mousse

It's extremely common in South Carolina's Low Country to make everything using shrimp. This recipe is a typical vintage shrimp appetizer, and it's great for a party. Chefs are rediscovering this old school kind of cooking, making whimsical plays off recipes with jelly or aspic like this one. Old school or new school, this mousse is delicious.

Ingredients
- 1 can tomato soup
- 27 ounces of cream cheese
- 2 Tablespoons gelatin powder
- 1/2 cup cold water
- 1/2 teaspoon Worcestershire sauce
- 1 cup mayonnaise
- 21 ounces of fresh boiled or thawed frozen shrimp, cut up in the food processor
- 1 1/2 cups celery, parsley, onions, green olives, chopped together (food processor, leave a little texture)

Method
- Heat soup to boiling point. Add cheese and gelatin dissolved in the cold water. Let mixture cool. Add shrimp and other ingredients—mold.
- Serves 8 to 10 depending on how hungry they are.
- This makes a wee bit more than six cups.

A Charleston-Style Artichoke Dip

Makes a 4-person serving for a dinner party.

Ingredients
- 1 can artichoke hearts, drained
- 1/2 cup mayo
- 1/2 cup grated Parmesan cheese
- 4 green onions, sliced, white and green parts (2 Tablespoons of the green parts reserved for garnish)
- 1 teaspoon apple cider vinegar
- 1 splash hot sauce

Method
- *Combine all ingredients in a bowl. Using a wire potato masher, roughly mash into a paste.*
- *Pour into a small ovenproof crock or baking dish.*
- *Bake in the oven for 15 mins or until heated and bubbly.*
- *Then broil on high until top is browned.*
- *Remove from the oven.*
- *Garnish with the remaining green onion slices.*
- *Serve with warm pita triangles.*

Baked Brown Sugar Bacon Crackers

These party crackers were the rage all over the South in the 1950s and early '60s at bridge and cocktail parties. They are like cracker bacon candy.

Makes enough for a small gathering.

Ingredients
    1 sleeve Club® crackers
    1 package bacon
    Brown sugar

Method
- Cut bacon strips into thirds.
- Wrap crackers in bacon until all bacon is used.
- Place on a wire rack on top of a sheet tray, seam side down.
- Spoon a small mound of brown sugar on each cracker.
- Bake at 270 degrees for about 1 1/2 hours.

Company Strata (Great for a brunch party)

This is a buffet staple and feeds twelve people easily. It's actually very elegant looking even today and easy to make ahead of time. The flavors in this dish are so indicative of the time I was growing up. Ham, broccoli, sharp cheddar cheese, and a rich "eggy" mustard sauce are the subtle flavorings of an entire American generation.

Ingredients

    12 slices of white sandwich bread
    12 ounces sharp yellow cheese slices (American or cheddar)
    10 ounces broccoli florets, blanched
    2 cups diced cooked ham
    1 jar red pimentos, chopped
    1/2 cup slivered almonds
    1/2 cup chopped scallion
    1/2 cup chopped Italian parsley (2 Tablespoons reserved for garnish)
    6 eggs, beaten
    3 cups whole milk
    1/2 cup cottage cheese
    2 Tablespoons dried minced onion
    1/2 teaspoon salt
    1/4 teaspoon pepper (white pepper if you have it, black will do)
    1 teaspoon dry mustard

Method

- Cut bread rings from bread slices by cutting large rounds from the bread and then cut a "doughnut" hole with a smaller cookie cutter so that the larger pieces resemble a doughnut. Reserve the bread scraps.

- *In a large bowl, combine the eggs, milk, cottage cheese, scallions, parsley, and spices. Mix well.*
- *When ready to assemble, tear up the bread scraps and place on the bottom of a greased 13-by-9 inch baking dish.*
- *Layer the cheese slices on top, followed by the broccoli and then the ham. Dot with the chopped pimentos.*
- *Shingle the bread rings on top in two rows on the top to the left and right side of the dish, leaving the center open. Pile the "holes" between the two rows.*
- *Pour mustard egg mixture over the dish.*
- *Cover with plastic wrap and chill in the fridge at least 6 hours to overnight.*
- *Heat oven to 325 degrees.*
- *Bake uncovered in the oven for 55 minutes.*
- *10 minutes before being done, sprinkle with the cheddar cheese.*
- *Garnish with the parsley.*
- *Let stand 10 minutes before cutting.*

John Shells' Beef Tartare

The Shells remained friends of my parents even after we moved away from Charleston. Officer Shells' favorite meal was steak, and his favorite dish for entertaining was beef tartare. When we returned to Charleston in the 1980s, John was still serving this '50s' classic. The dish can also be served as canapés on small bread rounds. It's a decadent delight.

Serves 4

Ingredients

- 3 medium, oil-packed anchovy fillets, rinsed and minced
- 2 teaspoons really sharp Dijon mustard
- 2 large coddled egg yolks (boil eggs for exactly 1 min then cool)
- 3-4 teaspoons vegetable oil
- 1 teaspoon good quality mayonnaise
- 1 teaspoon chili sauce (you could use ketchup)
- 1 teaspoon cognac or brandy
- 1 teaspoon lemon juice
- 1 teaspoon Worcestershire sauce
- 16 ounces of USDA prime beef tenderloin, cut into small dice, covered, and refrigerated for 30 minutes after slicing
- 3 teaspoons brined capers, drained and slightly chopped
- 1/4 cup finely chopped shallots or red onion
- 3 Tablespoons finely chopped flat parsley leaves
- 3 Tablespoons finely chopped cornichons
- Salt and pepper to taste
- A few dashes of hot sauce or some crushed chili flakes if desired, to taste

Method

- *Combine the anchovies, egg yolks, chili sauce, brandy, lemon juice, and mustard in a metal bowl. Using a whisk, mix ingredients until evenly combined. Slowly stream in oil while mixing. Add mayonnaise and combine.*
- *Use a wooden spoon and mix remaining ingredients into eggs and mustard mixture until thoroughly combined. Season mixture well with salt and freshly ground black pepper.*

To serve

- *If you have a metal ring mold, place it on a plate and pack 1/4 of the mixture into it and press down. Remove the ring mold and you'll have a perfect "patty". If not, using your hands divide the mix into four and roll into balls.*

- *Make all the servings and garnish plate with some more fresh chopped herbs.*

- *Serve the tartare with very thinly sliced and oven-toasted baguette slices.*

Chatham Artillery Punch

Makes 25 servings

Ingredients
2 ounces of tea leaves
4 large lemons
1/2 pound turbinado or light brown sugar
1 quart dark rum
1 quart brandy
1 quart rye or bourbon whiskey
3 bottles champagne

Method
- *Soak the tea leaves 8 hours or overnight in a quart of cold water. Strain the liquid from the leaves into a large container that will hold all the spirits (use wooden, porcelain, or glass; do not use plastic or metal). Juice 3 lemons through a strainer into the tea and add the sugar, stirring until it is dissolved.*
- *Stir in the rum, brandy, and whiskey. Cover and let stand at room temperature for at least 8 hours or for up to a week.*
- *When ready to serve the punch, thinly slice 1 lemon. To serve the punch, allow 6 cups of the base for every bottle of champagne. First pour the brew over an ice ring or large block of ice in a punch bowl. Add the sliced lemon and swirl in the champagne, being careful not to disturb its effervescence.*

CHAPTER EIGHT: COOK MEAT LIKE A MAN

As far as food was concerned, my father passed on his love of food and the community that is born out of it. As Southerners, we love gatherings and we love our BBQ, and my father loved to cook outdoors for a crowd. It's something that rubbed off on me.

Daddy's most favorite crowd he liked to have around him was his family, especially during dinnertime. Whenever Daddy was in town, he always made a point of coming home for dinner. Although a senior manager with much responsibility after leaving the Navy, he left work mostly on time; he would claim that if you had more work than eight hours a day either you had too much (and you needed to ask your boss for help) or you were really bad at managing your time. He told me once how, sadly, he saw other men become workaholics to avoid their families in the evenings. He confided in me that marriage and parenthood were often harder than staying at the office, but if he had wanted to avoid us, he would have remained single. He said someday I'd understand and also hoped I'd see how rewarding being a husband and father could be. Reflecting on his wisdom, I now realize that he came home every night for dinner because he knew there, at home, he, too, found a harbor in the storm.

And once at home after a long workday, one of his great joys during the warmer months of the year was to BBQ dinner in the backyard. Upon arriving home, he would change out of his suit, make himself a Manhattan with a cherry, and then head out back to light the BBQ and cook dinner. So many of my memories of my father's cooking center around our backyard grill. When we were living in Hawaii, we had countless dinners on our lanai in the backyard.

In Hawaii, my parents stumbled upon the BBQ smoker and cooker of *all* BBQ smokers and cookers—the Japanese kamado grill, which we later carried with us wherever we moved. It was a green clay tower about four feet tall and capped with a dome lid that would swing open to reveal the grill. The dome had a round, chimney-like vent with a topper that could be removed to let out the smoke or heat. (It was very similar to today's popular Big Green Egg.) It produced a taste that I have found unparalleled in BBQ. It lent a really special flavor to meats cooked in it or on it.

Now, one of the staples of the American grill experience has got to be the burger. Oh, and by burger, I mean cheeseburger, 'cause what else is there, really? And I loved my father's burgers. He would light up the coals or, later, the gas grill and sail out onto the patio or deck with a platter of his special burger mix in hand. From the meat hitting the fiery coals to the sizzling of the fat on the hot flame to the eventual landing of the luscious patties on the soft rolls ready for toppings, grilling burgers was always a delicious time.

Another part of my father's culinary repertoire came about because my mother was a big fan of live theater and would arrange for our family to see things on a regular basis. The one type of production my father did not really like was musical theater. Whenever my mama would take my brother and me to a musical, my father would often stay home and make us dinner. When we came home from a matinee performance, we would have a great meal waiting for us. He had a particular dish, Veal Scaloppini and Musical Sauce, that became a staple in our home after seeing the musical *Evita*—the Broadway hit that made Patti LuPone a big star—in downtown Washington, DC. We enjoyed the dish often, even if theater was not involved, because it was so tasty.

Daddy's Famous Hedden House Burgers

I'm not sure who came up with the seasoning that went into the Hedden family burger mix. It could have been my dad or someone else, but thank goodness they did 'cause this seasoning makes some pretty darn good burgers.

Makes 10 burgers

Ingredients

    3 pounds of ground chuck 80/20 min fat content or butcher's mix of sirloin, chuck, rib eye and short rib if you want to be fancy.
    1/8 cup Worcestershire sauce
    2 Tablespoons soy sauce
    1 Tablespoon onion powder
    1 1/2 Tablespoons garlic powder
    2 teaspoons of black pepper
    2 teaspoons of dried dill
    1 Tablespoon oil
    salt to taste

The Cheese
    Slices of good quality American or Havarti cheese

Buns
    Good quality sesame burger buns or soft potato burger rolls

Toppings
    2 1/2 cups shredded romaine or iceberg lettuce
    1 cup finely chopped white onion
    30 slices of dill pickles, 3 per burger

Secret Burger Sauce (recipe follows)

Method
- *Mix meat gently with the spices. Don't over-mix.*
- *Form into 6 burger patties (I use a metal burger form).*
- *Before grilling, use your thumb and press an indentation in the center of each burger. This will keep them from puffing up during cooking.*
- *Over a hot grill, coals or on a griddle, cook 3 to 4 minutes per side for med rare, turning once. Don't press the juice out of the burger; just let them get a good sear on them. Melt the cheese 1 to 2 minutes before you pull them off the grill.*
- *Toast the buns with butter.*
- *Spread a nice smear of burger sauce on the bottom bun.*
- *When burgers are done, place on the bottom bun.*
- *Top with lettuce, onions, and pickles.*
- *Place a good smear of Secret Burger Sauce on the top bun and close.*

Secret Burger Sauce
1/2 cup ketchup
1/2 cup mayonnaise
2 Tablespoons yellow mustard
1/4 cup sweet pickle relish, drained
1 Tablespoon dried dill (the secret ingredient)
1 teaspoon garlic powder
Squirt of lemon juice

Method
- *Mix all ingredients together in a small bowl and refrigerate until ready to use.*

1970s'-Style Shish Kebabs

This is a classic and was often prepared on our BBQ. It is great with Saffron Rice Pilaf.

Ingredients
2 1/2 pounds top sirloin or tenderloin, cut into 1 1/4 inch or 1 and 1/2 inch cubes
2 pounds Campari tomatoes
2 green peppers, cut into square strips
2 red peppers, cut into square strips
2 red onions, cut into chunks
1 large zucchini, cut into half moons
2 large yellow squash, cut into half moons
1 pound white mushrooms caps, stems removed

Marinade
1 cup soy sauce
2 Tablespoons Worcestershire sauce
2 cloves minced garlic
1 teaspoon ground ginger
1/4 teaspoon cayenne pepper
1/4 teaspoon curry powder
1/4 cup olive oil
1 teaspoon dried oregano

Method

- *Mix all ingredients together and allow beef and mushrooms to marinate for at least 8 hours or overnight.*
- *Thread all the ingredients onto metal skewers, alternating each one to form a colorful display.*
- *Take reserved marinade and bring to a boil. Reduce by a quarter.*
- *When ready to cook, grill the kebabs over a hot grill, turning frequently, and baste with the marinade as they cook. Cook about 12 minutes for medium to medium rare or up to 15 minutes for medium well.*
- *Serve the kebabs with a traditional Saffron Rice Pilaf.*

Saffron and Curry Rice Pilaf with Currants

Ingredients
    3 cups of basmati rice
    4 1/2 cups of chicken stock
    1/3 cups olive oil
    1 cup slivered almonds
    1 cup dried red currants or cranberries
    3 to 4 cups diced white onion
    3/4 teaspoon saffron threads
    1 1/4 teaspoon salt
    1/4 teaspoon pepper
    1 teaspoon minced garlic
    1/4 cup chopped flat leaf parsley

Method
- *In a heavy-bottomed pot, sauté onion and garlic about 10 minutes until soft.*
- *Place the saffron in a dish and add 2 Tablespoons of hot water.*
- *When onion is soft, add the rice and stir to coat well.*
- *Let toast for a few minutes.*
- *Add the stock and the saffron.*
- *Bring to a simmer, then turn heat down. Cover and cook until water is absorbed, about 18 minutes.*
- *Stir in the almonds, currants, and parsley.*
- *Let the rice rest for about 10 minutes.*
- *Rice can be cooled and reheated later for serving.*

Veal Scaloppini and Musical Sauce

Ingredients
    4 veal (or pork or chicken) cutlets, pounded flat and cut into pieces by separating the connective fat
    Flour for dusting
    4 Tablespoons of butter
    1 Tablespoon olive oil
    1/4 cup white wine
    2 teaspoons of lemon juice
    1 pound sliced white mushrooms
    1 small onion, diced
    1 Tablespoon capers brine from the jar
    2 Tablespoons chopped fresh parsley

Method
- *Heat olive oil and 2 Tablespoons butter in the pan.*
- *Add onions and mushrooms and cook until softened.*
- *Remove from the pan and add 2 remaining Tablespoons of butter.*
- *Dust veal with the flour right before you are going to cook it.*
- *Cook veal on medium heat on one side for 3 minutes, then turn and cook another 2 minutes.*
- *Add the wine and then the onions and mushrooms back to the pan.*
- *Add the caper brine.*
- *Cover and turn heat to low. Simmer for about 15 minutes.*
- *When ready to serve, add the lemon juice and the parsley and serve flat country noodles with lots of butter and chopped parsley.*

CHAPTER NINE: MEDICAL STUDENTS, NUNS, AND GRILLED CHEESE... OH MY!

Grilled cheese sandwiches are perhaps one of the most iconic American comfort foods of all time, and are, unsurprisingly, no stranger to my family's dinner table. I mean, with a mother who grew up in the cheese-loving Midwest, you'd expect them to make an appearance. And, of course, they did, laden with cheese and mayonnaise (apparently, another Midwest addition). However, it was the connection my father had to grilled cheeses that made our love of them all the more personal.

In 1951, my father graduated Clemson University and went on to attend medical school at the Medical University of South Carolina in Charleston. As my father tells it, Charleston during the 1950s was a lovely place. It was still prospering from the post-World War II and Korean War booms, which had given the city enormous increases in port and military base activity.

This meant jobs and revenue. According to my father, the city bustled with activity, and downtown was the center of commerce and shopping. Middle-class migration to the west of the Ashley River suburbs had not yet begun, and, as a result, downtown was vibrant and full of life.

Charleston, at that time, was an integrated city as compared to other Southern cities. In the northern part of the peninsula, the city had blocks of blacks and whites living side-by-side in so-called salt-and-pepper neighborhoods. Of course, the city remained segregated in every other way, just like most of the South.

Among the many hallmarks Charleston had at the time—such as afternoon porch culture (a precursor to happy hour) and shady parks crowded with school children playing and running free—my father always said that one of his most potent memories of living in the city was the multiple church bells that would rouse him on the weekends from deep slumber after a late night. Many of those bell towers date back to the city's origins. You see, in the late 1700s, in part because of the vast number of steeples seen from the harbor, Charleston came to be known as The Holy City. That nickname also was due to the tolerance found in colonial Charleston, which allowed for a variety of Christian denominations to coexist in peace. The city remains a bastion of tolerance and more liberal thinking compared to the rest of the state. But, of course, my father remembers finding the bells not very tolerant of his late-Sunday morning sleep habits.

My father said that being a medical student in the 1950s forced economic trade-offs; students had to figure out what weekend activities were going on and what could be afforded. Medical students also often lived in frat houses—which were the hubs of student life—because there was no on-campus housing and rents in the city far exceeded the students' budgets.

In those days, local doctors had great empathy for the medical students. As such, many doctors had their wives send over care packages to the frat houses. These care packages would take the form of groceries or prepared foods and even sometimes (to the delight of the students) kegs of beer. Sometimes the care packages contained invitations to social gatherings.

The invitations were another welcome distraction from the students' studies. Sometimes my father's class would be invited out to Folly Beach or Sullivan's Island for an oyster roast, or from time to time they would receive an invitation from the bored wives or widows of doctors for a 5 p.m. drop-in (the term "cocktail party" was not yet in use). At these parties, my father and his classmates would find themselves in a house full of lovely older ladies and a few random husbands who had not escaped the occasion. As Daddy tells it, after the sweet ladies had gotten a head of steam from a few drinks, a few would each sidle up to one of the prey (a medical student) and put her hand on his back or even on his fanny. The gentlewoman would ask his name and where he was from. She would ask, feigning demureness, those famous Charleston questions: Who is your family? Do *I* know them?

For the students, these were great occasions because the parties always had a buffet of cocktail shrimp, ham biscuits, and tea sandwiches. Plus, the parties always had a bar with real liquor, not beer, and that was a treat. Everyone would get a little crocked, and a grand time was had by all. It was a fair social trade-off; the ladies got some attention, and the students got free food and booze.

My father told me about a time later in his life when he attended a similar party at a downtown residence. There, with my mother occupied chatting away with the other women, he had a crazy flashback to his medical school days. He realized that he had become, unfortunately, one of those random husbands, dragged along to the fête because he had no excuse for not being there.

Another medical school story he would tell often was about the time he had taken a young lady down to the drugstore on the corner of Calhoun and King Streets for dinner at its lunch counter and soda fountain. There, he bought the pharmacy's famous grilled cheese sandwiches with pickles and milkshakes to round out the meal. Afterward, they went to a movie. Walking home, they decided to stop by his frat house to see if anything was going on.

As my father and his date got to the corner of Ashley Avenue (about six blocks away from the frat), they heard a band playing. At first they thought it must be the nearby high school band, but as they got closer, they realized the music was coming from the front porch of my father's fraternity. His frat had created an impromptu jazz band and they were putting on an alcohol-charged concert for the neighborhood.

Settled on a stoop across the street to enjoy the performance with his date, my dad heard police sirens in the distance. He ran across the street and yelled for everyone to go inside. Most people went upstairs, but my father, his date, and a few others nonchalantly sat in the living room. Sure enough, a few minutes later, the police showed up, banging on the front door. They said that, after the tenth person called to complain, they had come to shut down the party. My father casually replied that they must have the wrong frat house because, clearly, there was no party there; he and his friends were all just relaxing in the living room. As soon as he finished speaking, some idiot on the second-floor porch screamed, "AIRBORNE!" grabbed the palm fronds of the tree next to the house, and swung down to the front lawn. The drunken thrill-seeker looked at the officers, saluted, and wandered off down the street. The officer looked drolly at my father and said, "Son, if I hear so much as another peep from this house, I'm coming back and throwing you in jail."

With that, the police left and the evening was over.

Now, the frat house happened to sit next door to a nunnery. That next Monday morning, as my father was leaving the house for class, he spied a group of nuns waiting at the gate. As my father approached, one of the sisters addressed him. "Boys, we rarely complain about your parties, but Friday night was really, really bad."

My daddy began to apologize, but she raised her hand and stopped him.

"Young man, all I'm saying is it was really bad. And furthermore, if you don't get another trumpet player for your band, we are going to stop praying for you." She continued, "I mean, let's face it, he's really, *really* bad and has got to go. You can do better, boys. Yes? Okay? Am I understood?"

My father stared for a moment, taking in what had just happened. He immediately agreed with the sister and assured her they would follow her admonition. After all, the truth was that the guy was a horrible trumpet player. My father assured her that they would replace him immediately and begged the nuns not to stop praying for them because medical students needed all the prayers they could get.

So, you see, there are several reasons Charleston is known as The Holy City. And apparently in the 1950s, jazz-loving nuns were one of them.

Homage to King Street Pharmacy: Colby Grilled Cheese Sandwiches with Dill Pickles and Milkshakes

Makes 4 sandwiches

Ingredients

> Eight slices of good quality, thick white bread, sour dough or pullman loaf
> 12 slices of Colby Jack or Colby cheese
> 1 small bunch chives, finely chopped
> 20 or so slices of good quality hamburger dill pickles
> Mayonnaise
> Dijon mustard
> Butter at room temperature

Method

- Heat oven to 350 degrees.
- Very generously butter each slice of bread, wall to wall on one side, then spread very thin layer of mayo (this keeps it from burning) and place butter side down on a sheet of wax paper.
- Heat a skillet to medium heat.
- Mix a few Tablespoons of mayonnaise with the Dijon and spread on all slices of the bread.
- Divide the cheese between the slices of bread.
- Place the buttered bread 2 at a time in the skillet and cook until each piece is toasted golden and the cheese starts to melt, then add a big dollop of the chives, blanketing both sides of the bread and cheese.
- When done, hold to the side, and repeat until all slices are toasted and buttery warm.
- Put sandwiches together.
- On a clear baking sheet place the sandwiches and lightly press down with the spatula.

- *Place the sandwiches in the oven and heat for about 10 to 15 minutes until the cheese is melted and heated through.*
- *Remove from the oven and let stand for about 3 minutes. Slice in half and serve with dill pickle chips, potato chips or dressed arugula salad and the milkshakes.*

Scarlet O'Hara Coffee Cantata Milkshakes

Ingredients
8 large scoops of coffee ice cream
1/2 cup buttermilk
2 spoonfuls raspberry jam or 1 cup fresh or frozen raspberries
2 big squirts of chocolate syrup
Canister of real whipped cream

Method
- *Place all ingredients except whipped cream in a blender and whirl, whirl, whirl!!*
- *Pour into 4 glasses, top with whipped cream, and enjoy!*

CHAPTER TEN: FAMILY DINNER IN THE ERA OF FROZEN DINNERS AND WHEN OPENING A CAN WAS A RECIPE

Let's talk 1970s' home dinners. As a kid, it seemed to be an unending wonderland of tasty treats, but as an adult looking back, many options were salt-laden and overly processed. Indeed, based on what we know today about healthy eating, there were a lot of well-intentioned but bad choices on the market shelves. Canned foods, frozen foods and dinners, mix-and-bake casseroles, and boxed dinners like Hamburger Helper or Shake 'n Bake and even Hidden Valley® Ranch dressing mix debuted in home kitchens and quickly abounded. Despite these newcomers, elements of tradition and home cooking—like roasted chicken and mashed potatoes, homemade lasagna, casseroles, and roasts—continued to be mainstays. And we can't forget the less notable vegetable dish of the day that would make an appearance on the family dinner table almost daily: fresh veggies boiled beyond recognition.

Like most mothers who cooked during this time period, my mama had an array of go-to dishes that she rotated in and out of our weeknight meals. She would plan out our family's bill of fare a month in advance with Grandma Irene. Meals were planned out in detail, lists were made, and groceries procured. (Mama's keen sense of organization must have rubbed off on me because, to this day, I never leave the house to run errands unless I have my to-do list!)

Mama shopped at the beginning of each month for many of the things we would eat throughout the month. This was what she called the "big shop." Perishable items were bought as needed, but all the meat, potatoes, noodles, rice, beans, canned foods, frozen foods, flour, grits, and bottled or jarred items were purchased during the big shop.

The big shop always was done at the nearest naval commissary to save money and my brother and I were often enlisted to help with the shopping. Running through the grocery aisles on an errand to retrieve something for my mother or grandmother, we often pretended to be spacemen or pilots—fancying we were flying out on some mission from a central base (the grocery cart) and then returning with our cargo (an item on my mom's list) in tow. Such was the life of a military wife with two young boys food-shopping on a tight, tight grocery allowance.

My friend Liz totally got this when I was first telling her about life on a military budget. She said growing up in Florida with her family on a public servant's salary was about the same—living paycheck to paycheck, with every penny accounted for. She told a story about how, once, she ate all the Push Pops in the freezer. Upon discovering the offense, her mother explained that those were for the whole family and were supposed to have lasted the entire month. As punishment, her mother made her break open her piggy bank and walk to the store to replace them. She said she ran all the way home, fearing that the Florida heat would melt the popsicles, but she and the popsicles made it back in fine condition. Phew!

Despite the processed foods that were abundantly available at the grocery store, Mama always wanted to fix us healthier meals. This prompted her to try to get us to eat more seafood and salad as part of our diet. She introduced various recipes over the years. Some of them, like the Mexican salad with canned tuna, were hits. Some, like a dish called Puffy Fish (white fish slathered with a tasteless meringue), were lesser successes. That does not even sound good!

The ocean and seafood have long been a part of my consciousness and a big part of my life. After all, I lived near or at the shore for the first eleven years of my life. Sun and sand and water and sky were all a part of my every day. One of my earliest memories is in fact related to the sea: I am standing on the seawall either at St. Augustine Beach or Jacksonville Beach, Florida, holding hands with Mama and Grandma Irene. I was only a toddler, but I can still remember the roar of the waves and their cool blue-gray colors. Mama often took me for walks along the seashore, as we lived right off the beach in a yellow, cinderblock beach house. Because of our proximity to the sea and access to fresh, daily catches, seafood was always a staple on our home dinner table—even when it did come out of a can for Mama's famous Mexican salad.

Another example of Mama's attempts at promoting a healthy diet was salad dressing. My mama and grandmother were never fans of bottled dressings. So they made a family salad dressing that we called the Hedden House Dressing. It was orange and it was creamy. And it was the '70s, so that couldn't be unhealthy, right? Well, truth be told, it wasn't the healthiest of dressings, but it was my mama's way of keeping us eating something green and raw every day. And that dressing did just that! It was good enough to eat almost daily for twenty years on. We had a tossed green salad with that creamy dressing at every meal where it was appropriate and even sometimes when it had nothing to do with the meal at all, like when Mama made Mexican food or a Japanese stir-fry.

Then there are certain recipes my mama inherited from friends that became our family's favorites. These days when I make those foods, I'm ten years old again. Certain Italian foods are like that. When we were in

Hawaii, my father met a junior officer in his command whom he took under his wing. Over time, that officer and his wife, Geoff and Louise, became close friends of our family. The Wilsons—as we came to refer to them—were some of my brother's and my favorite people. Geoff liked old English sports cars and roadsters, and Louise was an Italian from Rhode Island. She was quite the homemaker and cook.

Louise introduced our family to real Italian-American food. She cooked for us things like fried artichokes, antipasti, tomato panzanella, and dishes such as eggplant Parmesan with red sauce like we had never had before. Oh, and the garlic in copious amounts was so good!

I count myself lucky to have had both a mother and a father (and dear family friends) who valued family heritage and health so much so that they often cooked delicious homemade meals and offered those meals with a savory side of family history of meals and memories they recalled from their childhoods and young adult lives. What they passed on to my brother and me was an unconscious veritable history lesson, in both eating and living.

I must admit that some of those meals my parents prepared were not especially healthy (from today's standards) or even original to our family's cultural lineage, as with the Wilsons' Italian fare. Sometimes the meals even included ingredients that came out of cans or freezer bags purchased at the commissary.

But truth be told, more times than not, the foods prepared by my mother and father *did* come out of a box. It just wasn't a box we got at the store. They came out of the recipe box, a treasure box of handwritten and ingredient-splattered index cards that sat on my mama's kitchen counter. And believe you me, those made for some great "boxed" dinners, ones that I still fix today!

These recipes are a varied and diverse collection of my favorite dinner memories from my 1970s' dinner table. A random collection perhaps, but it is a hearty, homemade, delicious one. Many of these I still make to this day.

Hedden House Dressing

Family legend has it that this dressing was from a well-known Floridian restaurant during the 1960s. My Grandma Irene, when living in Florida, found the recipe in a local newspaper. My mama and grandma tinkered with it over the years, and it ended up being the dressing we had in the icebox all the time.

Ingredients

    3 eggs, hard-boiled, peeled and finely chopped
    1/2 cup prepared chili sauce
    1 Tablespoon garlic powder
    1/4 cup Worcestershire sauce
    3/4 cup sweet pickle relish
    3 1/2 cups mayonnaise
    1/4 cup white vinegar
    1/2 cup sliced California black olives
    1/2 cup finely diced red bell pepper
    Pinch of allspice
    Pinch of salt to taste

Method

- *Place all ingredients except egg, pickle relish, and olive into a food processor. Blend, then add in olives and pulse a couple of times. Pour dressing into a mixing bowl, then add egg and relish and mix well.*
- *Check for seasoning.*
- *Chill for at least 1 hour to allow flavors to marry.*
- *Serve over salad greens and desired toppings like tomatoes, red onion, slivered almonds, cheddar cheese, cucumbers, canned black olives, shredded ham, bacon bits, shredded carrots, purple cabbage, crumbled boiled egg, broccoli slaw, and, of course, crunchy croutons.*

Mama's Antipasto Salad

This is one of my mama's favorite dishes to bring to any buffet dinner or serve as a first course for an Italian meal. It's one of Louise Wilson's recipes I love.

Ingredients
- 1/2 pound pepperoni rounds, sliced in half
- 1/4 pound provolone cheese, cut into small cubes
- 1/2 (13 ounces) jar Italian pepper salad
- 1 jar (6 ounces) marinated artichoke hearts
- 1 small head of iceberg lettuce sliced into thin chiffonade
- 2 medium tomatoes, cut into wedges
- 5 ounces of canned tuna, drained and flaked
- 2 ounces of canned anchovies, drained
- 1/4 cup Italian salad dressing

Method
- *Prepare the following in advance:*
  - *In a covered container, combine the pepperoni, cheese, pepper salad with some juice, the artichokes and their juice. Toss. Cover and refrigerate at least 3 hours or, better, overnight.*

- *When ready to serve:*
  - *Prepare the lettuce as you would for a regular salad.*
  - *Combine the lettuce and tomatoes and chill until ready to serve.*
  - *When ready, add the tuna and anchovies and the refrigerated mix together and toss with the salad dressing. Pile high on a round platter as high into a pointed cone as possible. Serve.*

Louise Wilson's Spaghetti Sauce (Italian Sunday Gravy)

Everyone should know how to make good Italian-American red meat sauce. This is my version of her sauce.

Ingredients
- 1 pound ground pork
- 1 1/2 pounds ground beef
- 1 teaspoon olive oil
- 6 cloves garlic, minced
- 2 large Spanish onions, minced
- 1/4 cup red wine
- 1 6 ounce can of tomato paste
- 2 cans chopped tomatoes
- 32 ounces of canned tomatoes
- 1 envelope onion soup mix
- 1 small bunch Italian parsley, chopped
- 3 Tablespoons dried Italian Seasoning blend
- 1/2 teaspoon black pepper
- 1/4 teaspoon crushed red pepper (to start; if you like it spicier, add more later)
- 3 Tablespoons soy sauce
- 1 teaspoon sugar
- 1 package sliced mushrooms
- 3/4 cup plain bread crumbs
- 1/4 cup cream
- 1/2 stick butter
- Cooked pasta such as spaghetti or rigatoni (1 lb.)

Method

- *Brown the pork and the ground beef in a large pot with the olive oil.*
- *Remove from the pan.*
- *In the same pot, sauté the onions until soft and starting to brown, then add the garlic and cook until it blooms and you smell it strongly.*
- *Add wine and scrape the bits from the bottom of the pot.*
- *Add tomato paste and the tomatoes with their liquid.*
- *Add the herbs and spices, onion soup mix, and the fresh parsley.*
- *Reduce heat to medium low and simmer for 1 hour, stirring occasionally to prevent things from sticking.*
- *Then add the mushrooms, butter, soy sauce, and breadcrumbs and cook another 1/2 hour.*
- *When ready to serve, stir in cream. Cook for about 10 minutes, stirring frequently.*
- *Serve over the pasta with grated Parmesan cheese.*

Oven-Baked Festive Fish Filets

This really easy recipe is from Grandma Irene's cookbook. It beats my mama's puffy fish recipe.

Ingredients
    6 fresh solid white fish fillets (Cod, Halibut, Mullet or Bluefish)
    1 1/2 cups prepared creamy French dressing (yes, the orange stuff)
    1 cup Cheez-It® crackers
    1 cup Ritz® crackers
    1/2 cup grated Parmesan cheese
    Paprika
    1/2 cup chopped parsley
    1/2 cup melted butter

Method
- *Run crackers through a food processor until it becomes crumbs. Add cheese and parsley, and mix well in a bowl.*
- *Grease a baking dish.*
- *Pour dressing into a bowl.*
- *Place fish filets into dressing, coating liberally with dressing.*
- *Then dredge in cracker mixture until well and thickly coated.*
- *Place into dish and repeat until all filets are done.*
- *Sprinkle well with paprika.*
- *Cover dish and place into fridge for 10 minutes.*
- *Preheat oven to 500 degrees.*
- *Remove from the fridge and pour melted butter over the fish filets.*
- *Place into oven and cook for 10 to 12 minutes until fish is cooked through and flakey. Serve with mashed potatoes and sauerkraut tartar sauce.*

Sauerkraut Tartar Sauce

Scandinavians will put sauerkraut in anything, including tartar sauce!

Ingredients
1 cup mayo
1/2 cup jarred sauerkraut, drained
2 Tablespoons minced onion
2 Tablespoons lemon juice
1 Tablespoon capers
1 Tablespoon dill relish
1/4 teaspoon dill
Handful of chopped fresh parsley
1 teaspoon hot sauce
Salt and pepper to taste

Method
- *Place everything in a food processor and pulse, leaving a little texture from the sauerkraut.*

1970s' Ground Beef Casserole with Biscuits

This is a no-joke comfort food. My family used to eat this in the winter with salad and a green vegetable like broccoli or green beans.

Ingredients
    1 1/2 pounds ground beef
    1 large onion, chopped
    2 cloves garlic, minced
    10 ounces chopped mushrooms
    1 diced orange or red pepper (or green if you like green pepper)
    6 ounces cream cheese
    1 10 ounce can mushroom soup
    1 cup frozen or fresh peas
    1 cup cottage cheese
    4 teaspoons milk
    1/3 cup ketchup
    1 1/2 cups shredded cheddar cheese (half cup reserved for top)
    1/4 heaping teaspoon ground nutmeg
    1/2 teaspoon hot sauce
    Salt and pepper to taste
    4 cocktail or Campari-style small tomatoes, halved
    1 tube refrigerator flaky biscuits
    Black pepper, coarse ground if you have it
    Chopped parsley for garnish

Method
- Brown the beef with the onions in a skillet and then drain. Add mushrooms and peppers and cook until just softened. Add cream cheese in chunks and cook until softened and mixed in well.
- Mix the next 9 ingredients together in bowl and then add the warm beef mixture.

- *Mix well and place into a casserole dish. Place tomatoes in a line in the middle of the baking dish.*
- *Bake for 25 minutes and then remove from oven and place the biscuits on the top on either side of the tomatoes in a line but not touching. Sprinkle each with pepper and then sprinkle remaining cheese over the biscuits and the whole dish.*
- *Bake the dish for another 10 to 15 minutes or until the biscuits are golden and done.*

Excuse me, but do you have Dijon Chicken?

This recipe comes from the 1970s when Grey Poupon Dijon mustard first hit the market. In fact, everything about this recipe is so 70s. However it's a really easy and delicious dish. Served at room temperature, it makes a great picnic entree.

Ingredients
12 chicken pieces
Salt and pepper to taste
Garlic powder
1 8 ounce jar Dijon mustard
1 cup sour cream
Italian flavored breadcrumbs (Panko would be my choice these days)

Method
- *Preheat oven to 400 degrees.*
- *Sprinkle the chicken pieces with salt and pepper and garlic powder.*
- *Combine the Dijon and the sour cream.*
- *Spread each piece well with this mixture.*
- *Roll in the breadcrumbs.*
- *Place the chicken in a single layer on a baking sheet and cover with foil.*
- *Bake for 35 to 40 minutes at 400.*
- *Remove foil and bake another 20 minutes until the chicken is golden brown.*
- *This may be served hot, warm or cold.*

Louise Wilson's Magic Cake

A cake that is easy and so delicious, it's true magic.

Ingredients
Cake
- 1/2 cup flour
- 2 cups sugar
- 6 Tablespoons cocoa
- 1 teaspoon salt
- 2 teaspoons baking soda
- 2 cups cold water
- 2/3 cup cooking oil (corn/soybean)
- 2 Tablespoons cider vinegar
- 2 teaspoons vanilla

Frosting
- 2 Tablespoons flour
- 3/4 cup milk
- 1 cup sugar
- 1 stick margarine
- 1/4 Crisco® shortening (solid in a can)
- 1 teaspoons vanilla

Method
For Cake:
- In a 9x13 inch pan, mix the flour, sugar, cocoa, salt, and baking soda.
- Then pour the water, cider vinegar, cooking oil, and vanilla over the dry mix and combine very well.
- Bake at 350 degrees for about 40 minutes, when a toothpick comes out clean.

For Frosting
- *In a sauce pan over low heat, cook flour and milk until it's a paste.*
- *Add the sugar until incorporated and smooth.*
- *Cool to room temperature, then beat in the margarine, Crisco®, and vanilla.*
- *Frost the cake. Let set, then enjoy!*

SECTION TWO

ON BEING A GRANDSON

CHAPTER ELEVEN: OVER THE RIVER AND THROUGH THE YEARS TO GRANDMOTHER'S HOUSE WE GO

Grandparents are different teachers than parents, but they, too, are connected to the great circle of life. Young children often don't readily see the value seniors hold, and, instead, simply view them as old people or just outmoded. However, grandparents do impart meaningful lessons, lessons that seem to have more credibility than your mother's or your father's—because grandparents are from the great beyond of time and history.

Grandparents are the gatekeepers to our pasts, to those times that explain who we are and where we come from. For me, both of my grandmothers held this very important role. Stories they told, including stories about their families, helped me as a young Navy brat develop a sense of family history and centered me even though my physical world was constantly changing.

Like most families, my parents came together from two very different backgrounds. My father's side came from very old Southern tobacco, vegetable-farming, and pork-loving roots (transplanted from the British Isles and Germany). My mother's side hailed from Chicago. They were, as my father's mother called them, Yankees. Ethnically, my mother's family was Norwegian and Austro-Hungarian, immigrants from Northern and Eastern Europe. They brought smoked fish, pickled things, and sour cream with them across the Atlantic. And, like every family, both sides influenced my food heritage.

We called my father's mother Big Mama and my mother's mother Grandma Irene. They had nothing and everything in common. They were from different worlds, but they somehow taught me many of the same lessons through their varied lives. Their messages and morals matched those of my parents: be your own person, be of service to your community, work hard (it pays off), and gather as a family for dinner.

My grandmothers also brought a sense of humor into my life, and they helped me develop my own by passing on amusing anecdotes of interesting people from our family's past. The very first stories I remember about my extended family are those I heard from Big Mama. Her colorful Southern origins made it easy for her to pass on fascinating family history, as well as some delicious tidbits. One such tale is about a great-great-grandmother of note—a woman known to me in stories only as Grandma Barnes. And what's really important to know is that if it were not for Grandma Barnes, as Big pointed out, there would have been no me!

Grandma Barnes was Big's grandmother. And from what I gather from the stories, Grandma Barnes was a force of nature. In fact, in her older years, she looked kind of like that old picture of Carrie Nation, that militant member of the temperance movement, who, with her hatchet, smashed alcohol stocks of many a tavern. Grandma Barnes, like Carrie, wore nothing but long black dresses with black petticoats. Similarly, she wore a black lace scarf draped over her hair and shoulders or a large black bonnet.

The two women differed, however, on one very important matter. You see, Grandma Barnes was never one *not* to accept a drink. Every afternoon between four and five o'clock, Grandma Barnes drank three fingers of straight bourbon (no water to pollute the booze, please), which she called her "tea." She claimed it kept the blood vessels open. She would also smoke a corncob pipe—another activity Carrie Nation vehemently opposed—on the back porch, where the neighbors couldn't see. These habits must have stood her in good stead since she died at ninety-six! (Apparently, one evening she told my grandfather that she was too tired and old, and just couldn't go on. And by the next morning, she was dead. Cheers to going like that!)

Ensuring she could procure her medicinal drink during that unfortunate dry period of American history known as Prohibition, Grandma Barnes was friendly with the local bootlegger. The bootlegger, a lovely old woman, visited her customers in a horse and buggy, hiding her contraband beneath her voluminous skirts and lap blankets. Of course, just having an outside supply source wasn't enough for Grandma Barnes. She had my grandfather set up a brandy production in the barn every fall, when she would turn the local grapes grown on the nearby farms into wine and then further into liquor. And since the sheriff was a close family friend, she never had much trouble. In fact, the sheriff was known to attend "afternoon tea" at the house on many an occasion. Grandma Barnes's hobby must have rubbed off on her great-grandchildren, as several of my uncles made wine and brandy in their basements.

Now, Grandma Barnes's affinity to liquor may have also influenced her denomination of choice. Grandma Barnes was not a Baptist like most of her family. My daddy said she used to say she couldn't abide the Baptists with all that yellin' about sin and the evils of dancing, and their punch and cookies at parties. Instead, she told everyone that she was Episcopalian. How her conversion happened no one was really sure. In the South, as perhaps elsewhere, the "wealthy peoples" attended mass at the Anglican or Episcopal churches in town. Supposedly, Grandma Barnes belonged to her church not for the status it may have brought her, but for another reason. After church and at other events, the Episcopalians would serve cheese and wine at congregational meetings. She liked that.

According to my father, Grandma Barnes was reportedly also a "witch doctor healer." She had cures for every aliment. Daddy told me when he had a wart once on his pinky, she took his finger in her hand and spit on the wart. She then applied some ointment, said some mumbo jumbo over it, and wrapped it up. A week later, Daddy removed the bandage, and like magic, the wart was gone!

And according to Big, Grandma Barnes was a notable matchmaker. You see, in an attempt to marry off her granddaughter, Grandma Barnes figured out a way to introduce Big to her future husband, my grandfather. As the story goes, my grandfather Julius was returning from the West. There, he had tried his hand at being a cowboy and rancher, but he was not very successful. He did, however, succeed in catching malaria. Sick and destitute, he telegraphed the two maiden aunts who had raised him. He implored them to send money so he could return home; he wanted to either get better or die trying.

It so happened that Grandma Barnes was well acquainted with my grandfather's aunts, and upon hearing his sad tale, she told the aunts that she would be happy to take my grandfather up to one of the old German hotels near Walhalla so that he could take in the clean mountain air and "the cure." She even sent my grandfather a train ticket and arranged for his lodgings. And just guess whom Grandma Barnes sent to pick up my grandfather at the Walhalla train station. Yes sir, it was Big! And Grandma Barnes's plan worked perfectly. Big and my grandfather Julius fell in love, got married, and settled down, and he survived his bout with malaria, too!

Grandma Barnes was a simple philosopher. When my daddy was a young boy, he asked Grandma Barnes what the meaning of life was. Her answer shocked him. She beckoned for him to move close to her, and then, so as not to be heard, whispered under her breath, "Forrest, who gives a damn what life is about? It's what you do with it that matters."

My father never forgot that. Nor did he forget that while good Southern ladies don't swear in public, they certainly know how to swear to make a point.

Grandma Barnes is part of my family's history. She is part of how my family came to be. She's an interesting and humorous part of my past, and she inspires me to enjoy life. Her story reminds me that a life without the balance of a little spice is a little boring. That life is what we make it. So we had best make it something! Let's raise a glass to Grandma Barnes. Raise it to meddling when it's a good idea and to enjoying life a little bit, regardless!

Grown-Up Bourbon Milkshakes

Ingredients
    9 large scoops of vanilla ice cream
    1/4 cup buttermilk
    2 shots of bourbon
    Canister of real whipped cream

Method
- *Place all ingredients except whipped cream in a blender and whirl, whirl, whirl!!*
- *Pour into 4 glasses, top with canister of whipped cream, and enjoy!*

The Barnes Bourbon Brown Sugar Mustard Glazed Ham

You can use a pre-cooked spiral cut ham from the supermarket as the basis for this recipe or you can use a fresh ham. But a fresh ham takes way longer so I just don't bother. We use this recipe around the holidays. It's yummy.

Rub
- 1 Tablespoon allspice
- 1/4 cup Creole mustard
- 1/4 cup brown sugar
- 2 Tablespoons lemon zest (2 lemons)
- 1/2 teaspoon salt

Glaze
- 1/4 cup firmly-packed light brown sugar
- 1/4 cup honey
- 1/4 cup bourbon
- 1 Tablespoon Creole mustard
- 3 Tablespoons molasses

1 9 1/2 pound bone-in, pre-cooked spiral cut ham

Method
- Preheat oven to 250 degrees.
- Mix rub ingredients together and rub all over the ham.
- Place ham on a foil-lined baking sheet.
- Cover ham with foil and bake 10 minutes for every pound.
- In the last hour of baking, remove foil and slather the ham with the glaze.
- Bake uncovered for 20 minutes. Spoon glaze over the ham.

- *Remove ham from the oven and allow to cool.*
- *Continue to spoon glaze over the ham as it cools, making sure it gets into the folds of the slices.*

To serve
- *Reheat oven to 185 degrees.*
- *Place ham into the oven and cook for another 45 - 60 minutes.*
- *When ready to serve, remove from the oven and place on the buffet or the table and garnish with herbs, lemon halves and cranberries.*

CHAPTER TWELVE: BIG MAMA, NOURISHING STORIES, AND TOMATO PIE

My father's mother was a phenomenal woman. Her proper name was Belle. We called her Big Mama, a term of endearment she hated but later came to embrace. The nickname originally came from one of her handymen; he started referring to her as Big Mama because she had eight children and was the boss. My uncles loved the moniker. For years, she would tell my uncles not to call her that, but as time passed the name stuck and was shortened to simply Big.

By all accounts, Big was tough and fiery, and extremely proud and protective of her family. And even though she was direct and firm, she seemed as gentle as a summer rain to her grandchildren. These traits were revealed for all to see when Big's husband died and she was left with a houseful of young 'uns to care for and raise. A well-meaning cousin suggested that she should split up her brood among the various branches of the family. Well, Big told that cousin exactly what she thought of that idea and never spoke to her another day in her life!

Big's immediate family took priority over all else in her life, and this priority was clearly ingrained into my father. Like Big, Daddy always seemed to put my mother, brother, and me first; he would never compromise when it came to taking care of his family.

As Grandma Barnes did before her, Big passed away at ninety-five-years-old from, as they say in the South, just being tired. No disease and no drama. She passed the way we all wish we could go—quietly and in her sleep. And while she is no longer with us, the lessons she left behind—both in and out of the kitchen—influenced several generations.

Big was born and raised in Graham County, North Carolina, in the late 1880s. She was one of five children. Big had a much older brother and three younger sisters. Her family name was Farley. Her father's family was originally from Charleston, South Carolina. The family settled, years later, in the county of Seneca. Clearing land and farming were the hallmarks of their lives. Not very aristocratic, I'm afraid. We are a family of self-made people who carved out a life in the new and rugged world.

Her father, a tobacco farmer, smoked a corncob pipe and made his own whiskey. He had no love for store-bought liquor. "Never know what goes into it," he used to say. He died at ninety-six after taking care of his third and much younger wife who'd had a stroke. One day, he sat down in his rocking chair and just never got back up.

Big's relationship with her father was always strained. Upon learning of his death, Big told my father to go get the beef, wine, and iron tonic out of the icebox and to pour them both a drink. The tonic was a fortified wine of some kind that only Big knew the recipe for. But from the taste, my father would say it was a mixture of sweet wine and brandy. How the bottle got filled, Daddy never knew. And according to him, there was always a bottle in the icebox. Big and Daddy drank a toast to his grandpa. Big told him that her father was quite a rascal but a good man. Not a bad epitaph.

Now, Big's mother had passed away many years earlier, while giving birth to her fifth child when Big was only eleven years old. Her brother, Ted, died a few years later at the age of twenty from what Big called The Irish Curse. If my Aunt Leoah's family history is correct, Ted's end came when a train hit his buggy as he was coming home drunk from a tavern. He apparently tried to outrun the train at a crossing and lost.

Shortly after Big's mother died, Big's father remarried. The second wife was a horrible shrew who felt threatened by the children of the first wife and treated Big and her sisters with complete contempt. It fell on Big to take care of her sisters, including the infant child her mother died birthing. Big learned how to take care of her own during this trying time.

And I am sure she drew upon that experience when she later found herself with eight children to take care of after my grandfather passed on.

When the second wife fell ill, Big's father hired a housekeeper. When the second wife died, he married yet again. This time he married the housekeeper whom he was employing and had gotten pregnant!

According to my father, Big disapproved so much of her father's morally questionable behavior that, at the age of seventeen, she left home, leaving her sisters with their new stepmother, and moved in with her aunt's family (her mother's sister) in Walhalla, South Carolina. Also in that household was her grandmother, Bethana Barnes, known as Grandma Barnes. And we already know about her!

My father said Big considered herself a mountain woman; she liked to live off the land in the foothills of the Blue Ridge Mountains. She knew how to work the soil. She learned that from working her father's farm. But, she also made use of the indigenous knowledge she gleamed from the local Cherokees. She knew which native plants in the nearby woods were edible, which had medicinal properties, and which were poisonous.

Big, much like her grandmother, had cures for just about everything. My father confided that each of his siblings had one cure they hated the most. My Uncle John hated the buttermilk cure for GI track ailments, which consisted of basically being forced to drink glass upon glass of buttermilk; my uncle had such a hard time keeping that buttermilk down! My father hated the cure for colds and the flu that consisted of applying a flannel cloth to his chest that had been saturated with a mixture of kerosene and Vicks® VapoRub. One whiff, and he would want to pass out. He must have believed in it, though, because Daddy used it a few times on my brother and me when we were sick!

My father said that Big's thoughts on society were simple. She divided society into three groups. For her, there were white people and black people (no shame in being either in Big's eyes), and then way down there (below everyone else) were the morally irreverent—white trash. "Shiftless, good-for-nothing trash" was her most pungent and damning condemnation of someone. Our family was never one to think less of people because of the color of their skin or their social standing, but their diligence in living counted for a lot in my grandmother's eyes.

Once my father and Big were driving around the county on a family visit when they came across a house with an old washing machine and assorted garbage on the front porch and beat-up, abandoned cars in the yard. "Look at that!" she snarled. "What white trash! People just don't know how to be poor anymore." To her, being poor was not a sin. After all, we were never a wealthy family, by any stretch of the imagination. But to Big, not to care for or have pride in one's self and situation was what was a damnation!

My father told me these experiences with Big were the basis for the work ethic he developed for himself and passed onto my brother and me. No matter where we lived or how little my parents may have had, I never once thought of ourselves as poor. We were told that the way up in life was to go through. And hard work to achieve anything is better than achieving nothing.

Another thing Big could not abide was stealing. My father remembers a particularly humorous occasion when Big's denunciation was on full display. It was an autumn day and Big was bathing. Out the bathroom window she spied a man going through the larder on the back porch. She yelled at the top of her lungs, "Doris, get me the gun! There's a man on the porch stealing my food."

My Aunt Doris, who was standing next to my father in the kitchen, fainted dead away. Big opened the bathroom door to the kitchen, with no clothes on, and stared at Doris lying on the floor.

"Oh, for God's sake, Doris!" she exclaimed. "You are such a 'fraidy cat. Forrest, go get my gun NOW!" she roared.

My daddy was happy to have an excuse to escape the kitchen and the sight before his eyes. By the time my daddy returned, Big had wrapped herself up in her blue cotton bathrobe and her hair in a towel.

Taking the gun in hand, Big stepped onto the back porch and yelled, "Okay, boy, you better get gone 'cause I'm coming to get you!"

When Big got out there, the man was gone. And nothing had been taken. Big exclaimed that she was glad to have helped the lad see the error of his ways. My father said that the real irony of it all was that if the man had only asked, Big would have loaded him up to take food home to his family. But he didn't ask, and Big didn't tolerate stealing. She would say that the commandment is "Thou shalt not steal" not "Thou shalt not steal, except for…"

Big put a lot of love into doing for her family. When visiting her in Walhalla, I felt that love very strongly in her kitchen, eating the simple foods prepared for me with love and tradition. I think Big made her famous cornbread every day or, at least, it seemed like it. There were always home-canned foods and pickles, and, for as long as my father could remember, three-foot-tall crocks filled with fresh, delicious sauerkraut on the back porch. Big learned how to make that up in the mountains as well.

Farm-to-table was life for Big, not some heady idea. As little boys, my brother and I were always being recruited to help weed and pick vegetables from the garden next to the house. It was a lesson in what fresh really means. And, for little boys, playing in the dirt just seemed a jolly good time. That was, until it was time to wash up for supper, and our fingernails got inspected.

If there is one food that reminds me of Big, it would be the humble tomato. Whether stewed or cooked into some dish or eaten in sandwiches on white bread with copious amounts of mayo and fresh black pepper and maybe a slice of sweet onion, fresh summer tomatoes will always remind me of Big Mama.

Like tomatoes, these stories about her are a part of the heritage she has passed on to me. They are filled with lessons about working hard, asking for help when needed, never stealing, never judging one by color or class, and taking care of your family with all your soul. Indeed, these lessons are as bountiful and usable as any summer crop of tomatoes.

Big's Tomato Pie

Ingredients

    1 deep-dish biscuit pie crust (simple biscuit dough rolled thin and pressed into the pie pan and par-baked off). You can use a pie shell.
Oil for cooking
3 1/2 pounds small to medium tomatoes on the vine, cored, seeded, and diced into medium pieces—not tiny
3 or 4 very thin center slices of a large red tomato reserved for the top
1 small onion, chopped
1 small red pepper, chopped (Big used green)
2 scallions, chopped
6 fresh basil leaves, chopped chiffonade
1 teaspoon dried thyme
1 teaspoon garlic powder
1/2 teaspoon salt
1/2 teaspoon sugar
1/4 teaspoon black pepper
3/4 cup good quality mayonnaise (I like Dukes)
1/2 cup grated yellow extra sharp cheddar cheese
1/4 cup grated hard-aged white cheddar cheese
1/4 cup Parmesan cheese, grated
7 picked basil leaves

Method

- *Place the tomatoes in a bowl and salt them lightly.*
- *Place in a colander and let them drain for at least 2 hours or overnight into a bowl.*
- *Remove them and place between paper towels and blot to dry further. Do this to pull out as much liquid as possible. This will keep the pie from becoming mushy and is a very important step.*
- *Sauté onions until brown and caramelized, then add pepper and green onions. Cook until soft.*
- *Let cool.*
- *Combine the cooled onions and peppers with the tomatoes.*
- *Add in the salt, pepper, sugar, dried spices, and the fresh basil. Mix gently.*
- *Mix together the mayonnaise, cheddar cheese and Parmesan cheese.*
- *Mix 1/4 of the cheese mixture together with the tomatoes.*
- *Place the tomato-onion mixture into the shell and spoon the remaining cheese mixture over the tomatoes.*
- *Top with thin sliced tomatoes.*
- *Bake in the oven at 375 degrees for 30 minutes or until bubbling and the top is nice and brown.*
- *Allow pie to cool for 10 to 15 minutes, then slice and serve.*
  (It will be a little runny; don't worry. Just scoop it up. The cooler it gets, the more it sets up, but it is good at almost room temp as well.)
- *Garnish with basil leaves.*
- *Serve with a green salad or coleslaw and potato salad.*

Scalloped Tomato Casserole

(To me this is like a savory bread pudding.)
(Notes from my Aunt Martha: Serves 6. Easy to double for a crowd.)

Ingredients
- *1/2 stick of butter*
- *1 onion, sliced*
- *1 teaspoon of salt, or to taste*
- *Black pepper, to taste*
- *1 Tablespoon brown sugar*
- *3-4 large ripe tomatoes (a generous pound), sliced in rounds*
- *Bread, cut in large cubes. (I think my mother used a simple loaf of French bread, nothing fancy. She did cut the cubes large, like 1.5 inches x 1.5 inches. The goal is to have the bread cubes protrude out of the tomato mixture.)*

Method
- *Preheat oven to 375 degrees.*
- *Sauté the onion in butter until onion is wilted. Add to the pan the salt, pepper, brown sugar, and sliced tomatoes. Bring to a simmer. Let cook on low heat until thickened a bit—totally depends on how juicy the tomatoes are. Taste for seasoning and adjust to your taste.*
- *In a greased 9 x 13 casserole dish, cover the bottom with the bread cubes. Pour the thickened tomato mixture over the bread. Bake at 375 degrees for 30-40 minutes. The edges of the bread cubes should be lightly browned.*

Cousin Martha's Tomato Salad

(An American version of panzanella)

Ingredients

- 4 large ripe tomatoes, peeled and cut into wedges
- 1-2 Tablespoons apple cider vinegar (amount depends on acidity of the tomatoes; I've tried balsamic vinegar and red wine vinegar. I always go back to apple cider vinegar.)
- A handful of fresh basil leaves, cut in strips
- 2 Tablespoons good quality mayonnaise (Hellmann's is my favorite. Dukes is good, too.)
- Salt and pepper to taste
- 1 loaf of good, tough, hearty French or Italian bread, cut into slices.

Method

- In a large bowl, combine the tomatoes, vinegar, basil, salt, and pepper. Add the mayonnaise and mix well. Taste and adjust the seasoning as you prefer. If the tomatoes are not fresh summer tomatoes, perhaps add another splash of cider vinegar and a pinch of sugar. Let the mixture sit in the refrigerator until the juices appear.
- To serve, place a couple of slices of the good bread on a salad plate and spoon the tomatoes and plenty of the juices over the bread. This is good with anything in the summer— grilled chicken, steak, boiled lobsters, etc.

My sister Susan and I developed this recipe one summer when we were at the beach and had lots of tomatoes at the peak of ripeness.

Big's Summer Squash Casserole

Summer squash was everywhere during the summers in Walhalla, and this was my favorite decadent way to eat it.

Ingredients
    1 pound yellow crookneck squash, cooked and slightly mashed
    1/2 cup chopped onion
    1 cup grated extra sharp cheese
    1 teaspoon sugar
    1/2 teaspoon salt
    1/4 teaspoon ground black pepper
    1/2 cup mayonnaise
    1 egg, beaten
    1 stick butter, melted
    1 sleeve butter crackers, crushed

Method
- Combine squash, onion, cheese, sugar, salt, pepper, mayonnaise, and egg in a large mixing bowl. Stir to mix well.
- Pour into a greased 2-quart baking dish or 6 individual baking dishes.
- Combine melted butter and crushed butter crackers in a medium size mixing bowl. Stir with a fork to combine.
- Sprinkle cracker mixture over casserole.
- Bake at 350 degrees for 35 to 40 minutes.
- Let cool a few minutes before serving, Enjoy.

Walhalla Chess Cake

This recipe of a version of "chess pie" in cake form comes from a church cookbook and always reminds me of Big because I enjoyed chess pie for the first time at her house. This recipe is trashy Americana baking at its regional best.

Ingredients
Crust
- 1 stick butter
- 1 box yellow box cake mix
- 1 egg

Filling
- 8 ounces softened cream cheese
- 1 1/2 boxes powdered sugar
- 3 eggs
- 1 Tablespoon lemon juice
- 1 Tablespoon cornmeal
- 2 teaspoons grated lemon rind

Method
- Mix all crust ingredients and press into a greased 9 x 13 baking pan.
- Cream all filling ingredients together and top the crust with the mixture.
- Bake at 350 degrees for 40 minutes.

CHAPTER THIRTEEN: GRANDMA IRENE AND REMEMBERING NORWEGIAN MEATBALLS

My Grandma Irene was only five-foot-six which, in my family of giants, is relatively short. In my eyes, however, she was a formidable marvel. She was so personable and social; it seemed to me as I was growing up that she knew everyone. It also felt to me that there was no way she was only five-foot-six because she lived so large.

Grandma Irene was reportedly a feisty young girl. One of my favorite stories about her is from her childhood. Being good Catholics, my great-grandparents sent their children to parochial school. Apparently, one day in fifth grade, my grandmother was falsely accused of doing something by one of the nuns. As such, the nun disciplined her with a knuckle-rapping (teachers at that time had a penchant for striking students' knuckles with chalkboard pointers or rulers for punishment). After the incident, my grandmother asked to be excused to the restroom. She left the class and walked right out the doors of the school. She marched down the block to the monolithic public elementary school. She walked in, went straight into the main office, announced herself as a new student, and enrolled herself that day. She went home after school and told her parents what she had done. They were speechless but well aware that the daughter they were raising was destined to be a self-assured and self-reliant young woman.

Irene grew up the daughter of immigrants from Austria and Hungary who had settled in the Chicago area to start their lives anew. Her father owned a mercantile and grocery store on the corner of Cicero and Roscoe Streets. Her parents put her brother Clarence, her sister Martha, and her to work in the store and deli business. They cooked soups and large batches of goulash and noodles, made fried bologna sandwiches for workmen's lunches, and waited on customers at the grocery counter. Those days at the deli counter stuck with my grandmother. She put mayonnaise on every sandwich you could think of. Her abundant use of the condiment was so funny to my brother and me and was definitely something she'd picked up during her days in Chicago.

In her later years, Grandma Irene would always say that certain smells took her right back to those times of her life. For example, her parents' store had a blacksmithing farrier right next door. She said the smell of horses, leather, or metal smelting made her feel ten years old again. It must have been amazing for her growing up, when horses and buggies still predominately roamed the streets. The changes she saw in industry and technology during her lifetime are mind-boggling to me.

In Grandma Irene's late teens and early adulthood, life in Chicago was the epitome of the Jazz Age and the economic prosperity that defined the Roaring '20s. More importantly, however, my grandmother's coming of age occurred during a pivotal time for women's rights. The Nineteenth Amendment had just been ratified (on August 18, 1920), guaranteeing women the right to vote. Hence, it was a time when womanhood was being redefined. Women were now being seen as independent and confident. And Grandma Irene was never shy to tell her grandsons—and not without a little bit of pride—that she was one of those iconic flappers back in the day. She sported all the hallmark accessories of a young woman from that time: the short skirts, the short hair, the clutch purse, the red lipstick, and the cigarettes—accessories that helped recast the national perception of women. It was the basis of the self-confident attitude she would later impart to her grandsons.

Grandma Irene told me about being taken out to restaurants and nightclubs, always running with a fun set of young people in downtown Chicago. While she did revel at parties hosted and attend by Chicago's most rich and fabulous, she also, unfortunately, was witness to gangland violence in the streets where she saw gangsters shoot it out in an alley outside a nightclub one evening. It was a reminder of the dark and seedy side of the bright lights and big city she and others were enjoying.

And Grandma Irene was tough and protective of her family. I remember when I was seventeen, skinny as a rail and a cook at the local Bob's Big Boy, she took charge during a very scary incident. My parents had left town for a few days for one of the few vacations they took without us. On one of those nights after work, I was jumped by three drunk guys in the parking lot. They had earlier been thrown out of the restaurant for being disorderly. I fought my way to my car. Somehow, I got in and turned the ignition. It was then one of the guys kicked the driver-side mirror off with his boot. He began kicking in the window, while one of the others jumped on the hood. I put the car in gear and drove forward, then stopped suddenly, throwing the one off. I then gunned it to get out of there, unintentionally shoving the guy under the car and driving over him. Fortunately for him, it was a forward-drive K-car, and he went harmlessly under the chassis.

Upon arriving home, I was hysterical, crying and shaking as I told Grandma what had happened. Suddenly, she slapped me across the face and told me to focus. I did. She asked if anyone had seen what had happened. I said I didn't think so, 'cause it was so late. She then yelled at my brother to get the hose, a brush, and some soap; she told us to scrub any evidence off the car. She then looked at me, soaking and sobbing, and said that we would never speak of this. Not even to my parents.

"Those dirty birds got what they deserved," she snapped.

Eventually, she relented, letting me call my manager to ask if anything had happened in the parking lot after I left the restaurant. Nothing had. I guess those guys were okay or too ashamed to call 911. Either way, I learned that day not to mess with Grandma. And it made me wonder where in life, and under what circumstances, she had learned to be so tough.

In Chicago, Grandma Irene met her husband, my grandfather, Gilbert Gabrielson, and married him on the eve of the Wall Street Crash of 1929. In what felt like a single instant, all the prosperity and frivolity that Chicago and much of America had come to enjoy came to a screeching halt. Money was lost, businesses went under, and things got tough for a lot of people.

My grandfather had been part of his family's business, a company that built and finished the interiors of restaurants and bars throughout the city. The business never financially recovered from the ensuing deep economic downturn of the Great Depression. But Grandma never let that stop her from making a life. Like everyone at that time, you figured out how to make things work, make things last, and make things stretch. In fact, I don't think any of us today can fathom exactly what things were like back then, and I hope we never will. But she did pass onto my mother (and she, in turn, passed on to my brother and me) those skills of frugality and ingenuity.

My grandparents went on to raise my mother in the suburb of Logan Square, then a heavily Scandinavian neighborhood. The neighborhood was a collection of brick-and-wood row houses in the Chicago style. Mama said the houses had multiple stories and stairs climbing up the back of each. The houses faced a rear alleyway where laundry was hung and children played. It was a good community and remains so to this day, although the Norwegians are long gone.

As was typical of my grandmother, she was an active member of her community. She took on the very important role of a neighborhood preparedness director during World War II. She was responsible for monitoring the emergency readiness of her neighbors and for conducting bombing raid drills (it was thought that the country could be bombed by Germany at any moment, and everyone had to be prepared).

Grandma Irene was mostly a housewife during the years my mother was growing up. Grandma was a great home cook, and my mama has many fond memories of stewed and braised beef, roasted pork, and chicken dinners coupled with mashed potatoes, cauliflower, or rutabaga or some other vegetable prepared in the boiled-to-death Midwestern style of the day.

Irene, being an adventurous cook, expanded her culinary repertoire beyond the Midwest's standard fare. For example, she would make Delta-style tamales, which she learned to make from a woman from Mississippi. These tamales were corny, spicy, and cheesy and then smothered in a rich, red chili-beef sauce and more cheese. They were a labor of love to make but oh so good. Grandma Irene made them for us at home a number of times.

Of course, Grandma Irene also made a lot of the traditional Norwegian dishes my grandfather had grown up with, including Norwegian meatballs. Grandma learned the dish from her mother-in-law, and she then taught Mama, and, subsequently, Mama taught the recipe to my brother and me. It really is a comfort food and a meal I used to love as a boy. I can remember these delectable little orbs would always make an appearance around the holidays. In a chafing dish on a buffet table for a party or served as a course during a special dinner, they could always be counted on for some delicious fun.

As silly as it sounds, a shopping trip to IKEA—where the scent of Swedish meatballs (a very close cousin and rival to the Norwegian variety) from the cafeteria wafts through the air—always reminds me of my Grandma Irene. It is proof that certain foods and people we love can be forever tied to one another and live in our heads and hearts.

Norwegian Meatballs: A Gabrielson Family Recipe

You could say that the classic Midwestern meatball came from the Scandinavians who settled in the middle states. Traditionally, Norwegian meatballs are served with mashed potatoes. In our family, we also serve them with dilled cucumber salad and lingonberry jelly, a Swedish condiment.

Ingredients
For the Meatballs
- 2 eggs, beaten
- 1 cup whole milk
- 1 cup dry bread crumbs (I like crushed Panko)
- 1/2 cup minced onion
- 2 teaspoons salt
- 2 teaspoons sugar
- 1/2 teaspoon ground ginger
- 1/4 teaspoon ground nutmeg
- 1/2 teaspoon ground allspice
- 1/4 teaspoon pepper
- 2 pounds lean ground beef
- 1 pound ground pork

For the Gravy
- 3 Tablespoons butter and meatball drippings
- 5 Tablespoons all-purpose flour
- 4 cups beef broth
- 3/4 cup heavy cream
- Dash cayenne pepper
- A few dashes of white pepper
- 1/4 teaspoon ground nutmeg
- 4 ounces Norwegian brown cheese (optional)

Method

- *In a mixing bowl, combine eggs, milk, bread crumbs, onion, and seasonings. Let stand until crumbs absorb milk. Add meat. Stir until well blended. Shape into 1-in. meatballs. Place on a greased sheet pan. Bake at 400 degrees F until browned, about 30 minutes. Set aside.*
- *For gravy, melt butter and add the drippings over medium-high heat in a large skillet. Stir in flour and brown lightly. Slowly add broth. Cook and stir until smooth and thickened. Blend in cream, cayenne pepper, white pepper, and cheese. Gently stir in meatballs. Heat through but do not boil. Serve with really good mashed potatoes and lingonberry jam.*

Irene's Baked Cauliflower in Mustard and Horseradish Sauce

Cauliflower is an underappreciated vegetable, but with a little love and creativity, it can be awe-inspiring. I love it pureed, and I love it fried. Mostly, I love it in a stupidly rich sauce with cheese! Growing up, I remember Grandma Irene would make baked cauliflower in mustard cream. She usually made it when we had pork chops. I always thought it was a great pairing.

Ingredients

 2 heads cauliflower (or frozen 2-3 bags, about 3 lbs)
 1 Tablespoon cooking oil
 1/2 cup minced peeled onion
 2 cups heavy cream
 2 heaping Tablespoons spicy mustard (Dijon)
 1 1/2 teaspoons prepared horseradish
 1/4 teaspoon nutmeg
 1 Tablespoon freshly chopped rosemary leaves
 1 1/2 teaspoons salt
 1 teaspoon ground black pepper
 3/4 cup "hard" cheese grated (my grandmother used hard-aged Gouda)
 1/2 cup dried breadcrumbs (Panko works well nowadays)

Method

- Cut the cauliflower into small florets.
- Chop up the stems finely and reserve. (If using frozen cauliflower, chop 2 and 1/2 cups of florets)
- Blanch florets in boiling salted water 6 to 8 minutes.
- Quickly cool in a bowl of ice water to stop the cooking. Reserve.
- Sauté the onions in oil until soft, then add chopped stems and cream, and cook together.
- Bring to a boil and simmer until stems are very soft.
- Puree the mixture in a blender and then add in the mustard, horseradish, nutmeg, salt, pepper, rosemary, and 1/4 cup grated hard cheese.
- Mix together with the florets and pour into a buttered baking dish.
- Mix breadcrumbs and remaining cheese, then sprinkle on the top evenly.
- Bake at 350 for 20 to 25 minutes until top is golden and gratin is bubbling.
- Let stand at least 10 minutes before serving.

Lammekjøtt, "Lamb sticks" in Norwegian, is a recipe for lamb shanks with a sour cream dill sauce.

Ingredients
6 lamb shanks
Salt and pepper
3 Tablespoons butter
1 large onion, chopped
1 Tablespoon minced garlic
1 1/2 cup white wine
1 cup beef bouillon
3 Tablespoons flour
3 Tablespoons water
1 pinch of nutmeg, grated
1/4 cup chopped fresh dill, divided
1 Tablespoon turmeric
1 cup dairy sour cream
1/2 cup fresh peas

Method
- Trim excess fat from lamb shanks.
- Wash and pat dry.
- Rub meat with salt and pepper.
- Heat butter in a skillet and brown on all sides.
- Transfer shanks to a Dutch oven.
- Add the onion to the pan drippings and sauté.
- Add the garlic and cook until it blooms.
- Pour the onion with drippings into pot.
- Add wine, bouillon, and 2 Tablespoons of chopped dill, then simmer, covered, over medium low heat for about 1 1/2 hours. Remove shanks from the sauce.

- *Puree sauce and mix flour and water, then stir into the sauce and cook until thickened. Stir in the turmeric. Add the sour cream, nutmeg and dill, then place the lamb shanks into sauce and simmer (do not boil) until warmed through.*
- *Platter shanks and garnish with the sauce, remaining dill, and peas.*
- *Serve with new potatoes or herbed rice and peas and buttered blanched Brussels sprouts.*

Irene's Buttered Herbed Rice and Peas

Ingredients
2 cups water
2 chicken bouillon cubes
5 Tablespoons butter
10 ounces fresh or frozen peas
4 Tablespoons grated hard (Parmesan) cheese
4 slices of bacon, cooked and crumbled
1 Tablespoon white wine vinegar
1 1/4 teaspoons salt
1/8 teaspoon pepper
1/4 cup chopped parsley
2 Tablespoons chopped fresh dill
1 Tablespoon chopped fresh tarragon
3 Tablespoons chopped chives

Method
- *Place water, bouillon cubes, and 2 Tablespoons butter into a pot and bring to a boil.*
- *Stir in rice and cook 20 mins over low heat, covered.*
- *Stir in the next 6 ingredients and cook for 10 minutes until peas are tender and the bacon is soft and all the liquid is absorbed.*
- *Right before serving, stir in the herbs.*

Irene's Beet Salad

Ingredients
- 2 8 ounces jars marinated beet, drained and chopped into small cubes
- 2 red crisp sweet apples, diced same size as the beets
- 1/2 red onion, finely diced
- 6 ounces of Maytag Blue Cheese crumbles (or favorite)
- 1/2 cup chopped pistachio nuts (or walnuts)
- 1/4 cup safflower oil
- 2 ounces sherry vinegar
- 1 Tablespoon sugar
- 1 teaspoon salt
- 1/2 teaspoon black pepper

Method
- Mix the oil, vinegar, sugar, salt, and pepper together and beat until combined.
- Mix everything else in a bowl and add dressing until well dressed and serve into 4 to 6 portions as a first course or on the side with a meal

Norwegian Stuffed Cabbage Rolls with a Spicy Mustard Sauce

Ingredients
16 large Savoy cabbage leaves, blanched
1 large onion, finely diced
1 pound ground beef
1 pound ground pork
1 pound ground ham
2 eggs
1 1/2 cups milk
1 cup roughly chopped pistachios
1 cup bread crumbs
1 teaspoon dried dill
1 teaspoon garlic powder
1 teaspoon ground ginger
1/4 teaspoon nutmeg
1 1/2 cups chicken stock
1 teaspoon salt
1/2 teaspoon pepper

Method
- *Preheat the oven to 320°F (160°C).*
- *Mix all ingredients for the rolls together really well.*
- *Divide the mix between the cabbage leaves.*
- *Fold leaves around the filling and place the packages into a baking dish, seam side down.*
- *Pour the chicken stock into the pan.*
- *Bake for 45 mins in the oven.*

For the Sauce

Ingredients
    4 Tablespoons butter
    4 Tablespoons flour
    2 cups milk
    1 cup Colmans' English Mustard
    6 Tablespoons vinegar
    4 Tablespoons sugar
    1 teaspoon white pepper
    Salt to taste
    2 chicken bouillon cubes dissolved in 1/2 cup water
    4 Tablespoons chopped fresh dill, more to garnish
    Salt and pepper to taste

Method
- Add butter to a small pot and melt, then add flour and stir to make a roux.
- Cook for 3 minutes until the flour has cooked.
- Slowly whisk in the milk until combined, then cook until the mixture has thickened.
- Add mustard.
- Add vinegar.
- Add sugar.
- Add the chicken bouillon and seasoning.

To Serve
- 2 Tablespoons chopped dill for garnish
- Lingonberry jelly
- When the rolls are done, serve the rolls topped with the sauce, and garnish with the remaining parsley and a spoonful of the jelly.

Irene's Beef Liver with Bacon and Onions in Brown Sauce

For kids to like liver is an anomaly. This recipe will make kids and adults alike liver lovers!

Ingredients
   8 cups homemade chicken stock (a good quality purchased stock from a butcher can be used)
   1 bay leaf
   2 sprigs fresh thyme
   Worcestershire sauce to taste
   8 thin slices of calf's liver from the butcher (not frozen)
   Salt and pepper to taste
   1/2 cup flour mixed with some salt and pepper
   4 Tablespoons clarified butter or ghee
   2 to 3 Tablespoons cold butter, cut into small cubes
   4 strips of bacon, cooked and crumbled
   2 medium onions, sliced and cooked carefully in oil until caramelized and soft

Method
- Place chicken stock, the bay leaf, and thyme sprigs with a few dashes of Worcestershire in a pot and bring to a soft rolling boil. Reduce to simmer and cook the stock until it reaches a dark rich color and is reduced to about 2/3 of a cup.
- Watch the pot; you don't want it to burn. This could take 30 to 90 minutes.
- Dredge the liver in the seasoned flour and shake it get rid of any excess.
- In a large frying pan, heat ghee until hot, then add in the liver.
- Do not crowd the pan or liver will steam and not brown. You might have to do this in batches.

- *Cook until just done or the liver will be rubbery, which is what most people hate about liver.*
- *Put the cooked pieces on a warm plate until all are done.*
- *Bring the reduced stock to a boil, then slowly add in the cubes of butter, whisking until it forms a smooth, rich sauce. (This sauce is good on everything: chicken, beef, pork chops).*
- *Plate the liver, then top with the onions and bacon bits.*
- *Spoon the sauce over the top of the liver.*
- *Serve with mashed potatoes and garlicky green beans.*

Danish Layer Cake

This was one of my favorite cakes growing up because it was like jelly crack. It's super sweet and, as an adult, is great with a cup of coffee.

Ingredients
    2 cups all-purpose flour
    1 1/2 cups sugar
    3 teaspoons baking powder
    1/2 teaspoon salt
    1 cup milk
    1/2 cup vegetable shortening
    1 teaspoon vanilla
    1/2 teaspoon vanilla extract
    1/4 teaspoon cinnamon
    1/4 teaspoon nutmeg
    1/4 teaspoon allspice
    5 egg whites

Butter Cream Frosting
    1/3 cup butter
    1 pinch salt
    3 cups confectioners' sugar
    1 Tablespoon allspice
    1 teaspoon pumpkin pie spice
    1/4 cup milk or cream
    11/2 teaspoon vanilla extract
    1 small jar raspberry or blackberry jam
    1 small jar lemon curd
    1 small jar apricot jam

Method

- *Heat oven to 350°F. Grease 2 9-inch round cake pans with shortening. Lightly flour.*
- *In large bowl, beat flour, sugar, baking powder, salt, milk, shortening, vanilla, and spices with electric mixer on low speed until moistened, scraping bowl occasionally.*
- *Then beat on medium speed for 2 minutes, scraping bowl occasionally.*
- *Add egg whites. Beat 2 minutes longer, scraping bowl occasionally.*
- *Pour batter evenly into pans.*
- *Bake 27 to 35 minutes or until toothpick inserted in center comes out clean. Cool in pans for 10 minutes. Remove from pans and place on wire racks. Cool completely, about 1 hour.*

Prepare the frosting

- *In large bowl with mixer on medium-high speed, beat butter, salt, and 1 cup confectioners' sugar for 4 minutes or until pale and fluffy, occasionally scraping bowl with rubber spatula.*
- *Add remaining 2 cups confectioners' sugar alternately with milk, beginning and ending with sugar.*
- *Beat 6 minutes or until very smooth and soft enough to spread. Add in vanilla and allspice and pumpkin pie spice.*

To serve

- *Carefully slice each layer in half through the middle, making 2 separate layers.*
- *Place 1 cake layer, bottom side up, on cake plate. Spread with apricot jam. Top with second half layer, bottom side up. Spread a layer of lemon curd.*
- *Place second cake layer, bottom side up, on the lemon curd, then spread with berry jam. Top with second half layer, top side up.*
- *Spread frosting over sides and top of cake.*

CHAPTER FOURTEEN: FINDING SELF-CONFIDENCE AND A GREEK SALAD

Following years of living in the cold Midwest, my mother's parents resettled in sunny Tampa, Florida. Moving from Chicago to Tampa in the early 1950s meant trading in the big city for a smaller town and frigid winters for Floridian sunshine.

Tampa opened up new worlds for my grandparents, particularly for my grandmother. Yes, she was the daring sort, and that included experimenting with new culinary influences in her kitchen. It was in Tampa that Cuban, Spanish, and Creole foods, and even dishes with Greek origins, made their way into her recipe rotation. More significantly, however, it was in Tampa that the independent nature she exhibited as a young girl reemerged. And it is from this period in Grandma Irene's life that comes a story that taught me to not be afraid of trying, to think on my feet, and to trust in myself, regardless of the odds.

After living in Tampa only a few short years, my grandfather became ill, and Grandma Irene decided that she needed a full-time job to support them. She applied at Maas Brothers, an upscale department store chain. The open position was for an accounting clerk at their flagship store in downtown Tampa. She had some bookkeeping experience—albeit minimal—from working in Chicago, so she felt she could meet the requirements of the job.

During the interview, the hiring manager asked Irene if she knew how to use a new fancy adding machine. Without any hesitation, Irene looked the interviewer straight in the eye and declared she was an expert at using that particular machine. But there was just one problem. Grandma Irene didn't even know what the machine looked like, let alone how to use it. She wasn't going to let those small details, though, get in the way of getting that job. Well, after witnessing Grandma's stellar interview performance and taking note of her qualifications, the manager hired her on the spot.

While moving through the office on her way out, after finishing up all the new employee paperwork, she spied an adding machine that looked like it could quite possibly be the machine in question. She quietly asked one of the other office clerks to confirm that it was. It was!

As luck would have it, it was Friday afternoon. Grandma was to start first thing Monday morning. She would have all weekend to learn how to use that machine, but how? She needed to get her hands on one. So, what did she do? She left the department store and went straight down the block to an office supply company. She asked the sales clerk if they had the adding machine in stock. They did! She then asked if it would be possible for her to rent the adding machine over the weekend, along with its manual. And guess what? They indeed rented it to her, and she spent the entire weekend learning everything there was to know about using it. Monday morning, she went to work and operated the machine like an old pro. No one ever suspected that she had no previous experience with it.

Before my grandfather became ill, my grandparents would often venture outside Tampa, taking daytrips to Tarpon Springs (just an hour north) to spend the day relaxing and deep-sea fishing—a passion my grandfather developed upon moving to Florida.

Tarpon Springs, prior to reinventing itself as a fishing and tourist destination, relied heavily on its natural sponge industry. And because Greece was the birthplace of sponge diving, it is not surprising that many Greek immigrants settled in Tarpon Springs and along Florida's gulf coast in the early 1900s. In fact, to this day, Tarpon Springs has the highest percentage of Greek Americans of any town in the US. As such, Greek culture and culinary traditions strongly influence the region. So it was there, in Tarpon Springs, after a glorious day of fishing, that my grandparents first encountered Louis Pappas's Greek restaurant and the salad he made famous. His Greek salad was unique because, under the greens, was a rich potato salad and, because it was Florida, the salad was garnished with shrimp. The dish became well renowned, spreading quickly all along the Floridian gulf coast. And, in fact, if you order a Greek salad in this part of Florida today, you'll get a Pappas-style Greek salad.

It wasn't until I was a young adult that I encountered the standard Greek salad; it came to the table without the additions of potato salad and shrimp. But I didn't worry about the omissions, because, let's face it, a good Greek salad with all the sharp feta cheese, fresh vegetables, and a rich oregano-scented dressing is just plain delicious. I quickly realized that Greeks bearing the gift of Greek salad—Pappas-style or not—should always be welcomed!

Tampa-Style Greek Salad à la Forrest

This recipe is my version of the Papas Greek salad I grew up eating at home. The secret is the dressing. It is so rich and full and satisfying. The salad makes a great one-dish party meal with some garlic bread, and it can pretty much be done in advance so you can spend more time with your guests. Try to dice everything into uniform-sized pieces. That will make for an impressive presentation.

Ingredients

- 2 cups romaine hearts, finely chopped into a shred
- 4 cups of Greek potato salad (recipe follows)
- 1 red onion, finely diced
- 1 large English cucumber, peeled and diced into cubes
- 2 large tomatoes, chopped into cubes
- 5 Campari tomatoes, cut into quarters reserved
- 1/2 pound snow peas, finely chopped
- 1/2 can beets, drained well and diced
- 12 large shrimp, cooked and peeled
- 1 8 ounces jar Kalamata olives in juice, drained. Most of them sliced, reserve a few for garnish
- 3 radishes, sliced into discs for garnish
- 4 green onions, diced—reserve some for garnish
- 20 ounces feta cheese, diced into small cubes with 1/2 cup reserved for garnish
- 1 8 ounces jar Greek Salonika peppers, drained, 1/2 of the jar chopped, a few reserved whole
- 1 small eggplant, diced into cubes and fried in olive oil until soft and golden
- 1 cup fresh or frozen corn

Best-Ever Greek Salad Dressing (recipe follows)

Greek Potato Salad

This is the base of the salad and what makes a Pappas-style salad unique.

Ingredients
    6 large yellow potato, boiled and cut up
    4 green onions, diced
    1/4 cup parsley, chopped
    1/2 cup finely chopped Kalamata olives
    1/2 cup Greek yogurt or mayo
    1/4 cup red wine vinegar
    2 Tablespoons dried oregano
    2 Tablespoons minced garlic
    Salt and pepper to taste

Method for Potato Salad
- Combine all ingredients in a bowl. Mix everything gently and place in the refrigerator. (Best if made couple of hours before.) Chill well.

Best-Ever Greek Salad Dressing (Ingredients must be exact)

The secret to this salad is the dressing. It can be used for many other uses, including a cold sauce for fish or chicken or mixing into rice or potatoes or vegetables as a side dish.

Ingredients
    1 cup good olive oil
    1/2 cup good sherry vinegar

3 Tablespoons lemon juice
4 small finely chopped large shallots
2 cups finely picked FRESH oregano (must be fresh)
2-3 Tablespoons French's® Yellow mustard (must be French's® Yellow)
Salt and pepper to taste

Method

- Place everything but olive oil and mustard in a food processor and blend well. While running, pour oil slowly in from the top until creamy. Then add mustard by the Tablespoon and blend until emulsified. Taste until the mustard balances out the oil flavor and is bright and rich.

Method for Serving the Salad

- Use a large serving platter.
- Mound the potato salad in the center of the platter.
- Place all ingredients from salad list except the reserved portions of items from list above (green onions, whole olives, feta cubes), the tomato wedges, the radishes, and the shrimp in a bowl.
- In the bowl, dress and mix the salad fixings generously until dressed to your liking. (I prefer it well-dressed but not dripping.)
- Carefully cover the potato salad with the dressed salad, mounding it until the potato salad is hidden.
- Garnish the salad, with the shrimp, then the tomato wedges around as a border, then sprinkle the remaining feta, reserved olives, radishes, and green onions.
- Serve within 30 minutes. When you serve, make sure you dig down to get the potato salad underneath.

CHAPTER FIFTEEN: BIG MAMA'S BIG FAMILY TABLE, VEGETABLES, AND THE PIG

My father was one of eight children. Tail-End Charlie was one of his nicknames, being that he was the youngest of eight and his closest sibling was eight years his senior. Talk about an oops!

My father told me once that whenever he was traveling or away on business (and was feeling lonely or sorry for himself), he would think about his father and mother and the family dinner table. Their table was enormous and could amply fit his family of ten. In fact, it was so big, my grandfather always had Big set the dinner table for fourteen. That meant there were always four extra places at the table for anyone who happened by and needed a meal.

According to my father, those four extra seats were seldom empty. They were occupied by visiting distant relatives, friends of Daddy's brothers and sisters from the country or mountains who were staying with the family in order to go to high school, or stray children my grandfather would pick up by the railroad yard. (The railroad line ended in Walhalla and many runaways mistakenly ended up there while trying to escape whatever fate had pushed them to flee their homes.) Also, when Big's sisters were having troubles with their husbands, they knew they could always find refuge at Big's home (and her table) during the dark times. There were even weekly permanent guests in those dining room chairs. On Wednesdays, for example, there was always one particular gentleman from town sitting at the table. He had The Irish Curse (according to Big) and could not really care for himself. But every Wednesday, he had a hot meal and good family conversation. My father always remembered the kindness shown around that table and how generous his parents were to every person they knew. Charity began at Big's table.

My own memories from that table are strong. At Big Mama's, I remember we would have lunch every day in the dining room on English china with silver flatware. She carried on the grand Southern tradition of late-afternoon supper. Then, like clockwork, she took a nap every day.

You could bet that at every meal there would be some form of The Pig. Ham or sausages, BBQ or a sliced pork roast (usually served cold) were familiar porky friends on the bill of fare. And, of course, something made with buttermilk and Big's famous cornbread made almost daily showings. Looking back, we ate a lot of vegetables, too. Tomatoes, corn, field peas, green beans, greens, and yellow squash always found their way to the table. I think Big's diet was much like this since forever. And that diet served her well. She lived to be ninety-five years old!

When I think about Big, the stories about her and my times visiting her in Walhalla, my mind circles back to so many memories of being young. These memories reveal how our time in Walhalla and Big Mama's house helped my small family of four feel connected to the rest of my father's family, despite being separated from them by many miles for much of the year.

In Walhalla, there were mornings spent poring over the latest magazines, newspapers, and comics, while the adults drank cups of percolated black coffee and discussed the news of the day, my brother and I having breakfast at the big, dark cherry dining table covered with white lace tablecloths and surrounded by chairs with dark rose-and-paisley cushioned seats.

In the afternoons, there was the fresh smell of the bluegrass lawn just mowed—mowed by my brother or me with an old barrel-bladed, hand-pushed, rolling lawn mower. There was the smell of dirt and fertilizer under our fingernails from working in my uncle's garden next door.

I remember Big Mama cooking up the best lunches and suppers. For my brother and me, there were always beans to be snapped, potatoes to be peeled, corn to be shucked, or pecans to crack open.

I have memories of my Aunt Lucy, my dad's sister who moved in and lived with Big after her husband was killed in "Dubya Dubya Two" (as it comes out in a deep Southern drawl). I remember my father and mother sitting with Big, Lucy, and various adult friends, neighbors, and other relatives in the living room, visiting in the afternoons, memories filled with the cigarette smoke-filled living room's rose-colored walls, the dining room's patterned wallpaper, the coffee table with its pile of magazines and cut-glass candy dishes filled with nuts or peppermints.

I can see Big sitting in her large, off-white, wood-framed armchair with flowering branches on the fabric, her feet up on the brass-riveted, ribbon-wrapped footstool. I can remember my brother and I waiting for her to finish napping upstairs in the afternoon heat so we could do something together.

I would read from my aunt's copious collection of historical fiction under the soft, yellow light cast by old lamps with lacy shades well into the evening. We would discuss the stories the next day; Aunt Lucy would grill me about the details.

I remember the smell of stone and summer dew when I would sleep in the damp basement, lying in metal twin beds with faded cotton sheets and quilted blankets adorned with the images of cowboys. My brother slept across the room, and the old air conditioner whirred gently in the background.

For me, Big Mama's house was filled with laughter, grown-up conversations, tasty Southern food, excellent books, afternoon naps, and love.

I'm right back in Big's kitchen every time I catch the loping whirl of an electric mixer and that distinctive smell of burning metal and rubber that rises from an overworked motor when mixing batter, when I hear the crisping of bacon in a skillet on the stovetop or smell the cooking of cornbread in a cast-iron pan or detect the scent of a ham glazing in the oven on a holiday. These are the memories, along with the tastes and smells and stories, that are Big's food heritage to me. I see her (and my father) smiling down from Heaven every time I make one of these things. She is somehow present and still ringing the small, silver dinner bell that called her family all together. I just love the memory of being with her and the feeling of belonging.

Belonging to a past.

Belonging to a place.

Belonging to a family.

Oven-Smoked Pork Butt BBQ (Serves 30)

Few things say Southern more than BBQ. This recipe makes some amazing pork, and it could not be easier. It's how I learned to make BBQ at home without a fancy smoker.

Ingredients
Take 16 pounds of pork shoulder, bone in

Mix together
- 2 cups yellow mustard
- 1/2 cup brown sugar
- 2 Tablespoons smoked paprika
- 1/4 cup garlic powder
- 3 teaspoons liquid smoke
- 2 Tablespoons salt
- 1 Tablespoon pepper
- 1/2 cup water

Method
- Slather rub all over the pork shoulder and place in the fridge for at least five hours to overnight.
- Preset oven to 220 degrees.
- Place shoulder in roasting pan, fat pad side up, and cover with tin foil.
- Roast overnight for 12 hours (easy while you sleep; start cooking at 8 p.m., be done by 8 a.m. with your coffee).
- Remove from the oven and cool. Reserve drippings. (They are salty.)
- Remove the fat pad. Shred pork and remove bones. Skim fat off the drippings and use to moisten the pork.

- *Mix well with the some of the drippings, tasting for salt, then place in an ovenproof pot with a lid.*
- *Before serving, mix in 2-3 cups BBQ sauce of choice and heat in the oven until warmed through at 275 degrees for about 1 hour or so.*
- *Serve with good Southern coleslaw, more sauce, sliced dill pickles, and soft buns.*

A Tasty Southern Coleslaw

(Makes enough for 6 sandwiches)

You can use all green cabbage if you like to make this as a side dish, but I use a red cabbage mix when I want it as a topping for sandwiches.

Ingredients
Dressing
- 1/3 cup mayonnaise
- 2 Tablespoons buttermilk
- 1 teaspoon apple cider vinegar
- 3 Tablespoons dill pickle relish, drained
- 2 teaspoons horseradish, drained
- 1 teaspoon regular brown sandwich mustard
- 1/2 teaspoon sugar
- 1 teaspoon celery seed
- Salt and pepper to taste

Salad
- 2 cups finely shredded purple cabbage
- 1 1/2 cups finely shredded green cabbage
- 1/2 cup very finely shredded carrots
- 1/2 cup chopped parsley
- 1/4 cup finely chopped scallions

Method
- Mix all ingredients for the dressing together in a large mixing bowl.
- Add the salad fixings into another bowl and mix well.
- Toss with dressing right before serving.

Big's Baked Creamed Corn (Almost)

I added some spices and Panko bread crumbs because they are easier and crunchier than fresh ones. Big didn't use cheese, but I prefer the taste of the Parmesan in this dish.

Ingredients
- 8 to 9 ears of fresh corn (Can use frozen corn in off-season), about 4 cups
- 2 teaspoons minced garlic
- 1 pinch of dried thyme
- 1 bay leaf
- 1 small Vidalia onion or sweet onion, finely chopped
- 2 cups heavy cream
- 2 Tablespoons sugar
- 1 bay leaf
- 1 Tablespoon butter
- 6 ounces grated Parmesan cheese
- 1/4 cup Panko bread crumbs (Big's recipe called for soft fresh crumbs)
- 1 good dash of cayenne pepper
- 1/8 teaspoon white pepper
- Salt to taste
- 1 scallion, finely sliced for garnish

Method
- Cut kernels from the corncobs and scrape the "milk" from the cobs into a small bowl. Hold aside.
- Melt butter in a pot and cook onion and garlic and thyme until very soft.
- Add the cream, half the corn, the cobs, and the bay leaf. Bring to a low simmer.

- *Stirring mixture so it does not boil or burn, cook until the corn is soft and the cream thick, about 20 minutes. Remove the cobs and bay leaf.*
- *Remove pot from heat and place in a blender, blending until smooth.*
- *Return to pot and add the rest of the corn.*
- *Cook until soft, about 30 minutes.*
- *Season with salt and pepper.*
- *Mix crumbs and cheese together.*
- *Place in a casserole, top with the cheese and breadcrumbs, then bake until melted and bubbling and slightly browned.*
- *Top with the scallion slices.*
- *Serve hot.*

"Sufferin Succotash Salad"

Succotash is one of those iconic Southern vegetable dishes. These ingredients were always on Big's table. This is my version of succotash.

Ingredients
    2 1/2 cups corn, fresh or frozen
    2 cups lima beans, blanched and softened
    2 cans drained seasoned field peas from a can
    1/2 cup chopped bacon (don't use if you want this only vegetables)
    1/2 cup chopped red onion
    1 cup diced seeded Roma tomatoes
    1 seeded red pepper, diced
    1/2 cup finely chopped celery
    1/2 cup finely chopped parsley
    1/2 cup finely chopped scallions
    1 cup nuts (your choice)

Hot Dressing
    3/4 cup warmed bacon drippings
    1 large or two small shallots, very finely minced
    3/4 cup salad oil
    1/4 cup red wine vinegar
    3 Tablespoons Creole or brown mustard
    1 Tablespoon mayo
    1 Tablespoon sugar
    2 Tablespoons honey
    1 teaspoon garlic powder
    1 teaspoon salt
    1/2 teaspoon pepper
    1/4 teaspoon cayenne pepper

Method

- *Mix everything for the dressing really well and warm in a saucepot.*
- *Melt 2 Tablespoons of butter and 2 Tablespoons of water in a large pan and add corn and both beans. Drain before adding to other ingredients.*
- *Gently warm the vegetables.*
- *Right before serving, mix everything together and dress vegetables with the hot dressing. Add parsley and serve.*

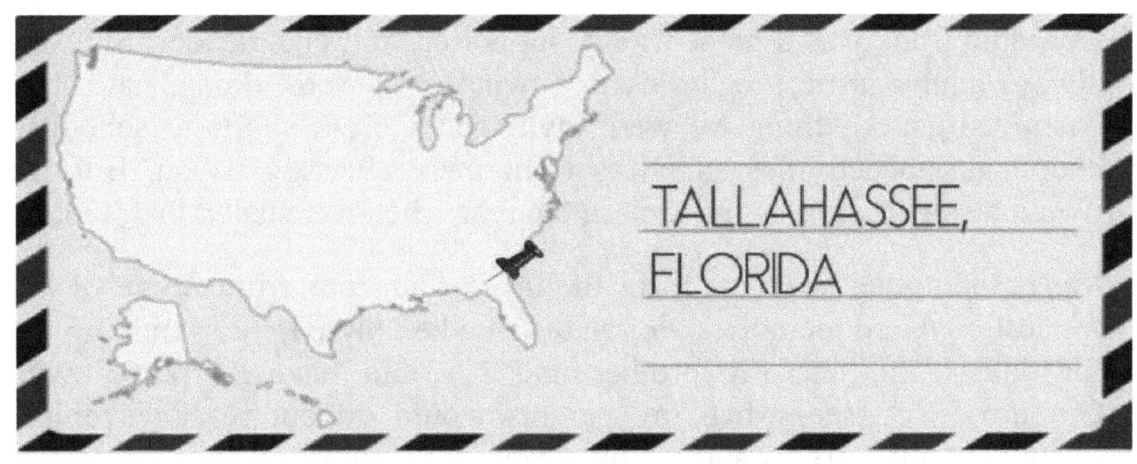

CHAPTER SIXTEEN: GIVING BACK AND FRIED CHICKEN WITH GRAVY

While Big Mama taught me about great Southern food and how the family table is an opportunity to share one's bounty with those less fortunate, Grandma Irene taught me lessons I hold equally dear. She taught me about the importance of self-reliance as well as charity. And because she was an integral part of our family (remember, she lived with us since I was in second grade), she conveyed her lessons daily—not through lecturing but by example.

Grandma Irene taught me how to make everything from amazing mashed potatoes to Norwegian Christmas cookies to the world's best pan gravy. Mama could never make gravy quite like Grandma could. Making good gravy is not about following an exact recipe. Instead, it's all about intuition, improvisation, and patience. Grandma knew exactly what to add to the pan, how much, and when. Never rushing, she would often equate gravy-making to life. She would tell my brother and me that things happen when they are supposed to and that we must be patient for the final result; the more effort, care, and love we put into something, the better it is in the end. Just like gravy!

Grandma Irene was a great friend, supporter, and cheerleader. She was always enthusiastic, regardless of what we were doing, and that energized us. Anything we were involved in, from sports to school to church group activities, she was right there cheering us on. But she would also give us a loving kick in the rear when we needed that, too.

My grandmother was just a lot of fun to hang out with. Some of my fondest boyhood memories are related to when my parents would go out for date night, and my brother and I would have "a party" with Grandma. You see, when my parents would go out for an evening, Grandma would fix us something yummy for supper. It was the 1970s, so sometimes that took the form of frozen TV dinners. My brother and I loved them, mostly because we never had them. All your food cooked up in a little metal tray at the same time in the oven. It almost seemed magical! Looking back, it's horrifying to think we thought those dinners were so good, but to us then they were really a special treat (probably because we never had to eat them day-in and day-out like some kids did).

After dinner, Grandma would pop popcorn with loads of butter and salt. She'd let us sit on her bed and we'd watch the weekend TV lineups with her, lineups that included *The Love Boat, Fantasy Island, The Brady Bunch, The Partridge Family*, and *Donny & Marie*. Or we might just play cards for hours, listening to big band music and telling silly stories.

As an adult, one of the things I learned about my Grandma Irene was that she felt that it's not just enough to have gratitude for the blessings in your life. Doing something to show what it is you are grateful for is also very important. It's about acting grateful not just being grateful.

And what she did before she came to live with us in Hawaii taught me one of the greatest lessons about giving back she would ever teach.

Shortly after my grandfather died, Grandma made a life-changing decision to give up that secure job as the bookkeeper for Maas Brothers in Tampa and to move to a place she had never been to, to do something she had never done. Change was part of who my grandmother was. She'd given up her longstanding relationship with the Catholic church for membership at the Bayshore United Methodist Church when she and my grandfather moved to Florida. Interestingly, that switch ended up playing a key role in determining where Grandma took her life after my grandfather passed. You see, at church one Sunday, Grandma Irene heard that a Methodist school for disadvantaged teenage girls in Thomasville, Georgia, was looking for a dietician. Upon hearing of the opportunity—despite never having been to Vashti (the school in need) or to Thomasville, for that matter—my grandma was moved to help. She explained to my parents that she had always wanted to do something to give back for what she had received in life. To be of service to those who were in need.

Now Grandma knew a lot about food and cooking, having grown up in the grocery and catering business in Chicago, and she knew a lot about children. But, she had never been a dietician. As you can imagine, this didn't stop my grandma. Taking a leap of faith, she applied for the position and got an interview. Grandma impressed the headmaster so much, she was offered the job.

For a recent widow in the 1950s to leave a secure job and do something so completely new in a place she'd never been just seemed crazy to most people. However, my parents were very supportive so off she went. It was a lesson in a walk of faith.

When you think of schools for wayward children, you probably have some Dickensian visual of gray-clad children shuffling about with military precision and factory-like buildings with chimneys belching smoke into overcast skies. Vashti was nothing like that. It was a shade-covered collection of stone-and-brick buildings, one-, two-, and three-stories tall. Old oak trees with Spanish moss hanging gently from the boughs and swaying in the breeze dappled the landscape. It was the nicest home a young girl without a family could have hoped for. And for a little boy, one visiting his grandma, it was equally as nice. Each visit meant lots of attention from those girls. I loved it!

Over time, Irene became an integral part of Vashti and its mission of caring for teenage girls who were having a rough time in life. She influenced her charges by putting them to work in the kitchen so they could find a sense of purpose. Grandma also offered a compassionate ear when a girl needed someone to simply listen. And, of course, Grandma also provided a good, swift kick in the rear, figuratively speaking, if it was so deserved.

One day, Grandma noticed that one of the girls who had come in to set up for dinner was very upset.

Grandma asked, "What's the matter?"

The girl answered, "I just received a letter from my mother, and she says that I can't come home for the upcoming holiday because her current boyfriend doesn't like me, and she needs to keep him happy."

The girl—turning away to hide the tears swelling up in her eyes—said, "Mrs. Gabrielson, I'm so mad I just want to hit something."

Grandma thought a moment and, looking around the kitchen, picked up a dinner plate and handed it to the girl. She instructed, "Take this plate outside into the backyard, behind the kitchen, and break it on that big rock near the woods."

The girl took the plate and left. Grandma noticed that one of the cooks was staring at her with a horrified expression. Grandma shrugged and said, "What's wrong? It's the cheapest therapy I could think of." The cook shook her head and went back to her business.

Moments later there was a scream and the sound of breaking ceramic.

Soon, the girl returned and from her expression, all her anger had dissipated. She thanked Grandma and went back to her task in the dining room.

I think everyone has felt like that girl before, and Grandma helped her get through it with as little damage as possible.

Grandma served at Vashti for years and consulted as a dietician with many other schools in the Methodist system around the country. She was well loved and respected. And even after retiring and coming to live with us in Hawaii, she continued to look for ways to make a difference.

In Hawaii, she discovered that there was no social club for senior citizens on the island of Oahu where we were living. Working with the local government, she started one. She announced it through an ad in the newspaper. Less than half a dozen people showed up for that first meeting. However, when we left four years later, that group had grown to over two hundred members. Grandma taught me that it's not where in life one may find oneself, it's what you do there that matters. It's a lesson that continues to humble and inspire me to this day.

Grandma Irene taught me much of what I know about showing love through food. She demonstrated that to our family as well as to the church groups to which she belonged, to her catering clients, and to the schools where she worked and consulted. She gave of herself—and made a difference—amazingly often through food.

Grandma Irene was a constant example of what strength and self-reliance can do for one's quality of life. My father said she was an honorary Southern belle, in the truest sense of the word. She was gracious, kind, and well-spoken; she never compromised her values and she always was thinking of family (and expanded the definition of family to include those with whom she worked and served).

Fried Chicken and Cream Gravy

It's funny my home-fried chicken recipe is from my Northern grandmother! This fried chicken was always made in the oven or fried in a countertop electric skillet.

Ingredients
    1 whole chicken cut up into 10 pieces (breasts cut in half on the bone)

Brine
    1 cup of water
    1 cup dill or other pickle juice
    2 cups lowfat buttermilk
    3 Tablespoons soy sauce
    1 stem of rosemary, very finely chopped
    2 Tablespoons salt
    1 Tablespoon garlic powder
    1 Tablespoon onion powder
    1 Tablespoon hot sauce (I use Frank's RedHot® sauce)

For Oven Frying:
    1 cup vegetable shortening such as Crisco®

Method
- Place chicken in container. Mix all ingredients and pour over chicken, making sure it's covered. Add water if you must. Let it sit in refrigerator at least 4 hours but best overnight.
- When ready to start, remove chicken from brine (discard brine) and place on a drip tray and let sit in the fridge for about another hour.
- Remove chicken from refrigerator.

- *Make wet mix*
    - *1/2 cup buttermilk*
    - *3 eggs*
    - *1 teaspoon salt*
- *Make dry dredge*
    - *1 1/2 cups flour*
    - *1/2 Tablespoon sweet paprika*
    - *2 teaspoons garlic powder*
    - *2 teaspoons onion powder*
    - *4 teaspoons white pepper*
    - *1 teaspoon lemon pepper*
    - *1 teaspoon salt*
- *Remove chicken from the fridge. Drain and pat dry.*
- *Next, dip a few pieces of chicken at a time into the wet mixture, then dredge in the dry. You can do this in a paper bag, shaking the chicken until coated. Shake off excess coating.*
- *Let sit on the drip tray at room temperature for no more than 30 minutes.*
- *Add 1 cup shortening in baking pan and place in oven heated to 425 degrees until melted. Remove from oven.*
- *Add chicken slowly, skin side down, to pan carefully, trying not to crowd the chicken.*
- *Cook in a 425 oven for 30 minutes.*
- *With metal spatula, turn and cook another 30 minutes.*
- *Watch chicken so it does not get too dark.*
- *Remove chicken from the oven and place on paper towels before serving.*

To make gravy
- *Transfer pan drippings to a pot, then add 1 cup milk and 4 Tablespoons butter to the chicken drippings.*
- *Mix 1/2 cup milk with 3 Tablespoons of flour and stir until smooth.*
- *Add milk mixture slowly to the pot and stir in.*
- *Add to this 1 Tablespoon white pepper and 2 teaspoons dried thyme. Add a big splash of sherry or Madeira wine.*

- *Cook until thickened and bubbly, about 5 minutes.*
- *Add salt to taste.*
- *Serve with warm chicken.*

Irene's Mashed Potatoes

Ingredients
    2 pounds of Yukon Gold or German Butterball potatoes (any thin-skinned potato will do), cut into 2-inch chunks
4 cups chicken or veggie broth, canned or bouillon
2 sprigs of rosemary, finely chopped
3 garlic cloves, crushed
1/2-3/4 cup heavy cream or milk
1/2 cup sour cream
4 ounces cream cheese at room temperature
1 stick of butter plus 2 Tablespoons
1/2 cup chopped chives

Method
- *Place the potatoes. garlic, rosemary, and cold broth in a large pot and bring to a boil. Cook about 25 minutes or until soft.*
- *Drain the potatoes and return to the pot.*
- *Add the butter, cream cheese, and the cream slowly, then the sour cream as you mash the potatoes with a masher until creamy. Season to taste with salt and pepper. Add the chives right before serving. Place in a large bowl and top with the leftover butter and let melt on top for a dramatic look of buttery goodness.*

Additions: If you want to change up your potatoes, you can skip the chives and add in dill, which is very Nordic. I like to add truffle oil (oil to taste), which is a decadent addition but a delicious one.

SECTION THREE

ON BEING A SOUTHERNER

Chapter Seventeen: My Southern Self and Pimento Cheese

I love being from the South, but it is a complicated relationship. As a modern, educated individual, I have my problems with some things associated with the South, her history, and her ideologies. But, equally, I have a problem with the way people from outside the South sometimes view her.

Every Southerner has a personal and private struggle, as well as an immense sense of pride about what being Southern means to them. Being from the South represents so many things. She's a multifaceted lady. People say she's been morally questionable, and that she's been good and gracious. She will embrace you in her mystery on the one hand, and then, with the other, slap you with her conservative backhand. She will dazzle you with her charm yet smother you in her history. And one thing is for sure, she will never bore you. As my cousin always says, "Yankees keep their crazy relatives locked up in an attic. Southerners like to trot them out into the middle of a party just to see what will happen." Keeps it interesting.

Plenty of folks have written about the South and Southern foods, and I can't pretend that I have something new or startling to add. I will say that, by exploring my personal food heritage, I have come to see that many of my stories and experiences are tightly connected to those of the South.

Of the many things you can say about the South (regardless of your take on her), she remains a truly unique cultural island in an America where commercialized experiences are encroaching on our unique and individual cultural fabric and are homogenizing people, places, and things. From ingrained rural dialects to the customs and the food, the American South has a rich and diverse history. It's perhaps that constant sense of history that keeps Southern people, well, Southern.

Being a Southerner gives me a sense of where I come from. I connect to the South's history and traditions. They are familiar and comfortable to me. This connection to history grounds me in a manner that is hard to describe. It has little to do with Dixie and the sad story for all Americans that led to the Civil War and more to do with having a compass point by which I can find my way to myself. Many a Southerner will tell you that it is this sense of past that somehow remains important to Southerners today. It is the starting point for self-definition.

As a Southerner, I have a love of old things. My hometown Charleston is considered very old by American standards. Some of the older buildings in Charleston appear to just sprout up out of the ground. Brick, mortar, wood, and stone rise up as if the earth itself was organically producing them. The masonry and architecture, giving the structures a life of their own, breathe life into a city that teems with history and tradition. That sense of age, time, and history is what is alluring about Charleston and the South in general. It gives me a sense that I belong to a great, very old, yet still unfolding story.

Southerners who move to other places, bringing their cuisine and hospitality with them, might have a story similar to this one. When I first came to New York, I was trying to be an actor. And I was poor, always. One weekend, my roommate and I decided to throw an early-evening cocktail party. After spending the majority of our money on booze, we found ourselves perplexed as to what kind of party foods we could serve that would be slightly more interesting than store-bought hummus and pita.

We had invited some twenty people, and knew the party would last well into the dinner hour. So I decided to make a bunch of pimento cheese sandwiches. My roommate was unfamiliar with this Southern staple. I explained that it's a dish that's traditionally served at celebrations and gatherings, and that some folks would consider it as iconic as deviled eggs and fried chicken are to Southern cuisine. Any real Southern cook should know how to make it. She was not impressed with my explanation.

Despite my roommate's lack of confidence, I made a batch of the cheese spread, got loaves of cheap white bread, and assembled the sandwiches. I cut off the crusts to be fancy, then cut them in quarters to make them fancier still—little tea sandwiches. (My roommate admittedly thought they were darling.) I made platefuls. And that, with bowls of potato chips and onion dip (concocted from dry soup mix, so good!), was the food for our gathering. Don't you know, every single one of those sandwiches disappeared? They were a real hit. Or maybe that living room was full of aspiring young actors and artists who were just drunk and hungry.

A Damn Good Pimento Cheese Recipe

I grew up around pimento cheese, which is sometimes referred to as "the caviar of the South" or "house pâté" by the famous Southern food icon, Natalie Dupree. At its best, it's a delicious concoction of simple ingredients that, somehow, when taken together, are amazing. It can be used in sandwiches and other cooked foods that use cheese as an ingredient, such as grits or casseroles. There is often debate as to what goes into the spread. I think almost everyone can agree that no matter how it's made, it's mostly just delicious.

Ingredients
1 1/4 cups shredded extra sharp yellow cheddar cheese
1 cup shredded yellow Colby cheese
4 ounces room temperature cream cheese
3/4 cups Duke's mayonnaise
1/4 teaspoon garlic powder
1/4 teaspoon cayenne pepper
2 good shakes of Worcestershire sauce
2 Tablespoons grated sweet onion
2 4 ounce jars pimentos, drained and diced, with 1 Tablespoon of juice reserved
Salt and pepper to taste

Method
- *Basically, place everything except the 1 cup of Colby cheese in a food processor and lightly pulse until just combined. Do not over-mix. Place in a bowl and mix in the last cup of cheese well by hand. Chill about an hour before serving.*

FORREST HEDDEN

"Pineapple Pimento Mess" or Scalloped Pineapple Casserole

Nothing else but this casserole goes with your Easter ham. This strange sounding collection of ingredients comes together to make something special. Many a Southern table is blessed by a version of this pineapple mess. Church and community cookbooks all over the South are full of different versions of this dish. This is ours. It's super delicious.

Ingredients

    1 15 ounce can pineapple chunks in juice
    1 15 ounce can crushed pineapple
    1 cup sugar
    6 Tablespoons self-rising flour
    1 jar red pimento
    2 cups shredded extra sharp yellow cheddar cheese
    1 sleeve Ritz crackers, crushed
    1/2 cup butter

Method

- *Preheat oven to 350 degrees.*
- *Toss drained pineapple chunks in a bowl with sugar and flour.*
- *Chop pimento and add to pineapple.*
- *Stir in crushed pineapple and then cheese.*
- *Pour into a 9 x 13 inch casserole.*
- *Mix crackers with butter and layer on top of pineapple mixture.*
- *Bake for 25 minutes and let stand a bit before serving.*

CHAPTER EIGHTEEN: SKELETONS IN A SOUTHERN CLOSET MAKE FOR SPICY STORIES AND A HOT CONDIMENT

I don't know about you, but I am pretty sure that every family has secrets. Sometimes, they are dark and unpleasant, and, sometimes, they are funny. Sometimes, they are the answers to questions that were always silently asked but never openly discussed.

In my family, questions about my daddy's father—his birth and childhood—had always raised eyebrows. Little was known about my grandpa's mother. My grandpa rarely spoke about her or his childhood. By the time he died, all his relatives had passed on.

So, the truth about my grandpa's background was never really known to his children until shortly before Big Mama's death. Before she died, she brought to light a story she had never shared about her husband's origins, putting an end to the secrets. As her story unfolded, an entire generation of truths—always previously shrouded in mystery—emerged.

Big Mama had been married to my grandfather for over twenty-two years when he died. And when he passed on, he left her with eight children to raise on her own. Somehow she did it—and got them all college-educated to boot! My father always said Big had more true grit than anyone he had ever known. She rode out the Great Depression better than most, including being able to always employ a cook and a handyman, but no one could quite understand how she had done it during those challenging years. Then came this revelation.

In late 1884, an English lord and his son, along with an entire contingent of other English gentleman farmers, made an agrarian tour of the American South. One of the large farms that they visited was the Hedden farm in northwest Georgia. Hedden was the surname of my great-great-grandfather. He was, by all accounts, a prosperous and successful agriculturalist in his own right.

Well, as Big recounted to my daddy and his siblings, the British visit left more than goodwill behind. Shortly afterwards, it was discovered that Hannah Hedden, my great-grandmother, was pregnant. The scandalous nature of this discovery sent the family reeling in defense of their reputation.

Hannah was immediately shipped off to relatives in Macon County, North Carolina, to have the baby in secret. To keep the family name intact, she returned without the child. The infant child, a boy, was eventually brought back home to Georgia and was raised by his mother Hannah and her sister, who, in society, were referred to as his aunts. His name was Julius Fredrick Hedden. His parentage was never discussed, and the family thus avoided scandal.

Hannah's father contacted the English lord to demand restitution immediately after learning his daughter was with child, requiring the lord to honor his obligation to the child his son had helped conceive. The English family set up a trust with a law firm in Greenville, South Carolina, stipulating that their name never be disclosed, and payments would be paid to the trust to support the child and his future family. The payments would cease upon Julius's death and the death of his spouse.

So for years, Big made the monthly trip to Greenville, always under the guise of "doing business." No one was exactly sure what kind of business she was doing nor did anyone ask, but somehow she always had enough money to see things through.

This was quite a revelation—especially because in the later years of Big's life, all her children had sent money to help support her. Little had they known the support she already got from the English family and how that support had kept the family afloat for all those years.

Before she died, Big Mama called her children together and told this very story. The story deflated my Aunt Leoah's accounts of our untarnished Southern family history. She had grand tales about how we were related to this person or that person. Her biggest point of pride was that we were linked by blood to Nathan Bedford Forrest, a famous Confederate general who was a somewhat infamous political figure and whose reputation is akin to the dichotomy that was the post-Civil War South. This and all her other stories were now debunked.

She and my Aunt Doris were also horrified by the fact that, if this story were true, we did not know our family's roots. Worse yet, their daddy had been a bastard child! They tried very hard to persuade their brothers not to say anything about it, but I think it's a better story than any that my very imaginative aunts ever came up with.

Southerners make me realize what an interesting and truly delicious heritage I have to draw from, and what a community of history and humor I belong to. Old, dark, and steeped in tradition and memory, it's either a great place to call home or a great place to be from. Regardless, it's a delicious place to call one's own.

Pepper Jelly: A Spicy Southern Condiment

While I believe this recipe is originally from Big, I am not 100 percent sure. I do know that my Aunt Lucille gave it to my mother. In any event, it's a delicious and spicy condiment, and can be easily canned and given away as gifts.

Ingredients
    1 1/2 pounds sweet peppers (green or red)
    1/4 diced hot peppers, seeds removed
    6 1/2 cups sugar
    1 1/2 cups apple cider vinegar
    1 bottle of certo (pectin)

Method
- *Place peppers in blender and add enough water to make a paste.*
- *Add the sugar and vinegar and, again, blend.*
- *Place into a stockpot and cover (careful of fumes).*
- *Bring to a boil for about 5 minutes.*
- *Add the pectin and boil another minute.*
- *Remove from heat and let sit for 5 minutes.*
- *Pour into sterilized jars (boiled and hot) and seal.*

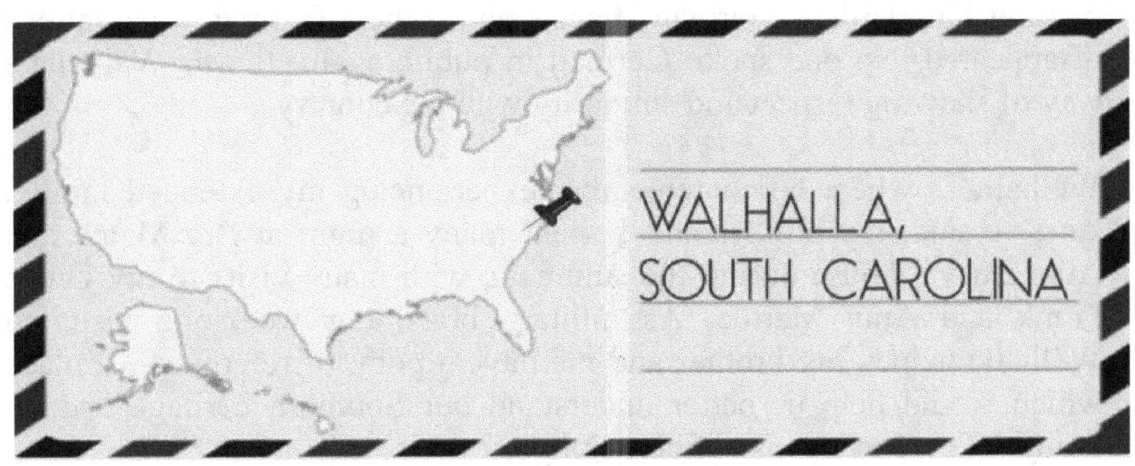

Chapter Nineteen: Walhalla, South Carolina, and Potato Salad

South Carolina is divided into three regions: Low Country (the coast and coastal plains of the southeast), Midlands (the middle of the state), and Upstate (the high plateaus and mountains of the northwest). They each have a rivalry with one another, but neither the Upstate nor the Low Country regions have much good to say about the Midlands. Columbia is the state capital and sits squarely in those Midlands. Big Mama, whose roots were in the Upstate, used to say that the only thing between Columbia and Hell was a screen door.

When Big and my grandfather, Julius, married, they lived and started their family in Walhalla, in the Upstate's Oconee County in the foothills of the Blue Ridge Mountains. There, my grandfather was a partner in the resort hotel business and an investor in the textile trade. Oh, and he was a veterinarian as well. Talk about multitasking!

Walhalla was a town settled by Germans and named after Valhalla, the home of the god Odin in German and Norse mythology. Until World War II, my father regularly heard German spoken in his town. Based upon my father's account, the day after FDR declared war on Germany (which was just days after the Japanese bombing of Pearl Harbor), all pictures of Hitler, German flags, and other German decorations disappeared. No one spoke German in public again. It was Walhalla's way of showing respect and solidarity with the country.

Walhalla is where I first remember experiencing my extended family. As I've said, my brother and I spent many a night at Big Mama and Aunt Lucy's house during the summers, with many visits to my Uncle Frank and Aunt Martha. As military brats, our weeklong visits to Walhalla helped my brother and me have a point of reference—a place which would help us better understand our Southern heritage and, in doing so, give us a sense of belonging.

Walhalla is one of God's great places, with natural beauty abounding. Just up the mountain from town is Oconee State Park with a lake for swimming, boating, and fishing. Nearby, there are mountains to explore and cool, dark swimming holes along the creeks for skinny-dipping. Long country walks were common in the late afternoons, and there were limitless blueberries to pick along the way for pie-making. And in late summer, the pecans would fall right off the trees into our eager hands.

Our days with my father's family were filled with trips to the homes of family friends, lunches, and dinners with people I barely knew but was somehow related to, trips to local historical sites with Aunt Lucy, gardening in the field next to Big Mama's house, or hikes with our cousins to waterfalls in the mountains. Uncle Frank would also sometimes put us to work, helping him bottle up wine he made in his shed. Sometimes, Aunt Lucy would take us to art shows or to the Dairy Queen for ice cream after dinner. On the weekends, there were BBQs at the local Veterans of Foreign Wars post and square dancing at a barn up the mountain near town.

My Aunt Lucy was an accomplished and somewhat known regional watercolorist. Many of her paintings—still lifes and local landscapes—grace the walls of my mama's house, as well as those of other relatives.

I can still see Aunt Lucy coming out of her bedroom for coffee and cereal in the mornings, wearing her white robe with pink flowers on it, her short, dark hair pulled back. Then sitting at the large, dark, and polished-cherry wood dining table, she'd light up a cigarette to go with her paper and coffee and eat her breakfast, commenting all the while (in her purposeful Southern drawl) about the news of the day.

After breakfast and before the other meals of the day, my brother and I often would sit on the worn, old wooden back-porch swing when tasked with snapping beans and husking corn. We would pick tomatoes in the garden and eat fresh corn and ham for lunch.

Besides spending time at Big Mama's, visiting Walhalla always meant time at my Uncle Frank and Aunt Martha's house. They lived in a charming blue-and-white house that had a big yellow kitchen, a white brick mantel around the fireplace, and a warmly colored dining room. My Uncle Frank had a farm—Big Garden—next door to Big's house. There, my brother and I learned from him all about basic farming chores, killing snakes and rats, and cursing. Uncle Frank also took us deer hunting in the nearby woodlands. We had a lot of fun, as little boys will.

Dinners at Uncle Frank and Aunt Martha's were always something special and unexpected for my brother and me. It did not have to be a special holiday for my uncle and aunt to put out an enormously wonderful meal. During the summers, one of the hallmark dishes that I remember was my uncle's yellow warm potato salad (it is the world's best, ever). We just called it "Uncle Frank's potato salad." In fact, when my mother got the recipe from my uncle, she often would fix it at home. When announcing dinner, she would proclaim, "We are having ham... and Uncle Frank's potato salad!" Upon hearing my mama's pronouncement, I knew we were about to have a meal that would take me back to my time spent in Walhalla with people who helped me to understand my Southern self.

Uncle Frank's Potato Salad

Uncle Frank, who was quite the gourmet cook in the family, made this extraordinary potato salad. It was a slightly warm, savory potato salad made with a generous amount of French's® Yellow mustard. The usual ingredients are there, but he added a few unique steps and ingredients. My cousin Martha, Frank's daughter, recalls it as a very spicy Southern potato salad. It was very good. The recipe that follows is from my mother's recipe collection.

Ingredients

    4 1/2 pounds Yukon Gold potatoes, washed and sliced into cubes
    1 1/2 cups diced large red onion
    1/2 cup dill pickle juice from a jar of pickles
    6 eggs, very finely diced (almost mashed up into paste)
    3/4 cups of celery finely, diced
    1/2 cup scallions, finely sliced (2 Tablespoons reserved for garnish)
    1/2 cup parsley, finely diced (2 Tablespoons reserved for garnish)

Dressing

    2/3 cup French's® Yellow mustard
    1 cup mayonnaise
    1/4 cup buttermilk
    3 Tablespoons apple cider vinegar
    4 Tablespoons hot melted bacon drippings (leave out if you want vegetarian version)
    4 heaping Tablespoons drained sweet pickle relish
    2 Tablespoons prepared horseradish
    2 teaspoons garlic powder
    1 teaspoon celery salt
    1 teaspoon turmeric
    2 teaspoons dried oregano
    5 dashes of hot sauce

Method

- *Boil potatoes until barely fork tender (15 minutes), then drain and return to pot. Add the onions and pickle juice. Mix gently. Let juice soak in and hold warm.*
- *Then, in a mixing bowl, mix all the dressing ingredients together.*
- *Mix the dressing into the potatoes.*
- *Gently fold herbs, eggs, and celery into potatoes. You don't want mashed potatoes, but they will break down a little.*
- *Mix until well combined and either serve warm immediately or cool and chill overnight. It's good either way.*

Walhalla Blueberry Peach Cobbler with Granola-Nut Crust

Here's a recipe that makes me think of my father's family. Every year during the summers, I went to Walhalla. My Uncle Frank or my cousins Martha and Susan and their boyfriends would take my brother and me blueberry picking. My aunt would make a cobbler from our harvest. I have made this recipe over the past few years to pay homage to Uncle Frank and his family.

Ingredients
- 2 pints fresh blueberries (fresh is better or 2 1lb. bags of thawed frozen berries)
- 2 cups sliced fresh peaches
- 3/4 cup sugar
- 3 Tablespoons lemon juice
- 2 cups oatmeal
- 1/2 cup crushed or slivered nuts (I like almonds)
- 1 stick butter, melted
- 1 cup light brown sugar
- 1/2 Tablespoon ground cinnamon
- 1 teaspoon ground nutmeg

Method
- Mix sugar, berries, peaches, and lemon juice in a bowl and pour into a 9 x13 baking dish.
- Mix the rest of the ingredients and top the berries with an even layer of the topping.
- Bake for 30 minutes at 350 degrees until top is browned and the berries are juicy.
- Remove from oven and let cool for about 20 minutes.
- Serve while still warm with good vanilla ice cream.

Martha's Baking Powder Biscuits with Ham

Makes 10-12 biscuits, using a 2 inch biscuit cutter

This recipe comes from my cousin Martha's (who is Frank's daughter) mother-in-law and was an adaptation of a back-of-the-box recipe. The adaptation: add some sugar and use cream or half-and-half instead of milk. Martha says her mother-in-law added sugar to lots of things and she was a darn good cook!

Ingredients
- 2 cups sifted all-purpose, bleached flour (my favorite brands are either Martha White® or White Lily®)
- 4 teaspoons baking powder
- 1 teaspoon salt
- 2 teaspoons sugar
- 4 Tablespoons vegetable shortening (like Crisco®)
- 2/3 cup half and half or cream, very cold

Method
- *Preheat oven to 450°.*
- *Sift together flour, baking powder, salt, and sugar.*
- *Cut in the shortening until mixture looks like coarse cornmeal.*
- *Add the cold cream a little at a time, mixing the dough just until it holds together. You may not need all the cream—it depends on the type of flour you use.*
- *Turn out dough onto a lightly-floured surface. Knead gently until the dough holds together in a ball, but handle as little as possible. Roll out to about ½ inch thick. Cut out biscuits to desired size.*
- *Bake on a lightly greased cookie sheet for 10-15 min. Watch carefully because the bottom can burn quickly if the cookie sheet has a dark finish.*

- *Serve split, and pile high with thinly-shaved ham, pickles, and mustard or pimento cheese or mayo, pepper, and turkey, or other of toppings of choice.*

CHAPTER TWENTY: THE STORIES OF SOUTHERN WOMEN AND A FAVORITE NEWSPAPER RECIPE

One thing that has always fascinated me about the South is the Southern woman. Southern women, like all women, are often placed in secondary roles when history is told. Although women are not often prominent in the more-well known stories of the South, I have found it is the Southern woman who truly defines and embodies the spirit of the South. Commitment to family, faith, community, hard work, and charitable causes are some of the hallmarks that define the amazing Southern women I know.

I personally delight in the fact that some of the Southern women in my life have had the most amazing experiences. Their stories are an inspiration. There are three women in particular who have influenced who I am today: One of these ladies taught me that talent is only as great as the amount you share it. One taught me that, out of questionable origins, one can find great gifts that uplift and multiply over time. And one taught me how to find passion in work and to live my life with style and enthusiasm.

First there's Nancy, the woman who taught me voice lessons as a young adult, as well as instilled in me a love for the dramatic, both on and off the stage. And she was the perfect person to have done this—she was on Broadway for years and was Angela Lansbury's understudy in the original production of *Sweeney Todd*. She sang opera all over the world, and her second husband, Jules Stedman, had been one of New York's largest talent agents. He even represented Bob Hope, among others.

Nancy liked to tell the story of how she met Jules. As Nancy recalls, she was called in to audition for Jules and his partner one afternoon in New York. She had made a reputation for herself in the opera world and was excited to potentially be opening up new work options by being seen by this agency. Upon her arrival, she was greeted and briefly interviewed by Jules's business partner. It was then that the partner noticed that the pianist who was supposed to be there was missing.

Jules's partner asked, "Honey, can you sing for us without a piano?"

Nancy replied that she could.

He then called for Jules, chuckling. "Hey Jules, come on in and hear this girl. She's going to sing for us, Acapulco!"

Well, apparently Jules saw more than talent in Nancy and married her not long after. Unfortunately, Nancy lost Jules too early. She eventually remarried again and retired to Charleston, where she taught voice and piano to hundreds of young people, passing on her love of music and theater with flair and love. No one is more positive and enthusiastic than Nancy. And while not originally from the South, she has the spirit of generosity that certainly makes her a Southern woman in spirit.

Then there's Miss Em, the woman who directed me in the symphony singing chorus. She had learned to play piano and sing while touring the South with her father who had been a tent preacher in the '30s and '40s. Apparently, he made a fair sum of money off the enterprise and left the ministry, went into real estate, and practiced all the sins he preached against, dying of syphilis and alcoholism. She went on to inspire thousands of students with her musical gifts. More importantly, she brought a sense of community and belonging to all the students she had in her choral groups. She lived out the faith her father abandoned, showing love and acceptance for all the students she taught.

Then there is my Aunt Lu. Like many in the South, we refer to women who are very close to our family, but who are not blood relatives, as "aunts." She lived out what she was passionate about and found ways to always bring a little beauty and grace to those with whom she worked. She is the embodiment of living life to the fullest.

Aunt Lu is now ninety-six. And like women of a certain era, she has a large portrait of herself hanging in her home near the front door. Commissioned by her late husband, the picture is of her in a beautiful jacket and with perfectly coiffed blonde hair, looking very much like a young Grace Kelly. Her slight smile and bright eyes are forever captured. The painting perfectly portrays Aunt Lu's fun and mischievous nature; her personality hits you from right off the wall. What's most surprising about this painting is that it was painted when she was already forty-six years old, but, in it, she looks every bit as youthful as a twenty-year-old.

You should see Aunt Lu's townhouse. It's all sorts of amazing. Dark green walls, muted brown and gold-striped wallpaper, and blond woven carpets set the stage. There are beautifully framed oil paintings of nudes and giant Georgia O'Keeffe-like florals. The furniture is mostly mid-century modern. There are also dark mahogany coffee tables and sideboards, and a pair of cheetah-print chairs.

When I'm visiting my mama, she and I often find ourselves at Aunt Lu's townhouse for dinner. Aunt Lu lives with her daughter, Wren, who is a lovely person and one of my mama's close friends. I look forward to these meals every year. Their dinner table is always set with crisp linen, French porcelain dinnerware, and crystal stemware. And dinner is always some creation out of an old food magazine or the local paper. I must say, the meal is always tasty!

It was during one of these dinners that I got Aunt Lu talking about her years in the retail and fashion industry as a buyer for one of Charleston's premier dress shops. She had been a buyer for the store for over twenty-five years. And because of that, Aunt Lu knew everyone in Charleston. As she tells it, she had either sold you a dress, sold your spouse a dress, sold your daughter a dress, or sold you down the river. It was a different time, when shops were still local businesses and tied intimately to the community. The local proprietors knew the wants of the people they served.

"I brought Halston to Charleston," Aunt Lu recounted that evening. "He was not being sold here, and actually almost no one knew about him yet in most places.

"Oh, those were good days! It was fun to fly up to New York back then, when flying was glamorous. We would stay at the Waldorf Astoria and go out for cocktails and fabulous dinners, and then to jazz clubs and nightclubs to top off the nights.

"During the days we would make the rounds, having personal meetings with Halston, Oscar, [de la Renta], Bill Blass, and the others. I'd get the latest pieces from them all, even before the shops in Atlanta had them. You know, Charleston has always been interested in having the latest and greatest.

"I still have so many of those gowns," she confessed. "They are each like little pieces of fashion history."

Aunt Lu continued to talk but then stopped. Suddenly, she ran into her bedroom, shouting for Wren to follow her. They were gone for a few minutes. Mama and I looked at each other. We didn't know what prompted their abrupt departure, and we were not expecting what we saw next: Aunt Lu and Wren swung open the bedroom doors and proceeded out into the living room sporting Halston gown after Halston gown and other couture pieces, walking the living room like a runway and giving Mama and me a trunk show. It was just like being in a private salon at Bergdorf Goodman, a luxury New York department store, back in the '60s or '70s. Each gown and cocktail dress came with its own unique pedigree. It was actually really fun to see these articles of clothing come to life and interesting to hear their back-stories!

After the fashion show was over, we delighted in a delicious dinner which I'm sure was from recipes clipped out of the culinary section of that Sunday's newspaper.

Best Newspaper Recipe Ever: Italian Chicken in Patty Shells

Like Wren enjoys cooking up newspaper recipes, this recipe comes from a newspaper and is down home delicious. A college friend's mother from Virginia made it for me several times. She got it from her hometown newspaper 30 years ago. I don't know which paper she got it from originally, but it sure is good.

Ingredients

2 small rotisserie chickens, shredded and cut into pieces
3 Tablespoons butter
2 Tablespoons flour
1 1/2 cup chicken stock
4 Tablespoons lemon juice
1/8 teaspoons mace (could use nutmeg)
10 ounces mushrooms, finely chopped
1/4 cup finely chopped sun-dried tomatoes
6 ounces soft goat cheese, crumbled and divided in half
3 Tablespoons finely chopped parsley plus one more for garnish
1 clove garlic, finely minced
White pepper
2 egg yolks, beaten
2 Tablespoons vermouth or white wine (optional)
3 Tablespoons fresh basil cut into ribbons

Method

- For the sauce, melt butter with garlic in a pan over low heat. Blend in flour and cook but do not allow to brown.
- Pour in chicken stock slowly, stirring constantly until smooth. Add mace.

- *Add mushrooms, sun-dried tomatoes, a dash of white pepper, one half of the goat cheese, lemon juice, and stir until combined and cheese is incorporated into the sauce.*
- *Add in chicken and heat through until hot.*
- *In a bowl, beat the egg yolks and add some of the hot sauce to the eggs and stir together. Add to the pot of sauce, blending well.*
- *Cook for 2 minutes, then stir in parsley and wine (if using), the remaining goat cheese, and half of the basil leaves.*
- *Serve right away in pastry shells or over buttered and crisped toast points or small biscuits. Garnish with the extra parsley and basil.*

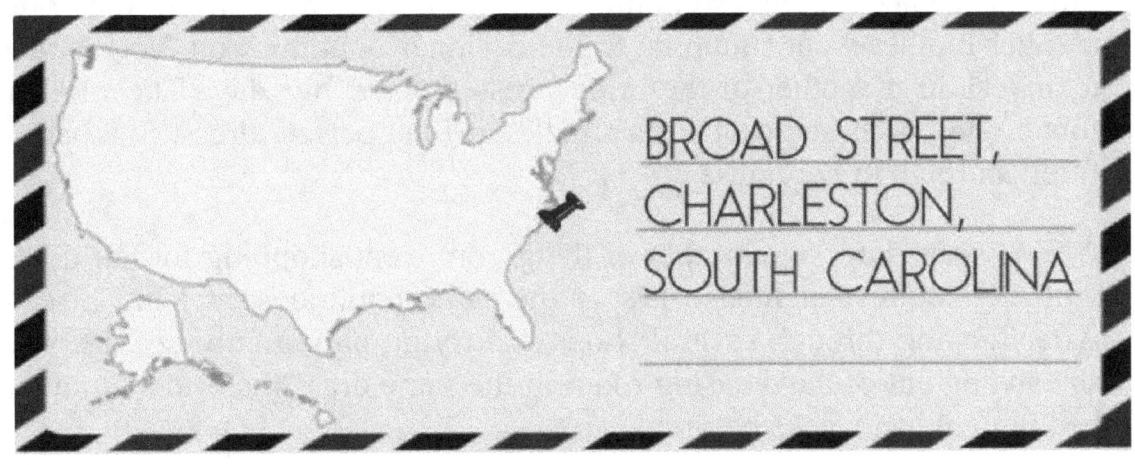

CHAPTER TWENTY-ONE: LADY BALTIMORE IS A BITCH, A SOUTHERN WEDDING STORY

My dear friend Karen from Charleston loves to tell this charming gem of a wedding story from years ago about her friend's sister. Karen even told it to her daughter as an example of how, especially as a Southern woman, one must sometimes stand up for oneself in the face of unfairness. I've carried the story around with me for many years, and have told it at many a cocktail party.

The story goes like this. Karen's friend's sister found herself engaged to a nice young man who came from a very well-heeled family from South of Broad. Being from South of Broad in Charleston amounts to being from Park Avenue or the Upper East Side in New York City. And the people who live there are humorously referred to as "SOBs" (South of Broad Streeters).

Although this bride's family was far from poor, they were not really part of Charleston's society set either. And the mother of the groom was the sort who had a hard time thinking anyone was going to be good enough for her son, especially someone outside of her social circles.

Since it seemed that this wedding was to be a very fancy affair, the bride and her mother went shopping at the designer boutiques on King Street to invest in a mother-of-the-bride dress for the big day. The mother found and purchased (not for a small sum) the perfect dress. She had it fitted and sent to her house.

A few weeks later, the mother of the groom went shopping for her dress with her future daughter-in-law at the same boutiques on King Street. After looking through several shops and trying on a number of dresses, she swung out of the dressing room in the same dress the bride's mother had bought just weeks before.

The bride saw the dress and informed the groom's mother that her mother had already bought that very dress. The woman looked at herself in the mirror, admiring the dress, and said rather flatly, "Oh well, your mother will just have to find another dress because *this* is the dress that I will see my son married in." The bride explained that her mother had already had it fitted and could not return it, but the woman was unmoved. She stated coldly that the mother of the bride would just have to find another dress. That was that.

Well, as you can imagine, this caused no small uproar and upheaval in the young lady's family. It clearly indicated the disdain the mother of the groom had toward her new in-laws, and the issue incited bad feelings all around.

As the wedding day drew closer, the bride found herself spending one last evening having dinner, drinks, and girl talk with her mother. Sitting in the garden of their favorite place at a high top table on stools, twinkle lights glowing in the warm Southern air, they drank wine, ate, and spoke about life in general. Of course, the subject of *the dress* inevitably came up.

"Mama," the daughter said, "I feel so terrible about this whole dress thing. I know you and daddy never go out to anything where you could ever wear it, and I'm your last child to be married. You won't have another wedding or occasion to use it."

The mother looked over her glasses, taking her daughter's hands in hers, and said sincerely, "Don't worry, honey. I went out to the mall and found myself another dress for your wedding, and I'm very pleased with it."

"I know, Mama," said the daughter, "but I just feel awful. You spent so much money on that first dress, and now you won't have an occasion to wear it. This drama is just so sad."

Again, the mother smiled and said, "Darlin', don't you worry about it."

The bride lamented, "I know, Mama, but I just feel terrible. If you had another occasion to wear that dress I'd feel better, but it's just such a waste of money and emotion."

The mother calmly said, "Oh, darlin', I'll find something to wear it to. Now you stop worrying about it."

"Really, Mama, really?" the daughter pressed. "When will you have something to wear that dress to?"

The mother sat back in her chair, picked up her wine glass, and said, smiling, "Oh, I'll wear *that dress*, darlin'."

"Where Mama? Where? Where will you wear that dress?" the bride exclaimed.

The mother, still smiling, leaned in close to her daughter and motioned for her daughter to lean in closer, too. Then taking a long slow sip from her wine glass, the mother let out a sigh, saying "Why to *your* rehearsal dinner, of course. Darlin', to *your* rehearsal dinner."

This gave rise to the saying among her family and girlfriends, "Sometimes in life—you've gotta wear the dress!"

Faux Lady Baltimore Cake (A Traditional Charleston Wedding Cake)

This is not a real Lady Baltimore Cake recipe. My grandma must have adapted it from a good ol' white cake recipe, frosting it with nuts and raisins. It's a good cake and pays homage to the Charleston original. It's sure a lot easier to make, though.

Ingredients
- 2 cups all-purpose flour
- 1 1/2 cups sugar
- 3 teaspoons baking powder
- 1/2 teaspoon salt
- 1 cup milk
- 1/2 cup oleo (vegetable shortening)
- 1 teaspoon vanilla
- 1/2 teaspoon almond extract
- 5 egg whites

Lady Baltimore Frosting
- 1/3 cup butter
- 1 pinch salt
- 3 cups confectioners' sugar
- 1 /4 cups milk or cream
- 1 1/2 teaspoon vanilla extract
- 1/3 cup chopped raisins
- 1/3 cup chopped dried figs or dates
- 1/3 cup chopped pecans

Garnish
- 15 pecan halves

Method

- *Heat oven to 350°F. Grease 2 9-inch round cake pans with shortening. Lightly flour.*
- *In large bowl, beat flour, sugar, baking powder, salt, milk, shortening, and vanilla with electric mixer on low speed until moistened, scraping bowl occasionally. Beat on medium speed 2 minutes, scraping bowl occasionally. Add egg whites; beat 2 minutes longer, scraping bowl occasionally. Pour batter evenly into pans.*
- *Bake 9-inch pans 27 to 35 minutes or until toothpick inserted in center comes out clean. Cool in pans 10 minutes. Remove from pans, place on wire racks. Cool completely, about 1 hour.*

Prepare the frosting

- *In large bowl with mixer on medium-high speed, beat butter, salt, and 1 cup confectioners' sugar 4 minutes or until pale and fluffy, occasionally scraping bowl with rubber spatula.*
- *Add remaining 2 cups confectioners' sugar alternately with milk, beginning and ending with sugar.*
- *Beat with hand or stand mixer for 6 minutes or until very smooth and soft enough to spread. Add in vanilla. Separate out one-third frosting to a small bowl and add in the raisins, figs, and pecans.*

To assemble the cake

- *Place 1 cake layer, bottom side up, on cake plate. Spread with fruit/nut-frosting mixture. Top with second layer, bottom side up. Spread frosting over sides and top of cake. Ring the top with pecan halves.*

SECTION FOUR

ON GROWING UP NAVY AND GEN X

CHAPTER TWENTY-TWO: KODAK COLORS AND THE FLAVORS OF GROWING UP IN THE EARLY 1970S

When I look back through the photo albums on the shelves in my mother's house, I see a world washed by soft Kodak colors. Creaky, faux-leather-backed albums give up their treasures as I turn the sticky and plastic-coated pages. There are photos from a time before I was even a twinkle in my father's eye. And there are plenty of pictorial memories that take me back to times when I was a kid. Family and personal histories are replayed as I leaf through those pages.

In the oldest volumes are somber-colored pictures of my father's early days in the Navy before he met my mother. On a jet fuel-stained steel deck of an aircraft carrier, against a backdrop of gray sky and dark waters, my father stands with his comrades-in-arms. Looking young and dashing, the men are wearing khaki uniforms, brown leather flight jackets with black fur collars, and aviator glasses. The promise of youth and the uncertainty of military service somehow elevate the images and their potency. And while I enjoy looking at these photos, comparing these images to the man I know as my father, I experience a sense of melancholy. I think this feeling is evoked with all photos of military men. We contemplate what sad histories may have befallen those pictured—the sacrifices they may have endured for protecting our country. Happily, for my father, there was no major conflict that involved the carriers on which he served.

There are also pictures taken of and by Mama from 1952 during her very extensive summer vacation all over postwar Europe with her friend Sylvia. With patterned and colorful designer scarves, white-rimmed sunglasses, and red lipstick, they posed smiling in front of all the must-sees for Americans abroad. From the Eiffel Tower in Paris to the Coliseum in Rome to Big Ben in London to the bombed-out ruins of postwar West Berlin, they visited every monument and significant historical edifice. My mother's artistic eye and camera captured moments in life and landscapes with prowess and style. There are also pictures of her giggling with men who are not my father. More pictures show her dancing on a terrace in Italy, vamping through Amsterdam, and lounging on an ocean liner deck chair in the harsh Atlantic sun. The photos look like stills from a Panavision motion picture. Dated and slightly amplified, the photos' colors match the palette of a 1950's Italian film, a slight shift in prism from that of the real world.

Then come the pictures of my brother and me; these photos begin with our first years on the planet, frolicking in the blue-gray surf of the Atlantic Ocean. I also find us with broad smiles in pictures from Christmas mornings, the photos capturing the moments we opened brightly-wrapped presents of G.I. Joe figures or other toy soldier sets, Matchbox® and Hot Wheels® cars, and sets of wooden building blocks. There are pictures of our family smiling, gathered around festively-set holiday tables, evoking a 1970s' corduroy-and-velour version of a Norman Rockwell painting.

As I continue to turn the pages of the photo albums, I find even more pictures of myself and my brother, of times spent singing in the school chorus, playing tennis and bowling, and participating in the church's youth group on Sundays. Then come the Polaroid prints of the mid-1980s. The shots bring me back to those birthdays celebrated at the local Japanese steakhouse, where the guest of honor is holding a "Happy Birthday" sign with a date scribbled on it. And, finally, there are the celebratory pictures of graduations—my brother and I proudly donning our graduation caps and gowns—and the bittersweet images of cars packed and hugs all around, marking the time my brother and I officially moved away to become young men on our own.

Yes, the images as well as the memories grow sharper, realer, clearer, and less faded as the years get closer. But it doesn't matter that the older photos—faded and slightly murky—are showing their age because the pictures tell the story of childhood. And each snapshot, while marking the passage of time, helps to etch the moment (no matter how long ago) into my memory. Good times are the only things in focus in those pictures. Any darkness, pain or challenges were left out of frame. Looking back at growing up, everything is purposely focused, rosy, and beautiful. And isn't that the point of nostalgia—to leave out the things not worth remembering? It provides hope that life will someday return to the imagined perfection it never truly was.

Ask anyone who grew up during the '60s and '70s—they would agree that our lives were substantially different from the lives of children today. We were Generation X. We were the first generation making our way after the baby boomers. We grew up during perhaps one of the most prosperous times in recent history. The world was full of promise and we had all sorts of opportunities. The technology boom, which would transform our world, was just beginning to find its feet.

The Gen Xers, for the most part, had great public schools to learn in. We also had television and movies to entertain and educate us, but not to the point of consuming us. We still had family dinners around the table, where life was shared and food was enjoyed (and ordinary chicken from the local grocer tasted like the best organic chicken today). We read books, and from the pages of those books, our imaginations were sparked and ignited. Imagination drove our worlds.

With their Camel cigarettes held high in one hand (their wrists bent slightly back) and their Tab or Fresca diet soda can in the other, our mothers threw us out of the house to play whenever the weather permitted. They instructed us not to come back until they called us for dinner, and we would instinctively hone our hearing to listen for our names in the early evening breeze. One of my friends would listen for a distinct and penetrating note, as his mother would summon him by whistling through her fingers. We could hear her calling for miles!

We were free and we were safe. Most of all, we had time. The world did not move as fast as it does now. We didn't have the over-sensory exposure to all things digital as kids have today, nor did we have an over-scheduled calendar of extra-curricular commitments. We had time to dream, to play, to ride bikes (without helmets), and to be a kid. In our time, things were simply *simpler*. My father summed it up best when he said to me that the greatest thing about my childhood was that we could be anything we wanted to be and still be home for supper.

Our family meals were also something we carried with us from place to place. And the familiar comfort food my mama and grandma cooked up kept us feeling like home was home no matter where it was.

Since my father was a naval officer, I had an additional layer of childhood experiences that most of my Gen X peers do not. I was a military brat, and being a military brat can be a difficult thing. I moved around a lot, which meant changing schools and making new friends every two years or so. I also had to find ways to carry a sense of home with me every time I moved because I didn't have the luxury of relying on a permanent neighborhood to give me that sense of familiarity and belonging.

As a military brat, life was about creating relationships. Relationships with peers and mentors at school were intense and real, albeit temporary. As a kid, you need friends so you made them even if you knew those friendships were destined to expire with the end of your father's billet. Family relationships, therefore, became elevated in their importance because they were the only constant relationships you could count on.

Despite the numerous moves and the burdens they brought, I have to say that we were stationed in some great places: northern California with its dappling of redwood groves along lushly gorgeous coasts, sunny Florida with its pure and soft-sand beaches, Hawaii with rainbows and spectacular green-flash sunsets, rural Virginia with its deep historical significance just outside our nation's capital, and South Carolina with, of course, its sense of home. These, along with a few other billet assignments, always positioned us on the coast, never far from the beach and the sun. Growing up was good.

Homemade 1970s' Beef Bourguignon Stew

Serves 6 to 8 really well

Ingredients
    3 pounds of chuck stew meat, cubed
    Oil for cooking
    Flour for coating the beef, heavily seasoned
    1 white onion, finely chopped
    2 carrots, finely diced
    2 stalks of celery, finely chopped
    4 cloves minced garlic
    2 teaspoons dried thyme
    3 bay leaves, dried
    1 small can tomato paste
    4 strips of bacon, chopped
    1 bottle rich red wine
    2 cups beef broth
    1 bag frozen pearl onions
    1 bag mini carrots, cut in thirds and boiled until just softened
    2 8 ounce packs of white mushrooms, quartered
    1/4 cup brandy
    2 teaspoons salt
    1 teaspoon pepper

Method
- Preheat oven to 325 degrees.
- In a large bowl, toss the beef with enough seasoned flour to coat very well.
- In a heavy enameled baking casserole, brown beef in batches.
- Add oil each time so each batch browns.

- *Don't overcrowd or the beef will steam; you want some browning and caramelizing.*
- *Hold browned beef to the side on a plate.*
- *Cook the bacon until just done. Remove from pan and leave the drippings.*
- *Cook the onions, celery, and carrots in the drippings until almost soft. Add 4 cloves of minced garlic.*
- *Add the tomato paste and combine with vegetables.*
- *Using some wine, deglaze the bits from the bottom of the pan.*
- *Add the beef, the bacon, the spices, the salt and pepper, and stir gently.*
- *Then pour in the rest of the wine and add enough beef broth until just covered.*
- *Bring to a boil, then turn off heat.*
- *Place in the oven for about 2 hours. At this point, add the mushrooms, the pearl onions, and brandy.*
- *Turn oven to 350 degrees and cook for another 30 minutes.*
- *Add in the cooked carrots right before serving.*
- *Season to taste with salt and pepper.*
- *Place on the stove over low heat until ready to eat.*
- *Serve with well-buttered mashed potatoes.*

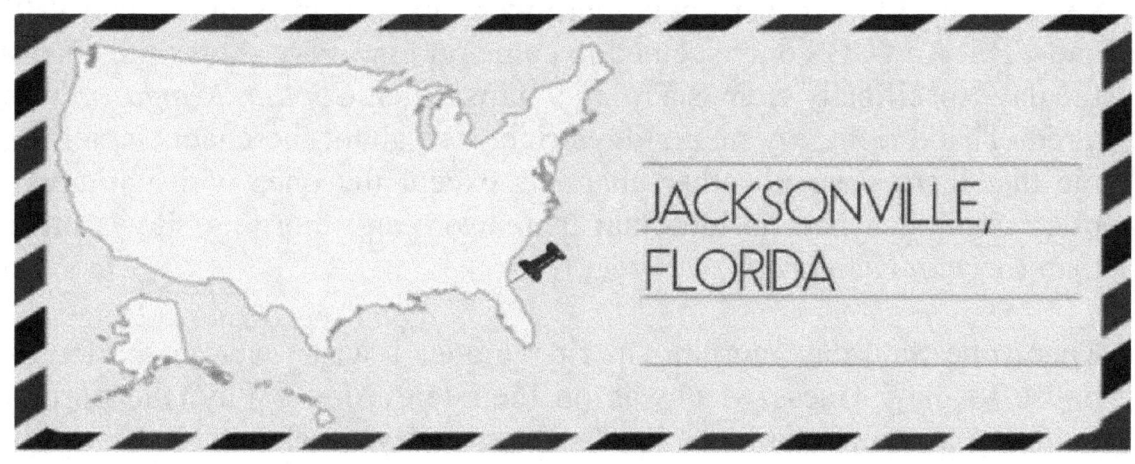

CHAPTER TWENTY-THREE: TV, FRIED SHRIMP, AND MORRISON'S CAFETERIA

Television, or the boob tube as my parents referred to it, found its way into every American home during the 1960s and 1970s. It became as much a part of the landscape of Gen X lives as the family dinner table, shopping malls, and church. In fact, it took the place of the family dinner table for many, becoming the focal point of attention. Family members would still spend their time eating together, but now they would do so hunched over individual TV trays, watching programs instead of talking and discussing their personal lives. Many thought television might bring an end to social interaction, but, like so many things, it has become a part of American life and is not the enemy to human connection it was once thought to be.

Among these early alarmists were my own parents. In fact, my mama tried hard to keep me from her feared evils of television. When I was very young, there were only about five or six channels on the television. Cable had not been invented. The three major networks were all we had, and a local station or two were added to the mix. And, of course, there was PBS. Because my mama was very concerned about the effects television could have on my young mind, for about the first three or four years of my life, I never knew there were any channels other than PBS and CBS. And CBS only seemed to come on for a very short time during the day, specifically from 8 a.m. to 9 a.m., when *Captain Kangaroo* was aired. That's right, my mama downright lied about the channels, telling me that there were no other channels except the ones with children's programming. I had no idea that there were any morning shows other than *Captain Kangaroo*.

Then, one Saturday morning in first grade, I went over to a friend's house to play. Guess what was on their television? Why, the normal Saturday morning cartoons that played every weekend! It blew my young mind. *Why did my family not know about this?*

So what did I do when I got back home? I excitedly tried to explain to my mama what I had learned. Apparently, in a follow-up conversation with Mama, my friend's mother filled in the missing gaps of the story and explained what she had told me. She told my mama that I was stupefied by the selection of cartoons on the set and that I asked her where all these programs were coming from. She explained to me that there were channels that you could turn to on the TV to see different programs. She asked if my parents had ever shown me that, and I declared that they had not! That is why, upon returning home, I regaled my mother with this story and excitedly showed her how to turn the dial. Mama was not pleased upon hearing this, and she had words with my friend's mom during that follow-up conversation; the next time I went there to play, the television was off.

Now, like TV watching, eating out when I was young—unlike for kids today—was always a special occasion. My father always joked that his limited paycheck reflected the Navy's opinion that if they wanted him to have a family, they would have issued him one. But living on a tight military budget didn't stop us from exploring and finding fun in our regularly changing hometowns. Albeit rare, sometimes that would include a dinner out. As a young officer's family, we didn't have money to splurge on restaurants too often, but when we did go out, my parents seemed to pick the most exciting places for my brother and me. When I was little and we were stationed in Jacksonville, Florida, that place was Morrison's Cafeteria.

The Morrison's Cafeterias I was familiar with as a youngster were those located at the new suburban mall complexes that were popping up in the mid-60s. As I remember it, each Morrison's was an amber-lit, cavernous place decorated in the latest cafeteria chic. The one in Jacksonville had pale-ivory walls framed in distressed-oak panels and carpet that slightly emanated the smell of stale grease and cooking. Square wood tables and chairs with green fabric backings occupied the center of the dining space. A row of quilted, camel-colored leatherette booths lined the long back walls where, as a child, I was convinced that only adults got to sit. If one word could have summed up my impression of Morrison's as a small boy, the word would have been "Wow."

The first thing that struck me when stepping from the parking lot into Morrison's was its entryway. You entered the front door and were immediately funneled down the long, dimly lit corridor with its over-handled wallpaper and dented wainscoting. The corridor was crowded and filled with a line of hungry patrons, mostly adults. And since they were tall and I was little, I couldn't exactly see what was coming, but the anticipation was palpable.

Walking into a Morrison's was like getting on an amusement park ride, like the Pirates of the Caribbean at Disneyland, where you float down a canal inside a tunnel, waiting for the waterfalls to take you down into the main portion of the ride. You hear the roar of the waterfalls before you ever come upon them, making the suspense that much more heightened. In the case of Morrison's, as you entered the line, there was a far-off but quickly approaching din resulting from the combination of the hustle and bustle of the kitchen and the chatter of the guests and servers. You heard the clinking of ice and the whooshing of sweet tea and soda being poured into amber plastic glasses and the *chortle-pop-drip* of gallons of hot coffee being percolated in giant urns. There were the scrapes of plastic trays along the metal cafeteria rails, the chinking of plates and serving utensils, the ringing of the cash registers, and the ticking of receipts being printed. The last noise emanating from the line was the tearing of the paper tape, finalizing the transaction. (The cashiers would wet the receipt with a sponge and stick it to your tray, which I always found gross.)

And of course, you could also hear the hubbub of laughter and conversation from the large dining room that was just beyond the main cafeteria line. People "eatin' and greetin,'" my Aunt Leoha would say about dining out at Morrison's on a Sunday or Friday night. There were waiters in maroon or white jackets and black bow ties, bussing stacks of trays and dirty dishes out of the dining room and conversing with guests about special orders while delivering drink refills. All of these sounds are part of my memory of the happy racket at Morrison's.

Like all cafeterias in the South I've been to throughout the years, including the famous Robertson's in Charleston, Morrison's in Jacksonville had a black letter board with white lettering positioned at the beginning of the diners' line. It detailed an overwhelming number of entrées from fried chicken to sole almondine, meatloaf to chicken pot pie, and on and on. On the letter board, I would see listed the fried shrimp with tartar sauce, the dish I loved the most. I believed it was seafood fit for a king. My love of fried seafood, which burns brightly to this day, was ignited by that entrée.

Once you were out of the corridor and officially in the serving line, you were overwhelmed with a vision. The first sight to greet you were cakes and pies as far as one's young eye could see. It was a brilliant marketing ploy, tempting you with sweets before you even got to your meal. Then there were tossed salads with house-made Thousand Island or blue cheese dressing and Jell-O® salad towers. Moving down the line, the offerings included coleslaw, squash casserole, green beans, mac and cheese (an unrivaled dish to this day with its soft elbow macaroni in a creamy, cheesy white sauce and a golden-cheddar cheese topping), and mashed potatoes, as well as many other side dishes. The garlic toast was a must, dripping in butter and crisped to within an inch of its life. In my experience, that bread has only been bested by Sizzler's (even David Chang knows that!).

Dining at Morrison's was a progressive meal experience. My mom or dad would get a tray for each of us from a stack, sometimes still hot and dripping from the commercial dishwasher. We would slide our trays (just like the school cafeteria) down the three long, parallel stainless steel rails. I would gaze with wonder through the glass sneeze guard at the panorama of foods right before my eyes. I would follow my Mama or Daddy down the seemingly endless serving line, making some selections along the way. When we got to the entrée section, a female server in a dress uniform with a nametag and hairnet would ask me, "Now, what do *you* like to eat, young man?"

I would look at my Mama, grin, and say, "Fried shrimp, please?" The lady would hand us a plastic number stand and let my mama know the shrimp would come to the table. They were always cooked to order. Boy, did that feel special!

After finishing in the line, we were off to find a spot in the dining room which was always filled with a sea of diners at tables in casual or, depending on the day, their Sunday best. (Cafeterias were a definitive after-church-going place on Sundays in the South.) We'd find our way to an open table, placing our trays down carefully so as to not upset the filled-to-capacity plates, cups, and bowls. After removing the various food-laden monkey dishes from our trays, Mama or Daddy would return them to the tray deposit against the wall. And when they returned, we would dig into an amazingly satisfying meal, each of us enjoying our most favorite dishes. I would wait on the shrimp until they came to the table.

Morrison's was indeed a delicious culinary amusement park ride of an experience for a young boy such as myself. From the entryway anticipation to the journey through the line with its array of succulent temptations to the meal finally landing on the table, it was a ride worth taking. And the fried shrimp were the best part. They would arrive at the table fresh and hot, and were placed down in front of my wide-eyed, smiling face.

My parents were somewhat stunned the first time we went to Morrison's by my gusto for these deliciously crisp, butter-flied and battered, deep-fried gems. And Mama (who was a little over-protective in my early years) was horrified. You see, not knowing any better, I devoured the whole shrimp, tail and all, with a giant smear of tartar sauce. A nearby waiter, seeing my mother's distress, came over to the table, and while refilling our water glasses, looked at my mother and said, "It's okay, ma'am. Don't you worry about the boy; shrimp don't have no bones." The diners around us chuckled as they overheard this commentary about my devouring those shrimp with such unbridled joy. And when the servers would come to the table to check in, they stood there and smiled broad, toothy grins, amused, I'm sure, to no end by the little boy who loved the fried shrimp so much he ate the whole thing—tail and all!

Morrison's Cafeteria-Inspired Fried Shrimp

Morrison's used a batter to make their shrimp. I opt for a double batter dry dredge at home.

Ingredients
  3 lbs shrimp, cleaned and tails left on (about 3 dozen medium to large)
  Peanut oil (for deep frying)

  Dredging Mixture
  1 1/2 cups flour, sifted
  1 cup corn flour
  1 teaspoon onion powder
  1 teaspoon garlic powder
  1 teaspoon white pepper
  1 teaspoon lemon pepper
  1 1/4 teaspoons salt

  Batter
  2 Tablespoons baking powder
  1 1/4 teaspoons salt
  3 teaspoons paprika
  1 teaspoon garlic powder
  1 teaspoon hot sauce (Crystal)
  2 cups all-purpose flour
  1 egg, slightly beaten
  1 cup milk
  1/2 cup buttermilk
  2 Tablespoons white or cider vinegar

Method

- *Blot shrimp dry with paper towels and set aside. Heat several inches of oil to 350 degrees in a deep, heavy pot or deep fryer.*
- *Combine the dredging mixture in a bowl.*
- *Combine the batter ingredients by whisking the baking powder, salt, and seasonings into the flour.*
- *Whisk in the egg, milk, buttermilk, hot sauce, and vinegar, blending well. Batter should be a bit thinner than pancake batter. Add more milk if necessary.*
- *Place shrimp in a large bowl and pour in just enough batter to heavily coat shrimp.*
- *Toss to coat, then pour in the dry dredge and toss with your hands until all shrimp are coated. The mixture will be clumpy.*
- *In batches, pull out shrimp and slip into hot oil.*
- *Fry a few at a time just until batter is golden. Drain on paper towels. Serve hot.*

Morrison's-Style Tartar Sauce

This recipe was printed in various newspapers. It makes a thick tartar sauce that is exactly the texture I see at the S&S Cafeteria in Charleston today. It's the addition of the cabbage that makes the difference. I've added carrots to my version; they give it a nice look.

Ingredients
- *1/4 cup green cabbage*
- *1 small white onion*
- *2 strips green pepper*
- *1/4 cup dill pickle relish*
- *1/4 cup shredded carrots*
- *1 1/4 cups real mayonnaise*

Method
- *Place cleaned cabbage, onion, green pepper, and carrots in a food processor and pulse to a fine pulp. Add relish and mayo; stir to blend. Place in a covered container and refrigerate overnight. Makes 3 1/2 cups.*

Morrison's-Style Macaroni and Cheese

Along with the fried shrimp, the mac and cheese at Morrison's was legendary. I've been told that old school Southern mac—like that found at Morrison's— always had eggs and white sauce often made with evaporated milk.

My Aunt Lucille gave this recipe to my mama. It's supposedly from her housekeeper who got it from working at a famous cafeteria in Columbia, South Carolina. It's pretty much what I remember growing up. Try this version for a real taste of down-South flavor.

Ingredients
- 16 ounces of elbow macaroni, uncooked
- 1/2 cup unsalted butter
- 1/2 cup all-purpose flour
- 3 1/4 cups evaporated milk, warmed
- 1 1/2 teaspoons dried mustard
- 1 teaspoon white pepper
- 1/4 teaspoon nutmeg
- 2 teaspoons salt
- 1/2 teaspoon freshly ground black pepper
- 2 eggs
- 2 1/2 cups grated extra sharp cheddar cheese
- 1 1/2 cups grated Monterey jack cheese (Gruyère if you want more flavor)
- 1/2 cup grated hard cheese like aged Parmesan (my addition)

Method

- *Preheat oven to 400 degrees.*
- *Cook macaroni per package directions and drain.*
- *Heat butter in a small saucepan over medium low heat. Stir in flour and cook 3 minutes.*
- *Use a whisk and add milk, stirring constantly, until sauce thickens.*
- *Add spices, salt, and pepper.*
- *Beat eggs slightly and add small amount of sauce to eggs so they don't turn into scrambled eggs.*
- *Then add egg mixture to sauce.*
- *Add Parmesan and stir.*
- *Taste sauce and adjust seasoning; it should be highly seasoned. If it is too thick, add milk; it should be a pourable sauce.*
- *Set aside 1 cup grated cheddar cheese for top.*
- *Add 1/3 of the macaroni to a buttered 2-quart casserole. Top with 1/3 of the remaining cheese.*
- *Then continue alternating layers of macaroni and cheese. Pour sauce all over. Then top with the reserved cheese.*
- *Bake 25 to 30 minutes and serve.*

CHAPTER TWENTY-FOUR: CHURCH POTLUCK SUPPERS FOR BODY AND SOUL

You never know what life will bring you. When I was in first grade, my father contracted Meniere's disease, an affliction that causes vertigo—a dizzying lack of balance. In order for him not to be discharged from the service, his friends in the naval command in Washington, DC, arranged for him to be given a tour of duty at Camp Smith near Pearl Harbor, Hawaii. They also arranged for him to stay there for four years instead of being transferred every two which was the norm. And so, in 1969, our family found ourselves leaving Jacksonville, Florida, and moving to Pearl Harbor on the island of Oahu. We had little clue that we were embarking on a cultural, spiritual, and culinary journey that would change each of us forever.

Oahu was a total cultural change for us as a family. At the center of our culture shock was the new wave of foods that we were introduced to while we were living on the island, foods that eventually became part and parcel of our family dinner fare. And later, when moving back to the mainland, we carried with us the recipes for these foods from Hawaii and the memories associated with them. My brother and I both still make, and share with our friends, dishes we enjoyed in Hawaii.

Hawaii is probably one of the most ethnically mixed places you could imagine. Nowhere was this more evident than at the church we came to call home: Trinity United Methodist Church in Pearl City. This vibrant congregation included individuals of Hawaiian, Chinese, Japanese, Filipino, Tongan, and Korean backgrounds as well as whites, blacks, and Latinos from the mainland, the latter three groups mostly brought to the Islands by the military. Through our association with the church and the relationships we built with our fellow churchgoers, we learned a lot about other cultures and cultural traditions, including culinary heritages. Our church community fed not only our souls but our stomachs as well!

Our new church taught and truly lived the fundamental Methodist concept that God is love. And this congregation was a wonderful place for living out that idea. That precept shaped how our family saw religion from that time on. Prior to moving to Hawaii, our family had always belonged to a church (my father joined the Methodist church when he married my mama); it was in Hawaii, however, where my parents came into their own as believers, discovering newfound involvement as church supporters, leaders, teachers, and choir members. For example, my father became a deacon of the church, helping with fundraising and budget administration, and my mother taught Sunday school and started a summer-vacation bible school for the kids in the congregation. Our church had not only a robust youth education program but one for adults as well. And lots of events for the whole family were held throughout the year; my favorites were the beach camp week and the Christmas crafts market.

It was also here that the terms "church potluck dinner" and "covered-dish supper" took on new and exciting meanings. With a congregation representing over sixty different nationalities and cultural backgrounds, we had some amazing church suppers. There were no ordinary dishes on this buffet. No, here there were lumpia (Filipino egg rolls) and beef dishes made with kimchi (Korean pickled cabbage), along with amazing fried rices. These were, of course, peppered by the normal Anglo-mainland dishes offered up by the naval wives and other good folks, like fried chicken, green bean casserole, rolls (homemade Parker House rolls and Hawaiian or Portuguese sweet rolls), and an array of salads—green leafy, potato, and Hawaiian-style macaroni, complete with chunks of Spam®. And, of course, there was a bounty of yeasty baked goods, Jell-O® molds, cakes, and pies. The spirit of fellowship that those meals created within the congregation was a lovely thing, and it was here that the concept of food and fellowship first made sense to me.

Our church also held a Huli-huli chicken dinner every year, which is a traditional Hawaiian BBQ event. Many churches and civic organizations often use this meal as a fundraising tool. When the large roadside grills were brought out of storage and set up in the parking lot, everyone knew an important and festive fundraiser was in the making. The main feature that drew the crowds was, of course, the chicken, which had been deeply marinated for hours in a bath of flavors from the Islands and the Orient. The chickens were then slowly grilled in large rotating cages on the spit. The dish is actually named for this part of the preparation: "huli" means turn in Hawaiian!

I remember great clouds of dark charcoal smoke engulfing the grills as the chickens turned in their rotisseries in the parking lot of the church, slowly roasting the marinated birds to perfection. And I can also remember the delicious aroma that would soon spread far and wide as the chickens cooked, calling to those who may not have even known that a fundraiser was taking place. People would head over with money in hand because Huli-huli chicken raises taste buds and funds! Our church's Huli-huli fundraiser was always such a delicious and successful affair!

Easy Huli-huli Chicken

Huli-huli chicken was the brainchild of one man if you listened to him tell the story. In 1955, Ernest Morgado of Pacific Poultry debuted his version of a teriyaki roast chicken at a farmers' gathering. This method for cooking chicken was such a hit that it became a favorite Hawaiian fundraising tool, raising perhaps millions over the years for schools, churches, softball teams, and hula groups.

The recipe is enough for about three chickens, split in half. You can use chicken pieces. Marinate your chicken for at least a half hour up to 3 hours.

Ingredients
  Marinade recipe
    1 cup pineapple juice
    2/3 cup soy sauce
    1/4 cup brown sugar
    1/4 cup sherry
    1-2 Tbsp. sesame oil
    1-2 or more pieces ginger root, crushed
    3 cloves garlic, minced
    1 Tablespoon Worcestershire sauce
    Lemon juice, about 1/2 a lemon
    1 cup water

  For BBQ Sauce
    1 cup hoisin sauce
    1/2 cup teriyaki sauce
    1 cup hickory BBQ sauce

Method

- *Brush the chicken with the marinade while cooking over a grill. Cook until almost done, then slather with BBQ sauce a couple times and let get sticky and thick. Sprinkle with sesame seeds for garnish if desired.*

OR

- *Bake chicken for 35 mins in the oven at 350 degrees. Slather with sauce and bake again another 20 mins or so until done and add sauce along the way to give it a very thick glaze.*

Divine Chicken Divan

While there were exotic dishes at our church dinners, the one dish that always reminds me of potlucks at Trinity United Methodist is this classic, totally from scratch, American casserole. Found at church potlucks everywhere, it's a sure-fire crowd-pleaser.

Ingredients
  2 pounds chicken breast, chopped into bite-sized pieces
  1/4 tsp each of salt, pepper, paprika
  1 16-20 ounce bag broccoli florets
  3 Tablespoons unsalted butter, divided
  2 Tablespoon olive oil, divided
  1/3 cup all-purpose flour
  2 cups low sodium chicken broth, divided
  2 cups milk
  3 Tablespoons sherry
  1 Tablespoon cornstarch
  2 teaspoons chicken bouillon
  1 1/2 teaspoons Dijon mustard
  1 1/2 teaspoons Worcestershire sauce
  1 tsp each of onion powder, garlic powder, dried parsley
  1/4 teaspoon ground cumin
  1/4 teaspoon ground nutmeg
  1/2 teaspoon pepper
  1 cup grated yellow cheddar cheese
  1/2 cup grated Gruyère cheese, divided
  1/2 cup grated Parmesan cheese
  1/2 cup sour cream
  1/4 cup sliced almonds, crushed with your hands
  1/2 cup Panko bread crumbs
  1 Tablespoon melted butter

1 Tablespoon extra virgin olive oil
Salt each step to taste

Method

- *Preheat oven to 350 degrees F. Lightly spray a 9x13 baking dish or 6 individual dishes with nonstick cooking spray.*
- *Toss the chicken with 1 1/2 teaspoons salt, 1 teaspoon pepper, 1 1/2 teaspoons paprika. Let marinate while you cook broccoli.*
- *Add 1 Tablespoon olive oil to a large skillet and heat over medium high heat until very hot. Add the broccoli, season, and sauté for 30 seconds. Add 1/2 cup chicken broth, cover pan, and lower heat to medium.*
- *Steam broccoli until tender but not limp, about 2 minutes.*
- *Transfer broccoli to baking dish in one layer.*
- *In same skillet, melt 1 Tablespoon butter over medium heat. Increase heat to medium high and add chicken in a single layer. Sear for three minutes, then continue to cook and stir chicken until cooked through. Layer the chicken on top of broccoli in the baking dish. Sprinkle with the almonds.*
- *In the same skillet, melt 2 Tablespoons butter with 2 Tablespoons olive oil over medium heat.*
- *Whisk in flour, then cook, stirring for 1 minute. Turn the heat to low, then slowly whisk in the remaining 1 1/2 cups chicken broth and 1 cup of the milk.*
- *Combine cornstarch with remaining 1 cup milk. Stir into the sauce and then add the Dijon, Worcestershire sauce, chicken bouillon, and all spices.*
- *Bring sauce to a boil, whisking constantly, then reduce heat to a simmer, whisking often until thickened. Remove from heat and whisk in 1/2 cup of Gruyère cheese until melted, followed by Parmesan cheese until melted. Taste and make sure it is well seasoned with salt.*
- *Whisk in sour cream and sherry until blended.*
- *Pour the sauce over chicken and broccoli and spread into an even layer. Top with the remaining cup of cheddar cheese.*

To top
- *Melt butter in olive oil over medium heat in a medium skillet. Add Panko and stir to coat. Continue cooking until crumbs become golden brown. Evenly sprinkle over cheese. Cover Chicken Divan with foil and bake at 350 degrees for 30 minutes or until hot and bubbly and cheese is melted.*
- *Serve the Chicken Divan with mashed potatoes, noodles or wild rice.*

Chinese Noodles with Pork and Peanut-Sesame Sauce

In Hawaii, my Grandma Irene took a Chinese cooking class. We have her cookbook filled with recipes she tried out on us. In the book is a recipe from Gladys Pang, a church member, who made this for potlucks. It was one of my favorites.

Ingredients
For the Sauce
- 1/2 cup smooth peanut butter
- 1/4 cup low sodium soy sauce
- 2 Tablespoons boiling water
- 2 Tablespoons mirin
- 3 Tablespoons toasted sesame oil (hold until end)
- 1 Tablespoon honey
- 1/4 teaspoon black pepper
- 1 teaspoon ground ginger
- 1/2 Tablespoon Asian chili sauce
- 1 Tablespoon mixed black and white sesame seeds

For the Noodles
- 1 lb thin Chinese or spaghetti noodles
- 1 cup shredded carrots
- 6 or 7 Thai red chilies, chopped in slices (or red jalapeño)
- 1/4 cup cucumber, cut into rectangular batons
- 1 cup chopped scallions, sliced on the bias (2 Tablespoons held back)
- 1/4 cup chopped cilantro, sesame seeds for garnish

For the Pork
- 1 pound fresh ground pork
- 2 Tablespoons soy sauce

2 Tablespoons minced chives
1 Tablespoon minced garlic
1 Tablespoon minced ginger
2 teaspoons dry sherry
2 Tablespoons Chinese hoisin sauce
Hot chili sauce and salt and pepper to taste

Method

- *Stir-fry pork with all ingredients. Cook until dark and crispy. Hold warm. Boil noodles according to the package directions.*
- *Add all the sauce ingredients into a bowl except peanut butter and sesame oil.*
- *Place peanut butter in the microwave for about 1 minute.*
- *Mix the peanut butter into the remaining ingredients until smooth.*
- *When the noodles are finished cooking, drain and add hot noodles to the sauce mixture. Mix to coat.*
- *Add the vegetables, pork mixture, cilantro, and sesame oil and toss well to combine.*
- *Place in a serving vessel and garnish with some scallion slices and sesame seeds.*

CHAPTER TWENTY-FIVE: HARD LESSONS ABOUT HISTORY, AND HAWAIIAN CURRIED-CHICKEN SALAD

Robert Louis Stevenson was one of my favorite authors when I was a kid. He wrote a lot of books about adventure—adventures which took place in faraway places and in historical settings, that featured freedom fighters, evil counterparts, dashing knights and fair maidens, pirates, and young heroes. His stories, for kids like me who spent lots of time reading, were greatly loved and devoured with ravenous abandon.

I came to love stories like *Treasure Island*, *The Black Arrow*, and *Kidnapped*, whose young-boy protagonists were, within the realms of my imagination, just like me. I was transported to exotic islands in the Pacific or the Caribbean, the dark smoky fields of Scotland, or onto ships filled with pirates. These books were easy to read and were classic adventure stories that were an inspiration for boys and girls sailing away in their imaginations to amazing places.

The other kind of books that captured my interest at a young age were historical novels, stories based on a period of time gone by and peopled with famous characters I had learned about at school or seen glamorized by Hollywood actors in the movies. The characters in those books were much like those seen on the screen; they were larger than life and came alive on the pages, moving across chapters through times long since passed. The pages I read only hinted at the horrific, tragic, painful, and scary circumstances of their lives. And from the safety of my bedroom, I further romanticized these figures as I read by lamplight.

Many of the historical fiction books I read were about cultural and military struggles, and I thought that I understood what I was reading. However, it wasn't until I was in Hawaii that the adventurous war stories and the romantic notions surrounding them came to be examined in the harsh light of day under the warm Hawaiian sun. This discovery came from exploring the real and darker side of some of the war stories laid out in the history books I was fascinated by. Little did I know at a young age that hard clues to that history lay directly outside the door of our house in Pearl Harbor.

Living in naval housing on the Pearl City peninsula, my brother, our friends, and I had up-close encounters with the relics of the area's military past. Not far from our house, right near the beach, was an old seaplane base, long deserted and overgrown with foliage and trees. Unbeknown to our parents, we explored and played in that defunct station with its seawall along the harbor. Large concrete slabs marked the former floor space and were surrounded by the remnants of walls and metal fixtures long rusted and bent under time. These abandoned spaces were transformed into forts and clubhouses in our minds. Running and hiding, climbing trees, and hunkering in trenches, my friends and I pretended to be soldiers and sailors protecting our nation from the Japanese.

Outside the crumbling walls of the station right by the water was a placard denoting the place where US naval officials spotted one of the Japanese mini subs entering Pearl Harbor. The placard explained that the sub was sunk by US artillery. I sometimes wondered about the sub's sinking and about the fate of the men on that vessel, but I never let my mind stay too long pondering the unimaginable.

As I played among the overgrown ruins of the old naval facility with my friends, I didn't understand the gravity of what happened to our nation that infamous day Pearl Harbor was attacked. And it wasn't until one spring day during our second year in Hawaii when our family visited the USS Arizona Memorial that my romantic notions were supplanted by stark reality. That week, Aunt Lucy, her friend Bobbie, and my cousin Pricilla came to visit from the mainland. My parents decided that taking them on a tour of the harbor and its historical past would be an interesting and meaningful excursion, particularly because the Navy offered special tours for military personnel. The military tours were separate from the crowded public boat tours offered in the harbor; we weren't to be lumped together with loads of clamoring tourists.

So off we went with the three ladies. My father brought us through the main gate of the harbor base, and, instead of heading in the same direction of all the tourists to the visitor center, we walked to a small dock. There, on the water's edge, we entered a building where we watched a documentary film that depicted the events of December 7, 1941. It was a tough film to watch, and it pulled no punches in describing the horrific human and naval carnage that befell Pearl Harbor.

I remember the first scenes of the film: the visions of a quiet Sunday morning. I remember pictures of shirtless military boys sporting caps playing ball and people walking near the beach or getting ready for church wearing suits, ladies in printed dresses and hats. Then the film turned to scenes aboard the Japanese warships and the waves of planes taking off from those carrier decks while the crew raised their arms and waved beanie caps and shouted, "Bonzai"! The movie detailed the planes' flight paths over the green, pointy Oahu mountains, and the US radar station trying to relay information to the sleeping fleet at anchor in the harbor below. The Japanese planes washed across the screen, darkening the skies on the film and casting shadows on the theater walls. Then came the devastation of the attack: the torpedoes and dive bombs slamming into the hulls of our battleships and the clouds of smoke and flames reaching into the clear Hawaiian sky. As the bombardment slowed, scenes panned the harbor, showing floating bodies among the naval wreckage. There were also images of the wounded Navy and Army boys, reeling in the aftermath of the attack. It was a lot to take in.

I remember the impact the film had on those around me. I think I focused on others in the audience because maybe that was easier than me thinking about what I was seeing on the screen. You know how when you are young and you are uncomfortable, and you don't know what to do, so you look to others around you? Well, I think that is what I did. I remember Aunt Lucy, who lost her husband in the war, her eyes welling up as the movie played. I remember that she (and others) wiped away the few tears that spilled over their lower lids. Other sniffled quietly. I also remember the room being extraordinarily and painfully still. These were people of a certain age who had lived through the war. They were moved as they silently remembered personal moments with the loved ones they had lost. Looking back at this experience as an adult, it was a sober and somber moment.

The hard and harsh reality of the war and its costs finally hit my young brain and heart when we boarded our tour boat and were shown around the harbor. We viewed many of the places the movie had spoken about. Seeing the actual locations where the events had occurred brought the realities of war to life in a way I couldn't grasp from my adventure books or any Hollywood movie.

The culmination of the tour was, of course, when we arrived at the USS Arizona Memorial itself. We disembarked from the tour boat and stood on a stark-white, floating platform in the middle of the harbor. The largest American flag I had ever seen flew overhead from a flagpole attached to the mainmast of the sunken ship. I approached the platform's railing and stared into the blue, lapping waters, waters that barely covered the huge smoke stacks of the defeated and majestic battleship. We listened to our guide's story of the Arizona's last moments before it succumbed to the Japanese navy and settled in its final resting place on the harbor's seafloor. Suddenly, all the pain, horror, and terror those young sailors must have experienced hit me. I was sick to my stomach and anxious. I reached for and held onto my father's hand more tightly as the guide continued to account the last moments our men saw daylight and breathed the air of the living.

That day brought hard lessons. And it brought up a feeling far more sinister than the adventurous notions of war my friends and I would so happily role-play in the old desolate base near our home. The trip to the memorial triggered feelings of fear, uneasiness, and sadness I never forgot. Yes, my interest in history continues to this day, however, whenever I reflect on the war stories I read about or watch depicted in films, I always think about the human cost that has been endured by the war's victims and their families.

There were many other historical sites besides the military ones that we explored in Hawaii. Beautiful waterfalls with stories tied to the ancient inhabitants of the Islands. Buddhist temples with grand gardens and peaceful interiors filled with the unfamiliar noises of prayer-chanting and the smell of incense. Historic Hawaiian hotels were visited for fancy lunches or elaborate luau dinner shows. And, of course, there was the Iolani Palace, the official residence of Hawaiian royalty in the late 1800s, and its citadel in the center of downtown Honolulu. And there was one site that even had a connection to my love of Robert Louis Stevenson's adventure books; that place was the Waioli Tea Room.

Looking for a warmer climate to help his weak respiratory system, Stevenson spent time in the Hawaiian Islands in the late 1800s. There, he became good friends with King Kalakaua and Princess Kaiulani, the king's niece. Stevenson and his family, as guests of the princess's father, lived for a time on the Ainahau estate. The guest house, a grass hut in which Stevenson resided, was eventually moved from Ainahau to its current location, a ten-acre property that also houses the Waioli Tea Room. The Salvation Army originally built the tea room in 1922 and provided vocational training to young girls under its roof for nearly forty years. In the 1960s, the property became a treasured destination where tourists could learn more about Hawaii's social history, appreciate the Islands' unique architecture, enjoy the lush tropical gardens, and partake of afternoon tea service and traditional Hawaiian hospitality.

We went to the tea room many times whenever we had family or friends visiting from the mainland. As a boy, the property was endlessly captivating, with great paths and historical structures to explore (including Stevenson's grass hut), and then there was the yummy food. Of the dishes that I remember well from the Waioli Tea Room, the house-baked breads and the curried chicken salad (supposedly based on the original tea sandwiches served in Stevenson's era) were the best. The chicken salad was piled onto wonderful toasted, homemade wheat bread and was served with delicious mayo, sliced tomatoes, and crisp lettuce.

In Hawaii, it became evident to me that history can be looked at from various viewpoints and that, through history, we can learn lessons which can help us to not repeat the mistakes of the past. The lessons about war and its cost certainly struck me hard. It was the first time I comprehended that my father and family were directly in harm's way should war ever arise. And I realized that the stories that are written about war and history can often make those realities seem less terrible than they really were. I appreciate the tough lessons history taught me as a boy.

However, in Hawaii, I also learned that history can provide us with happy memories and stories about adventure and discovery. It can provide us with delicious tastes from the past, either from our own past or from the world around us. So I'm also grateful for the fantastic stories and foods that are a part of my history. I have learned that sometimes all you need to experience history is a chicken salad sandwich and memories of a grass hut and adventure books that sparked ceaseless childhood dreaming.

Grandma Irene's Curried-Chicken Main Course Salad

This recipe for chicken salad is my take on a popular 1980s' spinach salad I know from growing up. It combines that salad with a curried chicken salad from my grandmother's handwritten cookbook. Eating it is always an opportunity to remember Old Hawaii, the Waioli Tea Room, and my time there.

Ingredients
    3 cups roasted chicken, pulled off bone torn into small pieces
    1 Tablespoon olive oil
    1/4 teaspoon curry powder
    1/4 cup water chestnuts, sliced
    1/2 cup white seedless grapes, halved
    1/4 cup toasted almonds, slivered
    1/4 cup chopped toasted walnuts
    1/2 cup pineapple chunks, juice drained
    1/4 cup raisins
    1/4 cup crumbled bacon
    1/4 cup finely diced red onion
    2 cups chopped escarole
    2 cups shredded napa cabbage
    4 cups fine, thin-chopped curly kale
    4 hard-boiled eggs, chopped
    6 ounces shredded sharp white cheddar cheese
    8 cups mature spinach leaves

Dressing
    3 Tablespoons champagne or white wine vinegar
    2 Tablespoons prepared horseradish
    1 Tablespoon plus 1 teaspoon Dijon mustard
    1/2 teaspoon honey

1/3 cup plus 2 Tablespoons olive oil
1/3 cup walnut or more olive oil
2 crumbled bacon strips
1/4 teaspoon curry powder
Salt, pepper, and hot sauce to taste

Method
- *In a bowl, toss torn chicken with the 1 Tablespoon of oil and the curry powder and a little salt and pepper, then massage into the chicken. Chill until ready to serve.*

Dressing
- *Whisk the horseradish, mustard, honey, and curry powder together, then add the vinegar.*
- *Slowly whisk in the oils, then add the bacon and season to taste with the salt, pepper, and hot sauce. Chill well.*

To Assemble
- *Toss the escarole, cabbage, kale, chicken, bacon, nuts, grapes, onion, and raisins with all the dressing. Season with salt and pepper as needed.*
- *Add in the pineapple, cheese, eggs, and spinach leaves, and toss to combine with the dressed salad. Season with salt and pepper as needed.*
- *Pile up salad in a large salad bowl and serve.*

Mamie Eisenhower's Quiche

Grandma Irene collected recipes from the rich and famous that were printed in newspaper and magazine articles. This was one of her favorite recipes, and she made it often. I found it in a handwritten cookbook she kept. It just seems like a recipe the tearoom would have served.

Ingredients
For the Crust
1 stick margarine (yes, margarine)
1 3 ounce package cream cheese
1 cup flour
2 Tablespoons ice water
Place in a food processor and combine
Press the into a 9-inch pie pan, prick with fork

For the Filling
3 eggs
1/4 cup grated onion
1/2 lb grated Swiss cheese
1/2 pound grated cheddar cheese
1 cup cubed ham
8 slices crisp bacon, crumbled
1 cup milk
1/2 cup sour cream
1/2 cup cottage cheese
1 Tablespoon flour
1 teaspoon salt

Method
- Combine dry and wet ingredients separately, then combine and pour into the pie shell.
- Bake for 45 to 60 to minutes at 375 degrees. Let cool for 10 mins before serving.

CHAPTER TWENTY-SIX: GROWING-UP MILESTONES AND STEAK DINNERS

Whenever we look back on childhood, our memories are comprised of moments or events that, in our mind's eye, define a larger period of time. We do not remember every moment of every day. Instead, individual experiences and milestones stand out and allow us a look into our past. These memories help define the very essence of how we recall our young selves. They are usually from one of two categories: the "firsts" or the longstanding rituals. Both fill the years of our youth. For me, the firsts include my first time at Disneyland, the first time I saw snow, the first time I rode my bike without training wheels, and, of course, for me, the first time I saw a fancy bakery cake (it was at my friend Byron's eighth birthday party). My childhood rituals involved going to eleven o'clock church service every Sunday morning with my family, playing in a youth tennis league every spring, and celebrating important family events at one particular Japanese steakhouse. And what makes these particular events stand out for me? I am not quite sure. They have one common thread, however: no matter how hard I try, I can never quite recapture their magic.

Among the many memories, I have three milestones that standout from boyhood, all of which occurred in Hawaii when I was between the second and fifth grades. They are simple things but momentous, particularly for a young boy. Perhaps they may make you think about what milestones you have experienced. And how life, while we like to think it should be remembered by big and exciting moments, is often remembered through nothing more than many little things that add up to a powerful memory.

My three childhood experiences all took place at Makalapa, a small base near Pearl Harbor that was mostly a residential and amenities station. And this makes sense, given our life in Hawaii centered so heavily around base life because the cost of living in Hawaii was so high, especially for military families. To my recollection, Makalapa had a medical clinic, a pool, a barbershop, an Officers' Club complete with a lounge and dining room, as well as living quarters for junior and senior officers. I'm sure other things existed but not in my young world.

The base was built on a sloping hillside, lush with rich Hawaiian vegetation, some of which was tamed into landscaping around the base buildings. For instance, I can remember the soft hot breezes moving the fronds of the banana trees that hung like botanical intruders over the pool fence. Other taller, leafy trees, casting shadows on the pool, loomed behind the tan cinderblock bathhouse with its tile roof. The trees and bushes wrapped the property in a blanket of greenery, giving one the feeling of complete seclusion and isolation from the outside world.

The lifeguards at the base's pool were mostly young women who wore whistles around their necks and red bathing suits. They sat high in tall, metal lifeguard chairs above the deep, blue-hued pool and the pool deck's teak chairs. Their lifesaver rings were always at the ready for any nonsense that might happen with the younger or teenaged patrons. Oh, I spent many a day in the sun under the watchful eye of blue skies, puffy clouds, and the lady lifeguards. Looking back, it was not a bad thing!

This pool is where I remember one of my first milestones—learning to swim and dive from the low and high diving boards. It started comically. On the day of my first swimming lesson, at age seven, the swim instructor asked her young Tadpoles—the name given to the class for the most inexperienced swimmers—who could swim. Just because I had been in a pool before, I raised my hand and plunged into the deep end, only needing to be rescued seconds later. Where is that shameless abandon now when taking on life?! Of course, I did eventually learn to swim and dive, which started a lifelong love for water recreation, but it was an ordinary lesson—with an initial big splash—that was the building block for many wonderful future experiences.

Another milestone at Makalapa was my first official haircut. My mother had always cut my hair at home, but when I turned seven, my father decided it was time he take me to the barber. I think for most men of my age getting a haircut is a primordial memory of some fellow with beefy hands smelling of talc and Barbicide®, standing behind you in a mirror. This fellow would set a wood block in the center of the chair for you to climb up onto so that you could be raised up to an adult height. He would drape a waxy, plastic cape over you, securing it around your neck with a snap collar. Using clippers and shears with unbelievable dexterity, he'd clip your young locks with manly vigor and precision. Sometimes scary and always intimidating, the barber was definitely an iconic figure in the pantheon of characters from boyhood. I was glad my dad was there for my first visit.

Haircuts at the barber may be a rite of passage for young boys, but they are also a gateway to male-bonding experiences. As a young boy, the Makalapa base barbershop was the first place where I realized there were places in the world that were solely the domain of men. It was a male sanctuary and a refuge from the world of women. It was a bastion of the military community and the center of manly conversation where sports, tours of duty, the fairer sex, and military gossip were all on the bill of fare along with hot towel facials, shaves, and haircuts.

The haircut became a ritual that, to this day, takes me regularly back into a version of my childhood experience. In fact, every time I smell the barber's talc on my neck, the barbershop I am in becomes Makalapa for me all over again. I still see its bright florescent lights, big mirrors, and tan-colored walls covered with framed prints of naval ships and commanding officers, past and present. I think about my dad relaxing in the old oak chair in the corner of the shop, reading a magazine or visiting with his buddies from the command, while I sat enduring the clip and snip of the barber. And I capture, for a moment, the boy I was and the wonder that time held for me learning an adult ritual.

My favorite milestone from that time in Hawaii and Makalapa is actually a food memory. Go figure! It is the memory of dining at the Officers' Club in the O. Club Dining Room. The O. Club was the scene of many a dinner for special family nights, for meals with relatives visiting from the mainland, and for special command occasions like my father's promotion to the rank of commander. It far surpassed the fanciness I had found only a few years earlier at Morrison's Cafeteria.

The O. Club was an old-school naval dining room built in the '40s. Its green walls were framed in polished bamboo accents and covered with paintings of former fleet commanders and famous warships. Low lighting washed over the dining room, cast from nautical-themed brass fixtures, and white linen tablecloths were set out with sparkling glassware and plates embossed with the gold-and-green Makalapa crest. The dining room was manned by an army of Filipino naval stewards, all with short haircuts slicked down with pomade. They wore starched, white waiter coats, while the maître d' and dining room managers donned dark blue. It seemed to me that the staff was always smiling and talking in thick accents, just like my best friend Francis in second grade. The O. Club staff moved about the dining room with military precision. For my brother and me, it was the grandest of dining rooms.

There, for the first time, I had a filet mignon steak. It came to the table wrapped in bacon and grilled to meaty perfection. It was a delicious and memorable food discovery. The potatoes that were served with it were stuffed and twice-baked. The asparagus spears made you want to stand up and salute. Eating that steak dinner made me feel all grown up. It was like I had finally arrived at the adult table.

And when I think back about our time in Hawaii and really reflect, I realize that we seldom got to indulge in steak dinners at the Officers' Club. In fact, most of my memories of steak dinners center around my father cooking a meal on the grill and us enjoying it on the lanai in our backyard. He would marinate the tough, grass-fed beef my mom would buy at the commissary with a Hawaiian marinade. It was a teriyaki-and-sweet pineapple sauce, which was popular in the 1970s. Today, I still love this sort of marinade, and I make this steak at home. One taste and I am transported back to those early steak experiences at Makalapa and our naval housing lanai and backyard. But I have to admit, eating steak at home on the lanai was never as impressive as eating that filet at the Officers' Club!

Like everyone, I have—on many an occasion—wanted to recapture my boyish awe of these childhood milestones growing up in Hawaii. But, try as I might, they allude me. I have been to amazing places with out-of-this-world swimming pools, but the pools do not rival my memory of the pool where my first almost-drowning occurred. I have received haircuts in the best of salons, but none have the soul of the barbershop at Makalapa. I have had phenomenal meals in steakhouse after steakhouse, even cooked by some of the most renowned chefs in the country, and I've made steaks at home, each time trying to recapture that same meaty goodness offered at the O. Club. But all those meals somehow pale in comparison with my succulent memories.

The pool, the barbershop, and the Officers' Club dining room were perhaps never the things I remember them being. But whatever really is? The important thing is that milestones become part of you and, hopefully, inspire you to build upon them. Through sharing the memories and enjoying life, we make new, fun, and tasty memories every day with people we love and who are important to us. We never really grow up; we just keep growing.

Steak Hawaiian

This is based on my daddy's recipe from the 1970s when sweet pineapple marinades were all the rage.

Ingredients
    4 8 to 10 ounce boneless rib eye (my favorite) or New York Strip steaks, 2-3 inches thick or even flank steak

For the marinade:
- *1/3 cup apple cider vinegar*
- *1 1/2 6 ounce cans pineapple juice*
- *3/4 cup soy sauce (low sodium)*
- *1/8 cup Worcestershire sauce*
- *1 Tablespoon sesame oil*
- *1/2 cup brown sugar*
- *2 teaspoons fresh chopped garlic*
- *2 teaspoons garlic powder*
- *2 teaspoons ginger powder*
- *2 teaspoons grated ginger*

Method
- *Season the steaks well on both sides with lots of salt and pepper.*
- *Place all ingredients for the marinade in a saucepan and heat on low for all the flavors to come together.*
- *Bring mixture up to a boil then turn off the heat and let cool completely.*
- *Seal steaks in a Ziploc® bag with the marinade and let sit in the fridge overnight or up to 48 hours. (I know commitment, right?)*
- *When ready to cook, let come back to room temp. Season again with pepper— no salt—then grill steaks over high heat for 2 to 3 mins on each side. (They are so marinated they do not need long on the grill.)*

Roasted Steakhouse-Style Tomatoes

Ingredients
    1/4 cup chopped flat leaf parsley
    2 teaspoons fresh-picked thyme leaves
    1 teaspoon minced garlic
    1/4 cup Panko bread crumbs
    1/4 cup olive oil
    1/3 cup grated Parmesan cheese
    1/2 teaspoon ground black pepper
    Salt to taste
    6 large ripe beefsteak tomatoes, halved

Method
- Preheat oven to 350 degrees.
- Combine the ingredients other than tomatoes in a bowl and mix well.
- Season with salt and then top the tomatoes with a mound of the stuffing mix.
- Place the tomatoes on a baking sheet and bake for 15 to 20 minutes until the tomatoes are done and the topping is browned and crusty.

Classic Roasted Asparagus

Serve these spears with Blender Hollandaise Sauce (recipe follows)

Ingredients
  2 bunches asparagus, trimmed
  1/4 cup olive oil
  Salt and pepper to taste
  1 lemon, halved

Method
- Pre-heat oven to 350.
- Place asparagus on a baking sheet lined with foil.
- Toss the stem to coat in the oil.
- Lay flat in one layer on baking sheet.
- Sprinkle with salt and pepper.
- Bake for about 15 minutes or so until the asparagus is done but not too soft.
- Place on a platter for serving and garnish with a squeeze of lemon juice and flaky sea salt.

Blender Hollandaise Sauce

Ingredients
  1 1/2 sticks melted butter
  4 egg yolks
  4 Tablespoon lemon juice
  Nice pinch of salt and of pepper

Method
- Pour eggs, lemon juice, and salt into a blender (that has been heated with hot water) and blend until combined.
- Then, with the motor running, slowly pour in the melted butter in a steady stream until the mixture becomes a thick sauce. Makes one cup.

Restaurant-Style Double-Stuffed Jacket Potatoes

Ingredients
8 medium baking potatoes
2 teaspoons vegetable oil
Coarse sea salt
4 Tablespoons butter
1/2 cup sour cream
4 Tablespoons chopped bacon
1 cup crumbled soft goat cheese
1/2 cup shredded white cheddar or Monterey Jack cheese
Milk as needed
Salt and pepper to taste
1/4 teaspoon garlic powder
1/2 teaspoon onion powder
1/2 cup finely chopped chives
1/4 cup of chopped scallions for garnish
1 cup shredded white cheddar cheese for garnish
2 Tablespoons chopped bacon for garnish

Method
- Preheat oven to 375 degrees.
- Wash and scrub potatoes until clean.
- Rub with the oil and sprinkle with the sea salt.
- Pierce with a folk and place potatoes on a foil-lined baking sheet.
- Bake in the oven for 50 to 60 minutes until soft when pierced by a fork.
- Remove and cool.
- When cool, slice the potatoes's top quarter off, exposing the flesh inside.

- *Carefully scoop out the insides, being careful to leave a little bit of the wall to prevent breaking the skin. Salt the shells before stuffing.*
- *Mash the potato pulp with all the remaining ingredients. Add milk a bit at a time if too thick or dry. Season to taste.*
- *Carefully re-stuff each potato until puffed out on the top.*
- *Bake at 300 for about 30 minutes until warmed through. To serve, garnish with cheddar cheese reserved bacon bits and with scallions.*

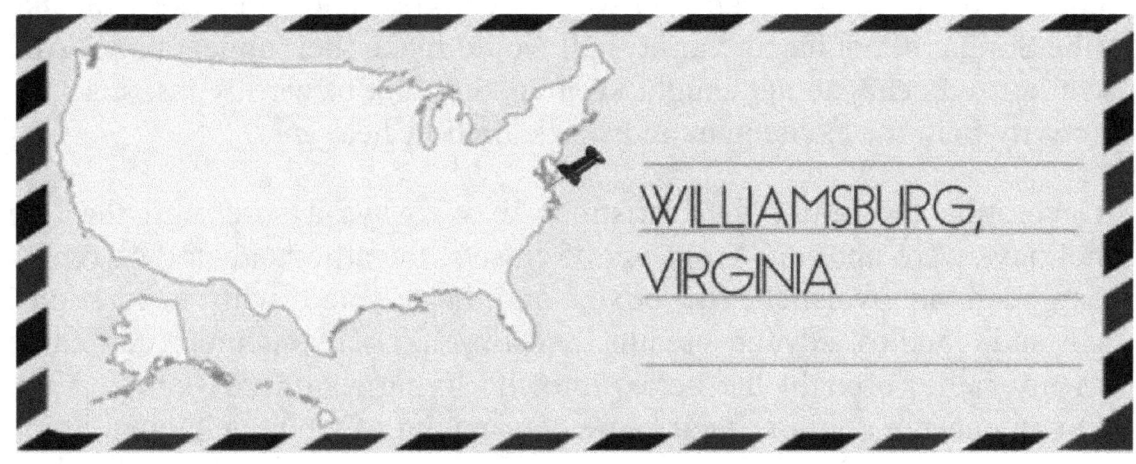

CHAPTER TWENTY-SEVEN: CHILDHOOD CHRISTMAS TRADITIONS, COLONIAL WILLIAMSBURG, AND STUFFED FLOUNDER

To me, Christmas is the queen of holidays. It is the most magical time of the year. And, as a child, the season was always heralded in with the appearance of the Sears Wish Book catalog in the mail. When that enormous book arrived, I knew my favorite time of year was right around the corner.

When you are little, time itself seems to slow down or even stand still around Christmas. For me, it was a season of great celebrating, of worship, and of family and friends coming together. Carols played on the radio and in stores, strands of lights were strung along eaves and around lamp posts, and twinkling evergreen trees were prominently displayed in almost every living room window throughout the neighborhood. And, of course, at the base of those trees, there were mounds of gifts beautifully and colorfully wrapped. All of these things made the season especially bright.

Christmas also meant church choirs, holiday pageants, parties, and, of course, food. Gingerbread, Norwegian cookies, and Japanese fruitcake (the Southern, not hated, variety) all would make their appearances. And while it was easy to get caught up in a whole lot of earthly tasks, all the activity built the excitement and was somehow heavenly.

Decorating the house for Christmas was always a sure sign that the holidays were upon us. From out of closets, the attic, and storage rooms exploded an avalanche of boxes and bags filled with decorations, garland, candles, advent wreaths, and tinsel. The excitement that came as my father brought the boxes into the living room was intoxicating. Ornaments not seen in a year came pouring out of their packaging. Some were in clear, plastic-faced boxes, where you could see the brightly colored ornaments nestled in their individual cells. Others wrapped in tissue were lifted gently out of their yearlong resting places. Garland and strings of lights were unfurled and found their places on the mantle or along the windowsills. The ceramic nativity set—cast by Grandma in a pottery class and hand-painted by my mother, brother, and me in garish primary colors—was carefully unwrapped and put into its place of prominence in the living room right next to the tree, reminding us what all the fun was really about. The advent wreath was placed in the center of the dining room table, and every week we lit the appropriate candles and remembered all the blessings we enjoyed all year long while sitting around the table and enjoying the tastes and flavors of the season.

Out of all the decorating being done, decorating the tree was my favorite part. When I was little, my parents always had a fresh tree. I would love to wake up in the morning or when I would come home from school, because our whole house smelled like a pine forest; it just smelled like Christmas. Later, we had fake trees that were less of a mess and much more in line with Mama's sense of good housekeeping (but to be honest, those fake trees never really lived up to the trees of my childhood).

Fresh or fake, we layered tons of lights and ornaments onto our tree. Some of the ornaments were extremely old, dating back to when my Grandma Irene had been a little girl. One glass ornament had even been brought over by family from Europe. Mama always made sure that ornament was hung carefully on the tree and in an eye-catching spot. One unique decoration that we put on our tree was a garland of paper doilies. Every year, sitting at the dining room table, Grandma Irene, my brother, and me would carefully cut the large lacy doilies into spirals and pin them together. The garland layered on the tree like snowdrifts. This was an old Depression-era decoration, and we just continued the tradition.

Now, of course, no tree would be complete without a sparkling tree topper. Our tree was crowned with a small silver foil star. It was an ornament my mama had from when she was a little girl. It was a Cinnamon Bear star. *Cinnamon Bear* was an old Christmastime radio program. Listening to the popular serial as a little girl was one of Mama's childhood holiday traditions, probably much like my brother and me watching *Rudolf the Red-Nosed Reindeer, Santa Claus is Comin' to Town,* and *The Year Without a Santa Claus* on network TV year after year. My brother and I were fascinated with the unique stop-motion animation of these programs, and, of course, the songs would stick in our heads for days!

Well, according to Mama, the story of Cinnamon Bear is the story of two young children who go looking for their missing silver star that is to sit at the top of their Christmas tree. The children find themselves in the Land of Maybe. In their search, they come across many enchanted characters. Some help the children in their quest, like Paddy O'Cinnamon (aka Cinnamon Bear). And of course others, like Crazy Quilt Dragon, Wesley The Wailing Whale, and the Wintergreen Witch, hinder their efforts.

Mama explained how she got her own silver star. Children in the radio audience could get their own Cinnamon Bear star by sending in a dime to the radio program. The station would then send you back your own star. My mama remembers her mother cutting slits in an index card to hold the dime. Mama taped the dime into place and then slid the card into an envelope. Mama recounted how she carefully addressed the envelope, mailed it, and then patiently waited. She told us she would wait for the mailman every day to deliver the mail, hoping the star would arrive. Finally it did, and that star has been with her ever since. It sits atop our family tree to this day.

The Cinnamon Bear may be a memory, but his mission to bring that star back still lives on today; every year we place it on the tree. Traditions like this one are not merely repetitive acts, they represent something deeper and symbolize something important to us. They, too, are missions. Traditions help us, in an outward manner, to remember an inward feeling—a feeling we want to recall and repeat. These family rituals help us to always remember and never forget our personal childhoods and our ancestral heritages.

Holidays are often times when we develop or adopt traditions, because customs can help us celebrate the larger message of a holiday in a more personal way. For me, finding a deeper meaning in Christmas has become important over the years. Christmas is about touching the ones I love in a special way. Gifts at this time of year, as well as gatherings, have a special place in the celebration.

During my childhood, my parents struggled, mostly financially, with how we could best spend the holidays. But I have to give my mom and dad credit because they gave us some wonderful moments and memories. When we got old enough to appreciate a more sophisticated holiday experience (and my father started making more money being out of the Navy), my parents decided to take us on a vacation to Colonial Williamsburg in southeast Virginia. Williamsburg, for those of you who don't know, was Virginia's center of government for eighty-one years during the 1700s. Additionally, some of our nation's founding fathers—Patrick Henry, Thomas Jefferson, George Washington, and George Wythe—all had personal and professional ties to Williamsburg prior to the American Revolution.

Today, Colonial Williamsburg makes up part of the historic district of Williamsburg, Virginia. It is also a living-history museum, where actors live out eighteenth-century customs and everyday life of colonial America. The town has been meticulously restored and is a realistic reproduction of a colonial village—with its homes, shops, taverns, restaurants, gardens, and other public spaces—as it was on the eve of 1776. Visitors can walk alongside our early compatriots and explore the time our country was being born.

For two young boys interested in history, Williamsburg during the Christmas season was a sight to see. Wandering along the pebble-paved streets lined with colonial buildings, we found ourselves immersed in the sights, smells, and tastes of the holiday season of another time. Period-dressed characters explained in detail about the architecture and history of the era. They even offered food to taste in bakeries, shops, and the kitchens of the larger houses. Greenery—wreaths and garlands decked with fruits, vegetables, and dried flowers—was draped everywhere. It was on doors and windows, along mantles and stairwell railings, and in the center of tables. And windows without wreaths often had lit candles, their flames dancing and twinkling in the evenings. Also at night, bonfires were lit for singing and storytelling, as well as lighting up the holiday nights. It was magical.

Our 1970s-dining experience in Williamsburg was varied. There were pancakes and waffles at the modern coffee shop at the Williamsburg Motor Inn and peanut soup and chicken potpie at the period taverns, like the Kings Arm, in the town. Prime rib and seafood were offered at the upscale Cascades Restaurant. My favorite meal, however, had to be a full-on Colonial feast with actors playing the parts of the hosts and servers, and us and fellow visitors playing the role of guests. It was very much like the family dining theater of Medieval Times, but instead of witnessing knights jousting, we were enjoying a meal in George Washington's dining room. There were so many different dishes to sample that night. Colonial foods such as corn chowder, stuffed chicken, shepherd's pie, pan roasts, wild game, spoon bread, and gingerbread abounded. What a great holiday dining experience!

Our Christmas in Williamsburg that year was very special, and it is a time I find even more special with each passing year. You see, growing up, we don't always understand that much of the richness we come to know about life actually comes from our parents. Parents can provide us with the opportunity to have experiences. Those experiences help us shape our view of the world. As an adult, I'm always amazed at how many wonderful things I have come to know because of the gifts my parents gave me—not just at Christmas all wrapped up with bows, but all year long in varied, little ways. As children, we are disappointed when we find out Santa Claus isn't real. But, from my adult perspective, mothers and fathers are indeed the real Santa Claus. A Santa Claus who gives tirelessly throughout the year!

East-Coast Style Stuffed Flounder

For a more modern and fine-dining experience in Williamsburg, my parents took us to Cascades. At the time, it was a very popular restaurant with a tiered dining room and windows that looked out on a waterfall, but it has since closed its doors. One of the dishes Cascades was known for was its stuffed flounder. My Grandma Irene made this flounder recipe often; the note in her cookbook reads, "As good as Cascades." It just might be the perfect stuffed flounder.

Ingredients
- 4 flounder filets
- Stuffing (recipe follows)
- Salt and pepper to taste
- Paprika
- Lemon butter sauce (recipe follows)
- 6 Tablespoons lemon juice
- Toasted tarragon bread crumbs (1 cup bread crumbs mixed with 1 Tablespoon dried tarragon)
- Some butter softened

Method
- Preheat oven to 375 degrees.
- Butter baking dish.
- Place fillets in the baking dish.
- Top each the fillet with 1/4 of the stuffing.
- Pour lemon juice over the fish.
- Season with salt and pepper.
- Top with bread crumbs, making sure each fillet is generously covered.
- Sprinkle with paprika.
- Dot with butter.
- Bake for 30 minutes or until fish is opaque and flakes easily with fork.

Seafood Stuffing

Ingredients
    1/4 cup grated onion
    1/4 cup finely chopped celery
    2/3 cup Panko bread crumbs
    2 Tablespoons chopped parsley
    Grated rind of one lemon
    1/4 cup melted butter
    The juice of one lemon
    1 teaspoon salt
    1/4 teaspoon pepper
    1/8 teaspoon nutmeg
    1/2 teaspoon Old Bay seasoning

    To this, fold in the following:
    1 finely chopped boiled egg
    1/4 cup chopped shrimp
    1/4 cup crabmeat

Method
- Melt butter, mix together all vegetables, cook until soft. Add spices and seafood, and stir until warmed and combined. Remove from heat.

Lemon Butter Sauce

Method
- *In a blender, drop three egg yolks and one small shallot, finely chopped.*
- *Melt 1/3 pound of butter.*
- *Warm 1/4 cup cream in a pan.*
- *In another pan, heat 1/2 teaspoon white vinegar with 6 Tablespoons lemon juice.*
- *With blender running and eggs inside, slowly add the heated lemon juice.*
- *Then add in 1 Tablespoon capers.*
- *Then slowly pour in the melted butter in a slow, steady stream.*
- *Then slowly add in the warm cream.*
- *Season to taste. Pour into small pan to keep warm or pour directly over fish when it comes out of the oven. Or serve on the side with fish.*

Japanese Fruitcake

Mama would often make this at Christmas. It was Big Mama's recipe.

Ingredients
    3 cups all-purpose flour
    2 teaspoons baking powder
    1/2 teaspoon salt
    1 cup chopped raisins or whole currants
    1 cup chopped pecans or walnuts
    1 1/2 teaspoons ground cinnamon
    1 1/2 teaspoons ground allspice
    1/2 teaspoon ground cloves
    1 cup (2 sticks) butter, softened
    2 cups sugar
    4 eggs
    1 teaspoon vanilla extract
    1 cup milk

Lemon-Coconut Filling
    1 cup water
    2 cups sugar
    1/4 cup lemon juice
    1 Tablespoon grated lemon zest
    About 3-1/2 cups freshly grated coconut or sweetened, shredded coconut
    2 Tablespoons cornstarch
    1/2 cup cold water

Method
- *To make the cake, heat the oven to 350 degrees F. Generously butter and flour four 8 or 9-inch round cake pans. Combine the*

flour, baking powder, and salt in one medium bowl. In another, combine the raisins, pecans, cinnamon, allspice, and cloves. Use a big spoon to stir the flour mixture well, then add to mix the raisins, nuts, and spices together.

- *In a large bowl, combine the butter and sugar, and beat with a mixer at high speed to combine them well. Add the eggs one at a time, beating to make a smooth, fluffy mixture. Stir the vanilla into the milk. Add about half the flour mixture, and then half the milk, beating at low speed after each addition to mix everything together well. Repeat with the remaining flour and milk.*

- *Divide half the batter between 2 of the pans, and set them aside. Stir the raisins, nuts, and spices into the remaining batter. Divide this spiced batter between the 2 remaining pans, and set all 4 cake pans in the oven.*

- *Bake at 350 degrees F for 20 to 25 minutes, until the layers are golden brown, pulling away from the sides of the pans, and spring back when touched lightly in the center. Cool the layers on a wire rack or a folded kitchen towel for 10 minutes, and then turn them out onto the wire racks or onto plates to cool completely, top side up.*

- *While the cake is baking, make the filling. In a heavy medium saucepan, bring the 1 cup of water to a boil over medium heat. Stir in the sugar, lemon juice, zest, and coconut, and bring to a boil. Adjust the heat to maintain a gentle boil, and cook for 7 minutes, stirring now and then. Mix the cornstarch into the cold water, stir well, and then add the mixture to the pan, mixing to dissolve it into the filling. Reduce the heat to a simmer and cook for 3 to 4 minutes, stirring often, until the filling is thickened and clear. Remove from the heat, transfer to a bowl, and cool to room temperature, stirring now and then.*

- *To complete the cake, place a plain, unspiced layer, top side down, on a cake stand or serving plate, and poke little holes all over it so that some of the filling will penetrate the cake. Spread about one fourth of the cooled filling over the layer all the way to the edges. Place a spiced layer over the filling, poke holes all over, and spread with another quarter of the filling. Repeat with the remaining layers and filling, placing the final spiced layer, top side up, and pouring all the remaining filling over the layer so that a little cascades down the sides of the cake. Let stand for several hours to firm up, and cover and chill overnight. If possible, remove the cake from the refrigerator an hour or so in advance of serving time, to return to room temperature.*

SECTION FIVE

ON RETURNING TO THE SOUTH CAROLINA LOW COUNTRY

CHAPTER TWENTY-EIGHT: BEACHES, NEW BEGINNINGS, AND BISCUITS AND GRAVY

My family moved back to the Charleston area, ending our sojourn in military life, when I was twenty years old. After living in so many different regions of our nation, returning to South Carolina was like coming home in an unexplainable way for me. I can still remember the trip. My brother and I—me at James Madison University, him at George Mason University—drove down from Virginia together during a Thanksgiving break. We were filled with anticipation, both of us excited to see our new home. Our parents had moved a few months earlier in the summer. My father had started a new adventure as director of the South Carolina Research Authority, founded to support the state's technology sector.

After our seven-hour drive, we neared the city at dusk. We could see the sun setting on the horizon and the twinkle of lights from downtown playing off the waters of the harbor. We saw a shadowed cityscape of low buildings, peaked roofs, and church spires popping out from the rest of the low-lying skyline. We followed the highway, driving across the long harbor bridge from downtown proper. We crossed the dark span of water, arriving in Mount Pleasant where my parents had settled. We made our way up the long, unlit stretch of Highway 17 for two miles or so, then turned at the solitary street lamp marking the entrance to our neighborhood, a golf course community far away from the city center.

Ancient, mossy oak trees illuminated by up-lighting greeted us as we drove down the street. When we finally found the house and pulled into the driveway, we were so glad to be home. And it was, without a doubt, home. Like every time we had moved in the Navy, our house was a new and different structure but unmistakably ours. There were the pictures, paintings, furniture, and the familiar trappings of our lives all around, just reordered in this new space. And wafting through the house was the all-too-familiar smell of my mother's chili bubbling quietly in the crockpot and cornbread warming in the oven. The Hedden boys were home and dinner was waiting.

We relaxed into the evening, catching up on all the news and being toured around the new family digs. And then we sat for our first family meal together after being months apart. That night, as I stood outside on the backyard deck overlooking the pool and watched the lights from the house dancing on the water, I breathed in the familiar Carolina air spiced by pine and damp vegetation and felt like I was, indeed, home.

The next day, upon waking in our new home, we came downstairs, the morning still fresh. My father wanted to take us out to the beach on Sullivan's Island—a nearby barrier island. He also wanted to treat us to a true Southern-style breakfast. He knew that, at the newly opened Sea Biscuit Café on the neighboring Isle of Palms, we could feast on, among other things, one of my favorite Southern-breakfast foods—biscuits and gravy.

We rode in his car across the causeway and the old steel drawbridge that separated the mainland from the barrier islands. The marshland, golden and fall-tinged, stretched out on either side of the elevated road. A thick, watery carpet of lush grasses were occasionally interrupted by egrets standing straight, white and tall, their heads peering over the top of the hedgerow of marsh grass.

We drove onto Sullivan's Island and turned, heading through its small business district of weathered buildings. We pulled onto a street designated Station 21 (the streets are all named after streetcar stops; a trolley had once run along the length of the island) and parked. Walking, we made our way down a beaten beach path between the looming edifices of two ancient, wooden beach houses. Both houses, badly needing a paint job, stood guard over the dunes under the chill of the gray morning. We rambled over the sandbanks, through the scraggly brush and sea grass, down to the beach.

At low tide, the beach stretched out wide and long, empty of all human visitors except us. The waves, gray and blue, lapped in slow rhythm, and the wind was coming off the sea. A feeling of the familiar suddenly seized me. I felt that I belonged on that beach and that, somehow, the beach was a part of me. Perhaps it was the memory of all the East Coast beaches I had been to as a child. Perhaps it was the sense memory of previous visits to Charleston. Whatever it was, it felt like I had been there before. There was a sense of belonging I can't really express, except to say it felt like a homecoming. And I was glad to be back.

What I connected to was silent and spiritual. My family's journey in this country had started in this coastal city in the 1700s. My ancestors had fought here in the war that divided this nation. My father had attended a university here. As a young family, we had lived here. My brother had been born here. But it was more than that. It was as if all my past family were reaching out, reminding me of my roots and calling me to sink my toes into the sand beneath my feet, to stand in this place and in the life that was to be had here and now. Here, in this spot, where others in my family had trod. This reflection was not just a nod to the past. It was a call to action—to embrace what life has to offer.

After we left the beach, we made our way to The Isle of Palms for breakfast. As I sat at the diner, enjoying the ocean breeze rolling softly through the screened-in porch and savoring the salty, creamy, porky, doughy deliciousness of those biscuits and gravy my dad wanted me to have, I reflected on my morning on the beach and knew, somehow, my next move would be back to Charleston.

And that's how my new beginning in Charleston began. The years of living there to follow would always come back to that moment when I realized, with my toes in the sand, that Charleston always was and always would be home.

Southern Biscuits and Gravy

I have to preface this recipe by saying that I did not grow up in a biscuit family. I grew up in a cornbread family. My knowledge of true biscuits and gravy came later on when I attended college in rural Virginia. There, in Harrisonburg, I encountered this tasty dish on a consistent basis at the local diners. This recipe is based on one given to me by my friend Phil, who managed the Howard Johnson's next to campus. Who would've thought that an aging chain restaurant would hold such culinary secrets? I've tweaked it over the years, but this dish is no joke. It is so delicious and decadent, and it's my elevated take on the classic.

Phil's Biscuits

These biscuits, made with cream, buttermilk, and cheese, come out so good. Back in the day, Phil used common Swiss cheese, but Gruyère or Fontina make excellent modern substitutions. I added chives and Parmesan.

Makes about 12 biscuits

Ingredients
    1 1/2 cups all-purpose flour
    1 1/2 cups pastry flour
    2 1/2 teaspoons baking powder
    1 1/4 teaspoons kosher salt
    1/2 teaspoon dry mustard powder
    1 pinch cayenne pepper
    1 1/2 sticks cold, unsalted butter, cubed
    1/4 cup finely chopped chives
    2 cups grated Swiss, Gruyère or Fontina cheese
    1/2 cup grated and loosely packed yellow or white cheddar cheese

1/4 cup grated Parmesan cheese
1 cup buttermilk
1/2 cup heavy cream
1 large egg
Flaky sea salt for garnish

Method

- *Put oven rack in middle position and preheat the oven to 425 degrees F.*
- *Whisk all dry ingredients together in a large mixing bowl.*
- *Blend in butter, chives, and cheeses with your pastry cutter or your fingers until mixture resembles coarse meal.*
- *Add heavy cream and buttermilk and mix together until dough just forms.*
- *Turn the dough out onto a well-floured surface and knead gently three times. Don't over-work the dough.*
- *Pat out dough into a rectangle on a floured board.*
- *Fold over on itself.*
- *Roll out slightly with rolling pin.*
- *Repeat folding four more times.*
- *Roll to 1/2-inch thickness and cut into 12 squares. (Love square biscuits!)*
- *Transfer to a baking sheet, placing them together on sheet that will help them rise.*
- *Brush the tops with egg wash and sprinkle with flaky sea salt.*
- *Bake until golden, 20 minutes, turning once.*
- *If biscuits look underdone on the inside, drop the oven temperature to 250 and continue baking just for a few more minutes. Serve warm.*

Cream Gravy with Sherry, Sausage and Thyme

The secret to this amazingly different cream gravy is twofold: thyme and sherry, both in two forms.

Ingredients
    2 pounds high quality ground sage-flavored pork sausage breakfast
    1 1/2 cups flour
    3/4 stick butter
    5 cups whole milk
    1 1/2 teaspoon garlic powder
    1 teaspoon onion powder
    1 Tablespoon Frank's RedHot® sauce
    3 teaspoons black pepper
    1/2 cup sherry cooking wine (yes, cooking wine)
    1 1/2 Tablespoons sherry vinegar
    1/4 teaspoon dried sage
    1 teaspoon dried thyme
    2 teaspoons fresh thyme, chopped
    2 Tablespoons fresh chives, finely chopped for garnish
    Salt to taste

Method
- *In a large heavy-bottomed pot, break up sausage and cook until done.*
- *Drain half of the rendered fat.*
- *Add butter until melted, then add flour and stir until cooked and the raw flavor is gone (about 3 minutes).*
- *Add spices and cook another 2 minutes.*
- *Slowly add the milk and stir constantly using a whisk.*
- *Add the sherry cooking wine and cook for about 10 minutes until the gravy is thick and has set up. If too thick, add more milk.*

- *Season to taste. It will take some salt; make sure it's not under-seasoned.*
- *Just before serving, stir in the vinegar.*
- *Serve over biscuits and top with chives.*

CHAPTER TWENTY-NINE: SHRIMP AND GRITS: IT'S NOT JUST FOR BREAKFAST ANYMORE!

For centuries, people who labored in the mostly agrarian South ate large, hearty breakfasts. And grits—a permanent fixture in Southern-breakfast fare—was the great equalizer. Big Mama told my father that when she was small on her father's farm, everyone from the foreman to the farm hands would sit down to breakfast together and eat from the same big pot of grits, cooked up over an open flame in cast-iron kettles. Breakfast was a nourishing meal often taken together, regardless of class, before beginning a long day of work in the fields.

As such, it is not surprising that generous breakfasts are a mainstay of Southern living and hospitality. And breakfast was always a good meal in our house. I grew up enjoying all sorts of morning dishes—savory and sweet—but grits were always on the top of my list. One of my first memories of Southern food begins with a serving platter heaping with grits at the breakfast table. I learned from a young age the joys of eating real grits—not the instant, watery kind served up in most diners, but the real thick, salty, and savory kind (the homemade kind) served with butter and love.

When my brother was about three, we went to my Aunt Doris's house in Atlanta for a family reunion. In the morning, she laid out a stunning breakfast of pastries and toast, eggs and sausage links, and, of course, grits. My mother almost never made sausage links because she got her sausage fresh from the butcher and made patties. Well, my brother, never having seen links before, just stared down at his plate with a confused and distressed gaze.

When my aunt questioned what was wrong, he looked up at her and in a woeful tone said, "Aunt Doris, I don't eat dog doo for breakfast."

You might have thought my aunt was going to keel over dead from laughing. It tickled her so much! But she quickly appeased my brother—removing the links from his plate and asking what he would like to eat instead.

He respectfully replied, "Could I have shrimp and grits, ma'am, please?"

My brother's request from so many years past seems to follow me wherever I go. Do you know that, in New York City, the number one request I get from friends is for shrimp and grits? It's funny to me that New Yorkers seem to have a love affair and a fascination with the dish. Truly, aside from fried chicken, I cannot think of another food item that is more iconic of the South to Yankees than shrimp and grits.

Indeed, the love of grits is strong. Equally though, like with many foods, some people—mostly those who did not grow up in the South—have a strong disdain for them. When we were in Hawaii, I became good friends with the son of the naval chaplain at Pearl Harbor. His name was Tad, and his family lived in a house right behind ours in naval housing.

They had been in Hawaii about six months when Tad came over one Saturday morning for breakfast. His eyes grew wide with surprise and joy when he saw grits on our breakfast table. He exclaimed how much he loved grits and had not had them since coming to Hawaii. With a confused look, he asked my mother where she got them.

"Why, at the commissary," she answered.

"That's funny, because my mom says she can't find them there." He returned home happily to tell his mother the great news that grits were indeed available at the store. She only needed to look a little bit harder for them.

A few days later, Tad's mother saw my mother in our backyard. She came out of her house, and they chatted over the fence. She told my mom how sad she was that my mom told her son about grits being at the commissary. My mother, of course, questioned why.

"Because I hate them and hate making them. My husband's family is from the South. He and all my kids love them, but, being from the North, I can't stand them. I thought I would be free of them for at least two years if I fibbed about them not being available at the commissary here."

My mother laughed at the thought of this mom lying to her family because she disliked grits so much. She thought it was especially funny because the woman was a minister's wife.

The dish we know today as shrimp and grits has its origins as a Low Country fisherman's breakfast. Originating in the fishing and shipping communities of South Carolina and Georgia, it was comprised simply of white grits and shrimp cooked quickly in a few ingredients. Onion, tomatoes, and green bell peppers were sautéed together in a pan with a little oil and cooked until soft. Then, some ketchup and water were added. The shrimp went into the pan, and the ingredients were tossed.

The mixture would be served over bowls of creamy white grits with a tad of butter. Sometimes a little bacon fat was used, and crumbled bacon was added. It was the breakfast shrimpers would have before they set out to sea for the day.

Today, there are just about as many recipes for shrimp and grits out there as there are cooks. Chefs all over are reinventing and adapting the dish for modern palates and adding their own unique twists. There are countless versions. And as this dish has evolved, it has come to include all sorts of other ingredients like okra, mushrooms, and other savory add-ins. That's the beautiful thing about this dish. You have an established starting point, but before you know it, you've developed your own unique version. That's the joy of cooking at home: *you* are the chef and *you* call the shots.

My version of shrimp and grits comes from a variety of places. My grandmother and mother's version is based on a recipe from *Charleston Receipts*, a cookbook first published in 1930. In the book's original edition, the recipe was titled, "Breakfast Shrimp and Hominy." In the 1976 edition, it is, "Breakfast Shrimp and Grits." Every time I go home, I have to have this dish at least once, and it doesn't have to be at breakfast! Although the dish was originally intended to be served in the mornings, our family has enjoyed it at breakfast, lunch, and dinner over the years.

Spicy Tarragon and Dijon Shrimp with Bacon-Boursin Grits

If you would like to try a modern take on shrimp and grits, I hope you will give this one a shot. I developed the recipe by taking a cue from one of my favorite pasta dishes, Shrimp Dijon and Linguini. I think it comes out rather lovely.

Makes 4 portions with extra grits

Ingredients
- 1 lb large shrimp, peeled and deveined, tail on
- 1/2 Tablespoon garlic flavored oil
- 2-3 Tablespoons Dijon mustard
- 1 teaspoon dried tarragon
- 1/4 cup butter
- 2 Tablespoons ketchup
- 2 Tablespoons Frank's RedHot® sauce
- 4 to 6 scallions, chopped
- 4 pieces of bacon, cooked and crumbled
- 1/2 of a red or green pepper, chopped into fine dice
- 1 1/2 cup 7 minute quick grits
- 6 cups chicken stock
- 1 bay leaf
- 1 whole package soft boursin shallot and garlic cheese
- 3 Tablespoons bacon grease
- 2 cups half and half
- Salt and pepper

Method

For the Shrimp
- *In a glass bowl, place the shrimp with the Dijon and the tarragon and combine until well-coated. Place in fridge, covered, for at least 2 hours.*
- *When ready to cook, place a small amount of garlic oil in a pan and cook the pepper and half the scallions until just done, then add the shrimp. Add the butter, ketchup, and hot sauce, and when shrimp is cooked, serve.*

For the Bacon-Cheese Grits
- *Bring the water to just a boil. Add 1 1/2 teaspoons salt and 1/2 teaspoon black pepper.*
- *Stir in grits with a whisk, making sure there is no clumping. Add in the bay leaf.*
- *Cook according to package directions until thick, about 7 minutes. Add the half and half and cook for another 30 minutes, stirring occasionally to make sure grits are not clumping, adding water if they get too thick.*
- *To serve, remove bay leaf, stir in cheese and bacon grease.*
- *Taste and adjust seasoning.*
- *Can be held for up to 2 hours. If too thick, add water and stir again until creamy.*

Serve
- *Place grits in the bottom of 4 wide bowls and divide shrimp among the four. Spoon butter and hot sauce mixture over the shrimp. Garnish with the bacon and the scallions.*

CHAPTER THIRTY: SAVORING SAVANNAH AND LOW COUNTRY CRAB STEW

Everyone loves a good road trip, and in 1979, Mama took my brother and me on a fantastic one. It was the summer between my eighth- and ninth-grade years. Friends of our family who had a beach house in St. Augustine, Florida, invited us to stay with them for a month. Well, my father was all tied up with business and could only commit to a weekend-long stay. But my mama was never one to refuse an offer for a good beach vacation, so she packed up the large Dodge Monaco station wagon and off we went, just the three off us. Our journey from Washington, DC, down to Florida quickly turned into one of those quintessential family road trips—the kind you never forget.

The trip started out joyously—the radio blaring Billy Joel, Elton John, Fleetwood Mac, and Doobie Brothers songs over and over, with my mother, brother, and me singing along. The lush, green woods of Virginia and North Carolina blanketed the car with shade, shielding us from the 98-degree summer heat. As we got further south and into the Low Country (a 220-mile stretch of coastal plains between South Carolina and Georgia), the tall oak and pine trees slowly gave way to scraggily conifers and sub-tropic vegetation. By the time we reached Georgia, the trees looked like shrubs interspersed among vast swaths of dead woody plants and tall marsh grasses. We drove over and through the old rice fields of the once-booming coastal rice empire. The sun and heat became punishing.

If you think driving down the East Coast in 98-degree weather in August is rough, believe me, it got worse. Just north of Savannah, Georgia, our usually trusty teal and wood-paneled station wagon began to make strange noises. The smell of burning wires wafted through the louvered vents of the air-conditioner panels. The car gave a great groan and then the air-conditioner sputtered and died.

Mama decided it would be a good idea to head toward Savannah, leaving I-95 behind, and get somewhere to see what was going on with the car. We slowly drove into downtown Savannah. Just as we pulled into a service station, the electrical system went *BOOM*! The three of us jumped out of the car, and Mom raised the hood. We stood there transfixed, staring at the ominous cloud of smoke rising from the engine. With each billow, our dreams of making it to the beach that night were slowly disappearing, and what was worse, we were in a strange town that smelled vaguely of burning rubber and methane gas (compliments of the nearby paper mill).

A knight in shining armor came to our aid in the form of a grease-covered and snaggletooth station attendant. In a thick Georgian accent, he informed us not only that he knew what the problem was, but that he could fix it. Our hopes briefly rose, thinking this would be a quick fix. Then, they slowly sank again when he told us that getting the part would take the better part of the day; if we were lucky, we would be on our way by 6 p.m. that evening, but most likely not until the next day. "Oh crap!" I thought to myself. My brother and I glanced at each other as we slowly sat down on a nearby bench like two deflated balloons. Our gazes then returned to the car. Oh how we wished it would magically come back to life.

My mama promptly called my father to fill him in on our car troubles. When she got off the phone, she told us we would have to make plans for staying in Savannah for the night. This is one thing that is great about Mama: she is the queen of making lemonade out of lemons. So, without so much as a *hello*, she led us off on a great adventure in downtown Savannah, a city rich in antebellum architecture and culinary history.

Now, we had stopped in Savannah before on family trips, but only to eat at the famous Pirate House Restaurant, a huge and rambling seafood house where the decor and the staff costumes celebrated the pirate history of the old city. It was a favorite family-dining destination, especially for our family with two young boys obsessed—for a time—with all things pirate.

During our previous visits, we never really had the time nor opportunity to explore the city. Having no idea where to go, my mother decided to head to the one place she knew would have the lowdown on what to see and do in town—the public library. On our way, we passed moss-covered squares and stately homes so unlike those found on the winding streets of Charleston or in historic Georgetown, DC. The Savannah library was an impressive, yellowish stone and faux-marble structure, covered on one side by creeping ivy and ringed all around by tall hedges and pretty flower beds. Much like the rest of downtown, the library seemed from another time.

On the self-guided tour route we obtained from the librarian, we encountered antebellum homes with black wrought iron gates and balconies, surrounding manicured squares and enclosing small gardens.

Many squares had tinkling water fountains or aged-stone birdbaths. Statues and gardens with flowerbeds and live oak trees draped with Spanish moss were everywhere.

In the center of the historic district was the massive Forsyth Park, its gushing fountains shooting into the air, flaunting their coolness in the stifling summer heat. And down by the city's newly redeveloped waterfront—peppered by novelty shops, candy kitchens, and cafés—we got a taste of the city's newest tourist traps. We snacked on delicious praline candies from a little bakery before my mama decided that lunch was in order. And she was right; we were all very hungry by this point.

Now, Mama had heard about a place called Ye Olde Pink House and thought we should try it. She had a knack of remembering cool landmarks and eating establishments that she had either heard or read about. As a result, we saw and ate at some pretty amazing places on our family vacations. Well, Ye Olde Pink House proved to be popular and hard to get into. We asked for a table, but I'm not quite sure what the host thought when he saw the three of us; we were sunburned from sightseeing, slightly crazed with hunger, and severely underdressed for the place. Nevertheless, he took pity on us and found us a table in the back. That lunch was so good. It was the first time I ever tried a Savannah-style crab stew. It was rich and crabby, salty and thick, with the subtle taste of sherry. I loved it. I can't remember what else I had at that restaurant, but I remember that dish!

After lunch and a couple more hours of hoofing it around town, it finally came time to check in about the car. As luck had it, the mechanic had secured the part early in the day and had been able to make all the necessary repairs! By 6 p.m., we picked up the car and were on our way. A mere three hours later, with our bellies still full from that satisfying crab stew, we arrived at Chez Kruse on the beach in Florida, the home of our friends.

Savannah Style-Crab Stew

Both Savannah and Charleston, the urban bookends of the Low Country, are cities with rich histories and culinary traditions. Each provides similar and competing dishes for the title of the most authentic and tastiest Low Country dish. Both are delicious! In Charleston, they are known for She Crab Soup. The soup was traditionally made with only female crabs, and as an extra flavor bonus, the roe of gravid crabs was included in the dish. Savannah has its own version: it's referred to as Crab Stew. It is definitely heartier than its Charleston counterpart.

Ingredients
    3 Tablespoons cooking oil
    3/4 cup finely chopped celery
    3/4 cup finely chopped carrots
    1 cup finely chopped white onion
    1 clove garlic, finely minced
    1 cup chopped cooked shrimp
    1/4 cup flour
    1 stick unsalted butter
    1 quart whole milk, heated
    1/2 cup dry sherry
    1 bottle clam juice
    1 pint heavy cream
    1 bay leaf
    1 Tablespoon white pepper
    1 teaspoon Worcestershire sauce
    1/2 Tablespoon crab boil seasoning
    1 teaspoon mace
    1/2 Tablespoon cocktail bitters
    1/4 teaspoon cayenne pepper
    2 lbs. jumbo crab meat picked over for shells

1/4 cup chopped fresh flat leaf parsley
Sea salt to taste

Method

- *Heat the cooking oil in large skillet. Sauté carrots, celery, and onion until soft.*
- *Add garlic and cook until garlic blooms, about 3 minutes. Turn off heat and hold.*
- *In large heavy-bottomed stew pot, melt butter and add flour slowly until a thick paste is formed and cook until golden brown, then whisk in warm milk slowly until blended and thick.*
- *Add clam juice and stir.*
- *Add sherry and all the seasonings and celery/garlic mixture.*
- *Bring to boil, stirring constantly, then reduce heat to a low simmer for 15 minutes.*
- *Add shrimp, heavy cream, and crab meat and heat through, but do not boil.*
- *Season to taste with salt.*
- *After about 7 minutes, remove from heat. Stir in parsley and serve.*

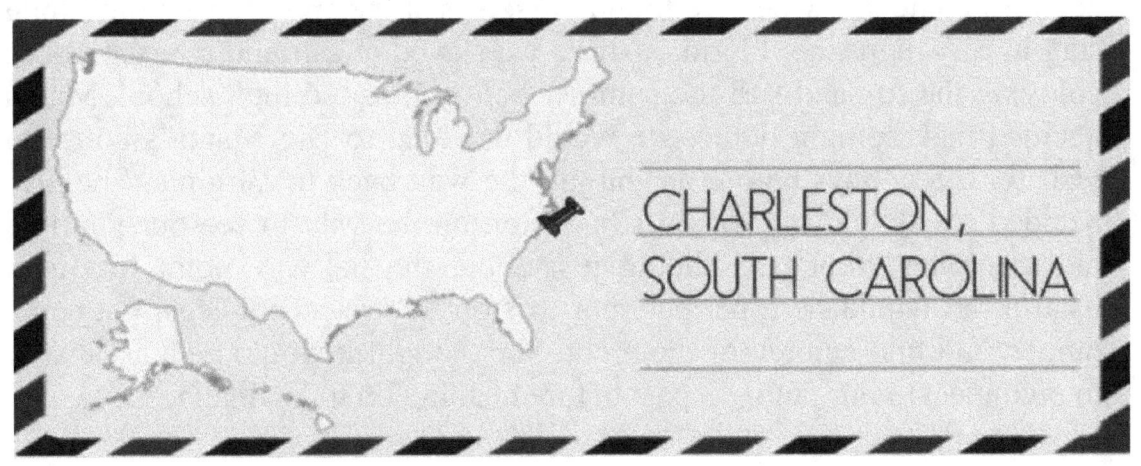

CHAPTER THIRTY-ONE: PARENTAL LESSONS, PERDITA'S OF CHARLESTON, AND CIOPPINO

One of the most important things parents can do for their children is to provide them the opportunity to have experiences that will help them navigate the waters of adulthood. Because my father worked a lot, my mother was often the parent who gave my brother and me exposure to new things. For instance, because the military bases offered access to a lot of recreational options, she made sure we knew how to play all the country-club sports, such as tennis and golf. She made sure we knew how to ride a horse, but she also was the one to teach us the more all-American activities, like how to bowl and play pool. In fact, I can still see her at the base's pool hall in Pearl Harbor, teaching her two little boys how to shoot a bank shot under the low-lying lamps that swung above the billiards table. Her blonde hair in a French twist, she would lean forward over the table to instruct us in how to execute the difficult shot. Her coaching was always spot on; so, as you can imagine, I was always confused as to why all the enlisted men kept coming up and offering to help.

Just like gaming activities, she also was often the one to take us on vacation, or to Big Mama's in Walhalla, when my father was busy and couldn't come. So, when we found ourselves at the end of our month-long stay in St. Augustine, Florida, where we stayed at a friend's beach house enjoying the sun and surf the summer before I started high school, Mama decided that, coming home, we would drive up to Big Mama's house to visit for a few days before driving all the way back to Virginia. She also decided we should stop off in Charleston on the way to see our family's old stomping grounds. It being just about the halfway point to Big's, Charleston would be a perfect spot to stop to stretch our legs, get some dinner, and find a hotel for the night. She thought it would be a good way to reconnect to our family's past before heading on to Walhalla.

Leaving our friends in St. Augustine, we drove north and rolled into Charleston about two o'clock in the afternoon. We did some sightseeing, checking out the Charleston City Market, one of the nation's oldest public markets, full of tourist-trap merchandise, and Rainbow Row with its brightly painted array of Georgian row houses built in the eighteenth century, and, finally, the Battery, Charleston's once-defensive seawall where majestic antebellum homes overlook the harbor and Fort Sumter, the historically notable sea fort, which is surrounded by the blue water of the harbor's mouth.

Hunger finally got the best of us, and we gravitated toward getting dinner. My brother and I wanted fried shrimp, but Mama had other ideas. She wanted to take us to a landmark restaurant named Perdita's. She and my daddy had gone there when we first lived in Charleston, and she wanted us to have the experience of eating there as well. So Mama pulled rank, and we drove around downtown until we came up behind the old Custom House to a narrow cobblestone street and sought out the restaurant and a parking spot.

Upon finding the restaurant, we saw from the sign that the place was just about to open for dinner. We peeked inside and two things became clear to me: we were going to be the only people in the place (not many people in Charleston eat dinner at 5 p.m., especially in the summer), and we would have to dress up because a coat and tie were required. Without hesitation, Mama told us to dig for our shirts, ties, and jackets in the luggage crammed in the back of the wagon. She had us change right there in the parking lot, in the heat and humidity, while she furtively slipped into a dress and heels! My brother and I were not amused.

Perdita's was one of Charleston's old-school dining establishments. Founded in the 1950s, it was one of the first restaurants to bring French, old-world cooking and dining to the city. With its louvered wood blinds blocking out the late afternoon sun, the restaurant was dimly and romantically lit by candles. I remember the air-conditioned room felt amazing after spending the day in the Charleston heat. The restaurant had mahogany wood accents, dark patterned wallpaper (it may have been purple), and velvet curtains that matched the upholstery of the dining chair cushions. It all had the patina of years of service.

When we entered, a battalion of veteran (think elderly) African American servers in black vests, starchy white shirts, and bow ties greeted us. Gleaming medals and colorful ribbons, marking the years of loyal service, were pinned to their vests and waistcoats. Aside from the three of us, the dining room was empty, except for the sea of tables draped with crisp, white tablecloths and covered in sparkling glassware and silverware set in anticipation of the crowd yet to arrive.

Looking around, my brother and I noted that we had never been in a restaurant as fancy as this one. As we moved to the table, chairs were pulled out for us and napkins were placed into our laps with a flourish. Large, leather-bound menus were handed to each of us, and as we looked through the handwritten pages within, we noted that, unlike the menus we had seen before, there were no prices listed. My mother stared over her spectacles at the menu, her eyes and forehead the only things visible behind the oversized tome. We looked to her for guidance.

The headwaiter appeared at the table to take our beverage order, as back waiters poured chilled water into the crystal water goblets and placed fresh French rolls onto our bread plates with serving tongs. My mother ordered a Manhattan for herself and asked if we would like a Shirley Temple or a Roy Rogers. Now, my brother and I had rarely ordered drinks like that before, maybe at the Makalapa O. Club (that place paled in comparison to the elegance of Perdita's), but we just went with it. You know, when in Rome!

When one of the back waiters returned with our drinks, the headwaiter reappeared to note the specials for the evening and to answer questions about the menu. As he walked away, my mother explained that she had brought us here so that we could have a full upscale-dining experience. She went on to say that she and our father wanted us to know how to navigate in a place like this, because at some point in our lives, we would need to know the proper way to eat like gentlemen at the gourmet level. She explained we would order four courses, which were to include appetizers, salads, entrée dishes, and dessert, all crafted in the old-world French style. When the headwaiter returned, we each told the waiter our choices. I remember I ordered the Fruits de Mer as my entrée, a French seafood stew and the signature dish on the menu. It was the one thing on the menu that seemed familiar out of many unfamiliar offerings. I knew what a seafood stew was and since it was noted as the house specialty, it seemed a good idea and a safe bet.

Now, up to this point in my short life, my only experience with seafood stew (aside from that tasty crab stew I had a few weeks earlier in Savannah) was with cioppino, a delicious San Francisco classic, which my mama made from a 1960's cookbook. (My folks probably got the book in northern California when my daddy was stationed in Monterey.) The dish was a family favorite especially in colder months. I've scoured my mother's cookbook shelves looking for that book, but I can't find it anywhere. Luckily, the cioppino recipe survived via a recipe card. The card is notated in several shades of ink and various handwriting styles. This family recipe clearly went through a number of changes and was tweaked over the years. I love the card because it has a few finger smudges as well as food stains and splatterings from long ago. It makes me think about who else may have referred to this exact card, holding it in their hands and using it to make a family meal. It's a reminder that recipes, like the stories that go with them, keep us connected to each other and to our pasts.

Fruits de Mer at Perdita's was not exactly like the cioppino I knew, but it was indeed an excellent choice. On the platter presented to me were baked flounder fillets as well as a delectable broth containing roasted oysters, mussels, clams, and sea squab (the tail of a puffer fish). The broth had undertones of bourbon, bacon, thyme, fennel, and a good dose of garlic. A ramekin of baked Crabmeat Remick accompanied the dish. The entrée was served with the buttery garlic bread I was used to, as well as a side of white rice accented with parsley. It wasn't the fried shrimp I had originally wanted nor the cioppino I had envisioned, but after one bite, I didn't care! It was delectable.

Overall, the dining experience at Perdita's was a little intimidating, but the deliciousness of the meal made all the stress of following fine-dining etiquette fade away. In fact, once the meal got going, it was like being in the middle of a ballet. Each course was served and cleared away by a team of waiters, and then the silver for the next course would be laid down. As the food was placed in front of us, the headwaiter would explain what each of us would be eating, and he would end these preludes with an invitation to enjoy. Water glasses were never empty, and being the only patrons in the place for about thirty minutes made us the focus of everyone's attention.

Although my brother and I did not know it at the time, that meal was a great memory in the making. True, we had been opposed to changing into our suits in the parking lot amid other cars and the sweltering heat, and we were both more than resistant to eating at a stuffy and old French place when all we wanted was fried shrimp at a seafood shack. But these days, I am glad to have had that learning moment and that meal. Every time I make cioppino at home, my mind circles back to that dining experience, those tableside lessons, and the time with my mother and brother in the dark and pampered cool of Perdita's dining room. That day, my brother and I not only had a lesson in manners and the finer things in life, but we got to partake of a little piece of Charleston's culinary history that no longer exists today. And, I must admit, that that lesson in elegant dining has served me well through the years as I ventured into social situations where knowing how to move through the menu, order a meal, and select the correct fork made me look all the wiser. My short visit to Perdita's as a child is something I always reflect back on. I enjoy replaying it over and over in my mind; it, too, is part of my personal food heritage.

Cioppino: A San Francisco-Style Seafood Stew

This is not Perdita's recipe for seafood stew, but, rather, it's my family's version of cioppino. Cioppino is a relic of the San Francisco fishing industry. My parents were introduced to it when they were stationed in Northern California.

Ingredients
- 1 28 can chopped tomatoes
- 1 4 ounce can tomato paste
- 1 4 ounce can tomato sauce
- 2 cups V8® vegetable juice
- 1 cup red wine
- 1 cup white vermouth
- 4 Tablespoons olive oil
- 2 leeks, white and light green parts chopped
- 2 heads of fennel and some of the leaves chopped
- 2 stalks of celery, chopped finely
- 1 1/2 Tablespoons crushed garlic from the jar
- 2 Tablespoons dried parsley
- 1 teaspoon each dried oregano, basil, tarragon
- 8 large shrimp in shells
- 8 to 12 clams
- 12 ounces of cod cut into 4 portions
- 4 to 8 diver scallops
- 1/2 pound bay scallops

Method
- In a large heavy-bottomed stock pot, heat oil until glistening.
- Add vegetables and cook vegetables until soft.
- Add spices cook until flavors bloom.

- *Add liquids and tomatoes and bring to a boil.*
- *Boil for 10 minutes.*
- *Reduce heat and simmer on low heat for 1 1/2 hours.*

To serve
- *Right before you are ready to eat, heat broth to boil, then reduce to high simmer.*
- *Turn timer on for 10 minutes.*
- *Add fish and clams.*
- *At 5 minutes, add scallops and shrimp.*
- *When timer sounds, check to see if clams are open and turn off the heat.*
- *Let sit 2 more minutes, then serve right away! (This is critical or seafood will overcook!)*
- *Divide seafood evenly and spoon broth to fill bowls.*
- *Serve with a Caesar salad and garlic bread toasts.*

Caesar Dressing with Fresh Herbs

This is the best Caesar dressing I've ever made. Toss it with baby gem lettuce hearts or chopped romaine, grated Parmesan, crunchy croutons, and some capers, and you have yourself an exceptional Caesar salad!

Ingredients
8 anchovies
2 heaping Tablespoons Dijon mustard
1/4 cup plus 2 Tablespoons lemon juice
1 Tablespoon sherry vinegar
1/2 Tablespoon Worcestershire sauce
1 cup grated Parmesan cheese
3 cloves minced garlic
2 coddled eggs
1 Tablespoon chopped fresh tarragon
1 Tablespoon chopped fresh parsley
1 Tablespoon chopped fresh chives
3/4 to 1 1/4 cups of good olive oil

Method
- *In a food processor, add everything but the oil and pulse until combined.*
- *Then add oil little by little with the machine running until the dressing comes together and you get a thick yellow dressing. You may not use all the oil. Will keep in the fridge for up to 3 weeks.*

CHAPTER THIRTY-TWO: CHARLESTON LIVING, SPOLETO FESTIVAL USA, AND LATE-NIGHT DINING

When I moved back to Charleston in 1987 to make it my home after college, I left behind my life in Virginia, my friends, and the connections that had sustained me throughout my adolescence and early adulthood. I came back to Charleston not only because my parents had moved there, but also because I felt that, of all the places I had ever been, it felt most like home. It is a feeling that has never left me, even in spite of my career taking me to New York, Europe, and other far-flung places.

So, after I arrived back in Charleston and found a job, I officially moved out of my folk's house in Mount Pleasant and into an apartment downtown on Montagu Street. It was an English basement apartment and part of a home built in 1852 by a Charleston family. An English basement is simply an apartment that is located on the ground level (perhaps even partially below ground level), with the main house one flight of stairs up; the apartment's front door, separate from the main entry of the home, typically opens onto a street-level garden.

The building I lived in was an interesting house because it was a duplex built by two merchant brothers. The building was unique because it looked like it was a single home that had been split down the middle. In warmer months, I would hear through my screen door the horse-and-carriage tour guides traveling by tell their tourist cargo, who were captivated by the guides' stories, about the nasty feud that erupted between the two brothers. Supposedly, that feud was the catalyst for splitting the house into two. (According to my landlords, that was just a grand tale; the building had always been two separate homes, built to share a common firewall. It was that firewall that gave the divided perception.)

My new life in Charleston centered around work and trying to integrate myself into the social fabric of the city. I met a few lovely individuals at church who introduced me into some great groups of people. And like any twenty-something, I found myself enjoying all the things the Low Country had to offer like the beach, sailing, oyster roasts, biking, and of course nightlife.

In 1989, the post-Hurricane Hugo Charleston was a city in the process of renewal. All the damage from the hurricane quickly drew in insurance and federal assistance dollars, and, within a few years, the city looked better than it had in the previous forty. With all this renewal came a host of new business opportunities, which was a draw for young, career-minded adults from all over the country. And, as a result, the music and nightlife scene began to boom. Every few months, especially in the late '80s and early '90s, it seemed a new bar club or trendy nouveau-Southern restaurant would spring up and garner much hype. It was an exciting time to be in the city, with its changing energy and food scene.

In addition to these new and exciting upstarts, there were also a few older and established places not to be missed, for Charleston's restaurant scene has a long and notable history. Those establishments included Garibaldi's, which always reeked deliciously of garlic and oregano; Henry's, one of Charleston's first fish houses from the 1930s, which offered a famously spicy cheese spread and its popular Seafood a la Wando (a dish preserved today at Hank's, a modern seafood house); Le Midi, a casual yet excellent French restaurant on King Street; and 82 Queen, the purveyor of the best She Crab soup in the city and, in those days, excellent pastas (today the menu has moved to Low Country modern). And there were still others: Bertha's Kitchen, named a James Beard America's Classic in 2017, where you could live out your soul food fantasies if you could brave the neighborhood back in the day; the Marina Variety Store, an eclectic waterfront diner from the 1960s; Colony House, a diverse establishment which offered traditional American steak and seafood upstairs in the main dining room and French cuisine and a robust wine list in The Wine Cellar; and the not-to-be-forgotten Philippe Million, a fabulously upscale-French restaurant with the famous Long Room (where George Washington was rumored to have dined), which is now McCrady's (another James Beard Award winner). My father took us out often to many of these places, and I had the opportunity to sample the city's restaurant scene up-close and personal.

Then there was Marianne's. Marianne's was a French restaurant that sat on the corner of Meeting and Hasell Streets. It is no longer there, but in its heyday, Marianne's had large picture windows and was brilliantly lit and bathed in soft colors by candles. Furnished with old antiques and oversized oil paintings, it was a stunning place to end any night out. Its menu offered classic bistro fare, and that complemented Marianne's elevated atmosphere. Further heightening the ambiance—setting a relaxed and elegant tone—was a woman who played the piano and sang softly throughout the evening. She would serenade the customers with cocktail standards by Ella Fitzgerald, Nina Simone, Judy Garland, and even Patsy Cline long into the night. To this day, her versions of "Crazy" and "Somewhere Over the Rainbow" still play in my memory. My discovery of Marianne's came about because of one of the most important events in Charleston's yearly calendar, the Spoleto Arts Festival.

For tourists, until recent travel magazines began touting Charleston's amazing allure, Spoleto used to be one of the most interesting and largest draws to Charleston. Founded in 1973 by composer Gianni Carlo Menotti, it's one of the largest municipal performing arts festivals in the United States. I am personally a huge fan of this seventeen-day event, which always begins the last week of May. Charleston comes alive with performances, concerts, operas, and art exhibits. Squares and parks are converted into outdoor galleries. Churches double as music halls. Every auditorium space is filled with a rotating repertoire of theater productions (both dramatic and musical). And the restaurant and nightlife scenes explode with patrons clamoring for copious amounts of local food and drink. It is a festive and convivial time.

In the 1970s, the festival brought cuisine-savvy tourists to town, beginning a trend of French influenced-restaurant openings like Marianne's, Mistral, and others, which sprouted up and gained in popularity until the current wave of nouveau-Southern restaurants took over. And during Spoleto in the 1980s, only a few of the local restaurants created late-night menus for hungry diners. Hotel bars and restaurants, like the Barbados Room in the historic Mills House Hotel, became popular late-night destinations for revelry, entertainment, and food offerings clamored for by hungry tourists, performers, and patrons of the arts. Even a makeshift nightclub and cabaret called the Coconut Club popped up annually during the festival and was a popular late-night option. The city's culinary scene was not remotely what it is today. These late-night dining options were unique and involved only a handful of establishments. And while popular during festival season, late-night dining was offered by only one restaurant all year round. That was Marianne's. My friend Diana introduced me to the place after an enjoyable day at the festival, and I instantly fell in love with it.

The two late-night dishes that kept me coming back to Marianne's over and over were the crab Oscar Benedict and the French onion soup. The first time they came to the table, I was smitten. My mouth waters thinking about the crunchy and buttery English muffin topped by a delicious mixture of fresh, warm crab salad and a layer of steamed asparagus crowned with a perfectly poached egg, blanketed in a creamy Béarnaise sauce. And the soup—cheesy hot and bubbly—was divine. I fondly think of my first years back in Charleston, my friend Diana, and our fun-filled Spoleto days (and nights) whenever I indulge in making these dishes now. Eating, chatting, and laughing late into the night with a good friend is always an excellent way to end any day!

Oscar Benedict from Marianne's of Charleston

Ingredients
    4 English muffins, split and toasted and buttered
    8 ounces fresh jumbo lump crab meat, 2 ounces per portion
    2 Tablespoons mayonnaise
    2 Tablespoons lemon juice
    1 teaspoon dried French tarragon leaves
    1 Tablespoon fresh chives
    2 Tablespoons grated Parmesan cheese
    6 Tablespoons grated Swiss cheese
    12 pieces of asparagus spears, uniformly cut and poached in water and lemon juice
    8 pre-poached eggs
    2 cups blender Béarnaise (recipe to follow)

Method
- Poach eggs in muffin tin by adding 1 Tablespoon of water to each tin, then adding eggs. Bake at 350 for 8 minutes.
- Place English muffin on plate.
- Mix next 6 ingredients together.
- Spoon on muffins.
- Place on broiler pan, sprinkle with the cheese.
- Broil until cheese is bubbling and browning and crab is heated through.
- Remove from broiler.
- Top with 3 spears of asparagus.
- Top with poached eggs that have been reheated.
- Spoon over the hollandaise.
- Dust with paprika.

Blender Mustard Béarnaise for Poached Eggs

Ingredients
    1 1/2 cups melted butter
    3 egg yolks
    2 Tablespoons white vinegar
    1 Tablespoon lemon juice
    Dash hot sauce
    2 teaspoons dried tarragon
    1 teaspoon Dijon mustard
    1/8 teaspoon salt
    1/8 teaspoon white pepper

Method
- *In a pot, reduce the acids down to half.*
- *Pour into a blender (that has been heated with hot water) and add seasoning and egg yolks.*
- *With the motor running, slowly pour in the melted butter in a steady stream until the mixture becomes a thick sauce.*
- *Pour over eggs.*

CHAPTER THIRTY-THREE: A WANNABE SON OF THE HOLY CITY AND LOW COUNTRY OYSTERS

When I moved to downtown Charleston, I realized one thing: while I might love and embrace the city—its history, culture, people, natural beauty, social scene, and of course its food—I would never actually be able to say I was a Charlestonian. Why? Well, I found out quickly that if you weren't born and raised in the city proper, despite having a deeply-rooted family history there, you could never call yourself a true Charlestonian. That's rough. Even New York City adopts you after living there for twenty years. No wonder people who settle in the area are sometimes referred to as being "from off"—meaning from off the Charleston peninsula.

I am a Southerner by both birth and heritage, and my family lives in Mount Pleasant right across the bridge from the city. My father's family even has roots originally in Charleston. I know a lot about the city. I spent my twenties and early thirties there, living downtown before my career choices took me away. I even have a brother who was born there, but there was one major roadblock to my total societal acceptance. I was not born in Charleston.

Now, of course, that didn't deter me from joining and enjoying membership in a variety of groups when I did live there, such as architectural and history organizations (most of which were thinly-veiled social organizations fronted by an intelligent guise), theater and fine-arts groups (including singing as a tenor in the Charleston Symphony Orchestra Chorus), and the Gibbs Museum of Art's group for young patrons. I was invited to great parties and, through our church, got to be involved with and got to know wonderfully exciting and intelligent people. Regardless of my involvement, memberships, and associations, one fact separated me from being a son of the city. I wasn't born there!

Now, while I say all this a little tongue-in-cheek, there is no denying that Charleston folk take this very seriously, historically at least. In fact, there is a famous Episcopal Church—St. Phillips—that has two graveyards: the one on the church grounds for people born in Charleston and the one across the street for people *not* born in Charleston. One side marking the resting place of the sons and daughters of the Holy City, the other full of dead folk from somewhere else. There are even some husbands and wives, enjoying their eternal life, forever separated by a street.

These days, Charlestonian exclusivity is often proffered in jest, but part of it is actually very real. Recently, while I was visiting home, my friend Karen got upset with a statement I made about Charleston. She told me in no uncertain terms I had no right to have an opinion about Charleston. Her reasoning? She exclaimed, "'Cause you weren't even born here!"

So, I'll just say that, while I'm commenting on Southern and Charlestonian things in this book, my thoughts and opinions are based on my personal experience and are not offered up as the gospel truth of the Holy City. Let me be clear, my dear Charleston friends, I am from Mount Pleasant, South Carolina. Not from Charleston. And as a neighbor from your most-yuppie 'burb, I understand that anything I say is purely opinion and not fact.

That all being said, I'd like to tell you what my favorite time of year was when I was living in Charleston, and it should come as no surprise that it is directly tied to a particular food season. That time of year is the fall and that season is oyster season. After the long and hot summer, cooler temperatures prevail in the fall, making it a prime time for people to come together for local events and, in Charleston especially, social galas. It also is the time for the return of the oyster roast—a get-together where the feast is based on the bounty of the oyster beds that line the offshore waterways of coastal South Carolina and Georgia. Traditional roasts take place outdoors, in the afternoon or evening, and always involve communal eating tables and lots of beer. Oyster roasts are the Low Country's fall version of a pig pickn' (A.K.A. a pig pull, where a whole pig is barbecued), a popular culinary gathering in the Piedmont region of the state.

Charleston oysters are usually brought up out of the water in big, crusty clusters and are placed in a large oyster roaster. The traditional roaster is typically a metal barrel laid on its side. It has a heating element under it or coals inside of it. A grate holds the oysters above the heat, and wet burlap is placed over the oysters. This process literally roasts and steams the edible nuggets in their own juices. Pretty spectacular as far as roasting goes! The oysters are then brought to the table in big, steaming clumps, and guests (supplied with hammers and oyster knives) are invited to feast on the bounty before them.

Today, oyster vendors have large mobile roasters, and they travel to wherever there is a party. They position their impressive ovens near the action, providing not only the services needed to cook the oysters, but also a bit of visual culinary drama for the event.

The roasted oysters are served up with cocktail sauce, hot sauce, saltine crackers, and copious amounts of beer. These meals are usually rounded out with a Low Country boil called Frogmore Stew (a one-pot seafood dish with shrimp, sausage, and potatoes), bowls of coleslaw and potato salad, and baskets of cornbread or biscuits. The real star of the show, however, is always the oyster.

Creamed Oysters, a Low Country tradition

My family's recipe for creamed oysters can be traced to my mama's James Beard cookbooks. These are often served around the holidays and traditionally for New Years. My version uses a roux to thicken the sauce.

Ingredients
- 1 qt oysters in their liquid
- 2 Tablespoons butter
- 1 Tablespoon flour
- 1 shallot, finely chopped
- Big splash of white wine
- 2 cups heavy cream
- Ground mace to taste (I like a lot)
- White pepper to taste
- Salt to taste
- Splash of dry sherry
- Chopped chives to taste (sometimes I add lots, sometimes none)
- Buttered toast points, cheese and herb and garlic biscuits or puff pastry shells
- 3 Tablespoons chopped fresh parsley

Method
- Bring oysters in their liquid to a boil.
- As soon as they plump, using a slotted spoon, remove them from the liquid. Add the shallots and cook through. Pour in the wine.
- Roll the butter in flour and add to the hot liquid in bits, vigorously whisking until all is incorporated and the sauce begins to thicken.
- Stir in cream, mace, and pepper.
- Stir constantly until smooth. Add the sherry. Reduce heat to low and simmer until thickened. Add chives just before serving.
- Add salt to taste.

To serve
- *Reduce heat to low and return oysters to the pan, discarding any liquid they left behind.*
- *Let them come to temperature in the sauce (do not cook or they will become like rubber) and then spoon into dishes and serve with toast points or biscuits or spooned over toast points or in a puff shell. Garnish with chopped parsley. Enjoy!*

SECTION SIX

ON FINDING THE FLAVORS OF FRIENDSHIP

CHAPTER THIRTY-FOUR: MEMENTOS AND MAGNETS, PERSISTENCE AND PERSEVERANCE, FRIENDSHIP AND RISOTTO

Friends are the family we choose. Sometimes they are around a lifetime, and sometimes just for a season. Friends who stay in our lives are, indeed, like family. They make indelible marks on us. When they are not immediately present in our everyday lives, their memory is etched in our minds. What they bring into our lives becomes part of our life's story.

As someone who defines much of his life by times, places, and people, I keep mementos to help me remember and celebrate those experiences and individuals. These markers take many forms: photos, bar coasters, postcards, a scrap of paper stuck in some book, ticket stubs, or entries in journals. With small magnets, each with pictures of places I've been or cheeky sayings on them, I actually (in a homespun manner) keep a collage of some of these varied items on my refrigerator door. Every time I open the fridge, I am reminded how rich and wonderful my life has been.

I also keep a special collection of recipes in a box. These recipes—scribbled on Post-it® Notes from my mama's desk or taken directly out of handwritten personal cookbooks—are pieces of the past. These recipes all state the same thing, each in their singular way: "I remember." One of these cherished recipe cards is for tomato risotto. When I see that card, it reminds me of one of the most exciting times of my life: my first few years in New York City. More importantly, it reminds me of Cristin Hubbard, a dear friend I met there who later became my roommate. We went through a lot together, from sharing stories and tears about dating and relationship disasters to lots of theatrical living on every level. We remained close friends long after we were no longer roommates.

Cristin was a Midwestern girl. She came from a small and tight-knit family. And although we were from different parts of the country, she and I held many similar core values. Family was of the utmost importance to us both. Similarly, we also both believed in the importance of fair play, hard work, and honesty. And we both had a shared commitment to excellence in our chosen fields (and at that time, it was musical theater). When either of us was leaving the house to go to an audition, the other would yell from the other end of the apartment, "Remember, try not to suck!"

While we were roommates, we shared recipes from our childhood. I shared pimento cheese and cornbread with her, and she shared with me tomato risotto. Cristin is actually the person who first taught me how to make risotto, a dish that requires almost constant attention. It is a dish she had grown up making with her mom. The original recipe came from some cookbook, I suppose, but her version came from the heartland and the heart.

I remember standing with her in our tiny apartment kitchen with the two-burner stove and the black-and-white tile floor. Cristin taught me how to slowly combine the risotto ingredients and the spices, layer by layer, to create the exact taste and texture. She also helped me find the enjoyment in taking the time it took to stir in the multiple cups of stock to achieve the creamy, delicious dish. There is a quality of Zen that is attained when taking time to do a task correctly. Stirring risotto is certainly like that. It took more than a few tries making this dish by myself until I got it right. It's just another example of how cooking imitates and instructs on other aspects of living: one must have patience and perseverance when working toward a goal.

When I moved out of our apartment, Cristin wrote out the risotto recipe on a recipe card, one of those index cards with cutesy sketches of wheat bales, roosters, and wooden spoons printed on them. Although I no longer need the card because I can make the recipe from memory, I keep it. The card is a reminder of a special time and a dear friend who made a mark forever on my life.

After I moved out, Cristin and I remained good friends. She went on to marry a great guy, and they began a family. I would enjoy running into her at the corner grocer or coffee shop after she had her first child. We would always spend a few minutes catching up and chatting about life. A few years later, I moved way uptown, and anytime I saw her, I always considered our meetings a nice reunion. Our encounters may have been short and interrupted by weeks or months at a time, but they were so very meaningful to me. We didn't simply exchange pleasantries; when we saw each other, we were honestly interested in hearing what the other was doing. Our friendship is a genuine one, standing the test of time.

Many years later, when I was going through a really hard period, I received a card in the mail from Cristin. It read, "'When you are going through Hell, Keep Going!'—Winston Churchill." The card was classic Cristin. She knew exactly what I needed to hear and when I needed to hear it; that is one of the reasons I cherish my friendship with her. That card summed up the lessons of life I first learned in the kitchen with my Grandma Irene making gravy that were then reinforced with Cristin making risotto. The good things in life cannot be achieved by shortcuts, and for a fulfilling life, one must rely on some key ingredients—time, persistence, and patience.

Cristin's Churchill card is one of the items collected on my fridge and sits squarely in the center of the mélange of items posted there, forever a token of our friendship. And whenever I am going through something tough these days, I always come back to Mr. Churchill's words and to the memories of a dear friend and tomato risotto. The combination of those three things helps to keep me going. Just goes to show how a helping hand or some kind words from a friend can have lifelong consequences. Friends are the family we choose, and I'm grateful to be reminded by my fridge (as kitschy as it may be) of my choices every day.

Cristin's Tomato Risotto

English Stilton and walnuts are the secret to this recipe. Garnished with tomato toppers, it looks very fancy.

Ingredients
    4 Tablespoons olive oil
    1 medium onion, finely diced
    3 cloves of garlic, minced
    1 teaspoon chopped fresh rosemary (or 2 teaspoons dried rosemary)
    1/4 cup chopped flat leaf parsley (1 Tablespoon reserved for garnish)
    2 cups Arborio rice
    3 plum tomatoes, seeded and small diced
    12 small tomatoes on the vine (for visual, they must be connected with the vine) and cut them into clusters of three tomatoes each
    1 cup dry vermouth wine (I think vermouth and tomatoes are a wonderful combo)
    4 to 6 cups warm beef broth (can use chicken or veggie)
    5 ounces English Stilton cheese
    2 ounces crumbled Stilton reserved for garnish
    1/2 cup toasted walnut pieces
    Salt and pepper
    2 Tablespoons butter
    Peppery extra virgin finishing olive oil on hand
    Maldon sea salt flakes

Method

For the Tomato toppers
- Place small round tomatoes on the vine connected in clusters of three on a foil-lined baking sheet.
- Rub with olive oil and season with salt and pepper.
- Bake in a 300-degree oven until slightly blistered and done, about 30 to 45 minutes.
- Hold warm.

For the Risotto
- Cook onion in oil in a large pan until translucent, then add garlic.
- Cook garlic until fragrant.
- Add rice and cook for about 3 to 4 mins. or until the rice is beginning to toast slightly in the oil and is well-covered. Add salt and pepper.
- Add rosemary and tomatoes. Cook another minute.
- Add 1 cup dry vermouth wine. Cook until absorbed.
- Slowly add stock, about a cup at a time, stirring until the risotto is thick and the liquid is completely absorbed. Then add more broth until all broth is used up or the risotto is just al dente (slightly chewy). You may not need all the broth. At this point, add the parsley.
- Add butter, stirring vigorously. Remove from the heat and add cheese and stir.
- When creamy, divide among 4 to 6 bowls.
- Garnish each dish with a cluster of three tomatoes and garnish with some Stilton and toasted walnuts. Add a splash of the peppery olive oil, then garnish with sea salt flakes and the remaining cheese and parsley.
- Serve right away.

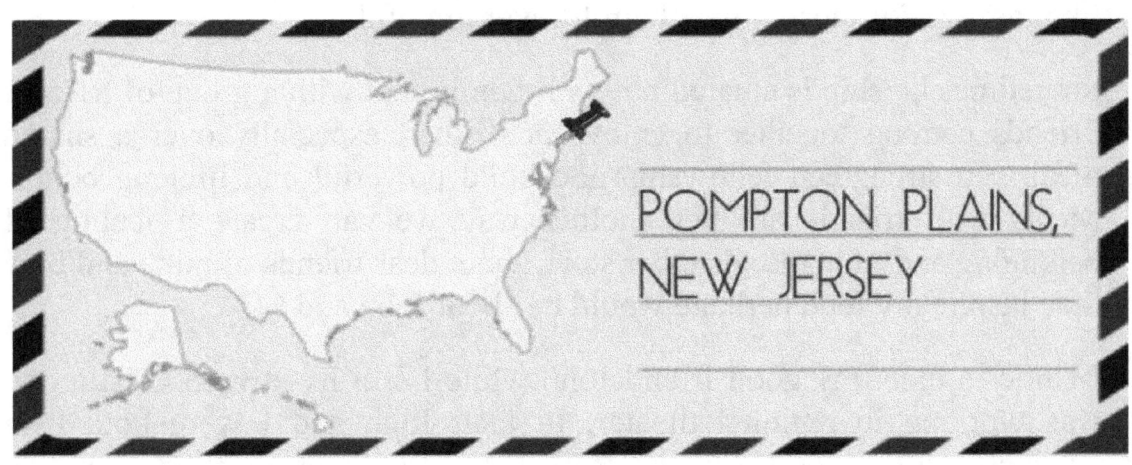

CHAPTER THIRTY-FIVE: THE DINNER TABLE OF FRIENDSHIP AND JERSEY MEATBALLS

As we have seen, dinner tables are magical gathering places. They are blank canvases waiting to be artfully filled with food and personalities, opportunities for shared experiences and memories. They offer a moment of togetherness in a way few other places do. By partaking of what is offered at the communal dining table, we fortify both our bodies and souls.

While dinner tables can become places of celebration for some of life's largest as well as most intimate moments, dinner tables can also be places of repose and refuge. I've talked about how my father, whenever he was traveling away from home and feeling lonely, would think back on Big Mama's dinner table, a table where people beyond the immediate family were always welcome. Similarly, I fondly remember when my friends would join my brother and me at our own family table. Often, they were friends whose mothers did not regularly cook dinner or whose families didn't gather but once a week for a meal together. My friends knew that there was an unspoken and open invitation at the Hedden home, an invitation not only to stay for a meal, but also to share in a sense of family created around our dinner table. And on many an occasion, I have been a guest at tables where I have been made to feel like family. For those times, I am forever grateful.

Sometimes kinship is created not with family, but with a group of friends. Friends coming together to enjoy each other, especially over a shared meal, can strengthen fellowship and build powerful and lifelong bonds. Meals with friends are yet another way we can create a feeling of belonging and of home. Another story about dear friends of mine and how they inspire my food heritage would be about John and Mike.

I came to meet my good friend John while I still lived with Cristin and was working in regional theater. In fact, John and I were both in a production of *Little Me* in the Berkshire Mountains in 1998. Yes, we became friends then, but our bond really became strong a few years later when he and I surprisingly discovered that we were neighbors in NYC. And by neighbor, I don't mean two people living in the same neighborhood; I am talking about two people living in the same apartment building and right next door to each other!

Sadly, John's mother passed away a few years after we became neighbors. Upon her passing, John learned that he had inherited his childhood home. John and his partner Mike decided it was time to move out of the city and to set up house back in Pompton Plains, New Jersey, a quaint little town forty-five minutes outside of New York City. They've made the home into a really lovely nest for themselves and the fortunate few who are invited to share it on special occasions.

The house was an original 1908 Sears Roebuck Victorian (one of the first prefab homes shipped and assembled on site). Now, it's the kind of home that, when you pass through the front door, makes you feel like you've entered a time warp; you feel as though you've stepped into the 1930s. Part of the reason for this is because John and Mike have done a tremendous amount of research on the era when restoring the home, using period wallpaper and paint hues. Additionally, they have inherited many antiques that have been in their families since forever. And John treats these cherished items with great respect and protects them against heedless abuse in the only way John can, as he is quite the character. Once someone put a cocktail glass down on one of his good tables. He handed them a coaster and remarked, "Use this please. It's got an 'H' on it [John's last initial], as in *HOW about you use a coaster?!*"

All joking aside, John and Mike love to share their meticulously restored home with family and friends. Of the many things I value about my friendship with Mike and John, it is perhaps being made to feel like part of their family in their home during the holidays (or whatever time of year it may be) that I value the most.

John and Mike entertain on a large scale twice a year. The first is two days after Thanksgiving, which happens also to be right around Mike's birthday. The second time is at Christmas. And how is food served in their warm and welcoming home? Why on their formal dining table, of course! A table so long that, when extended, it can accommodate every one of the up to twenty-six guests at Mike's birthday party or be handily used as a buffet table at Christmas. Whether covered in white, antique lace tablecloths and sparkling with glassware and dishes from the turn of the last century at Thanksgiving or laden with platters piled high with food at Christmas, it's a table to behold.

Working in catering and events as I do, I find that I work a lot during the holidays and don't have much time to celebrate the season. However, Christmas for me would not be Christmas without John and Mike. You see, Christmas is when John and Mike throw their largest soirée, and my one standing Christmas tradition is to attend. Having no family in the New York area and being made to feel at home and included in a holiday celebration is a powerful thing. It is a gift I treasure.

Now, no one does Christmas like John and Mike, and I think their Christmas party is a special present they give to their friends. All the colors of the season abound in every direction you look. Carefully curated holiday music is piped throughout the home. The house is decorated like a Norman Rockwell painting with equal parts class and kitsch. Antique ornaments mix with Santa mugs and heirloom Christmas china. Christmas throws and pillows adorn the furniture. There's even a leg lamp like from the *A Christmas Story* movie in their front window. A tall, fat, round tree, so huge it's supported by rigging, welcomes arriving guests; it fills the large entryway just off the living room. The tree is lit to within an inch of its life and its branches sag under the weight of the decorations. Snack trays are set out. Wine is drunk. Bread is broken. Carols are sung.

Every year there is a "family" portrait taken as everyone tries to fit on the staircase winding up from the first floor just past the tree, documenting the attendance for the evening and providing the cover of next year's invite (yes, they actually still mail out formal invitations in this digital age). Everyone attending is caught up in the spirit of love, family, and friends—the hallmarks of the Christmas season. And it's a homecoming of sorts. I see people there I only see there once a year. It's a lovely tradition.

As for the menu, it's a big Jersey Italian feast; there's a buffet set out on the long dining room table with lasagna, meatballs, pizza bread, and all sorts of antipasti and salads. There are Italian cookies and pastries and pies for dessert. No purchased stuff here! Mike even makes his own version of Italian meatballs and marinara sauce for these parties. He serves the meatballs on big Jersey rolls, making mouth-watering grinders. And if there is a splattering of a bit of red sauce from the marinara-topped grinders or gravy from the turkey, no worries! The linens all get sent off to a French laundry the next day.

And while all of this—John and Mike's home and the meals they serve—may sound impressive, the most important piece of these evenings is the wonderful cast of family and friends who gather to celebrate and spend time together in this enchanting environment. No matter what the setting, it's being together with people around the table who you love and love you, breaking bread, that really makes the memories.

Italian Meatballs in Tomato Sauce

Inspired by my love of Mike's meatballs, I took to making these little gems myself and have come up with my own version of these meaty wonders. The trick is in the choice of meat. I could never really get them to taste flavorful enough; they just tasted dense, until one day I made some with Italian sausage and voila! Flavor problem solved. Whenever I make these meatballs, I think of John and Mike, and their wonderful holiday gatherings.

Ingredients

    1 1/2 pounds ground beef
    1 pound of spicy Italian sausage
    1/2 cup Pecorino Romano cheese (not Parmesan)
    3/4 cup dry Panko Italian bread crumbs
    1 cup ricotta cheese mixed with 2 teaspoons dried basil
    4 large eggs
    1/2 cup minced cooked onion
    1 teaspoon garlic salt

Method

- In a large mixing bowl, combine all the ingredients and mix together with your clean hands really well. Then shape into golf-ball sized meatballs and place on an oiled tray (makes about 40 or so).
- Place on the counter and let sit to marry all the flavors for about 1 hour.
- Heat oven to 350 degrees and place the meatballs in the oven for about 20 minutes or until just browned.
- Remove from the oven. Place the meatballs and their juice into the pot of sauce (recipe follows). Let cook on low heat for about 40 minutes.
- Serve on club rolls as a sandwich or, as I prefer, on rigatoni garnished with freshly chopped basil.

Super Meatball Sauce

This is an easy sauce to make. It's a basic marinara to which I add pesto and Frank's RedHot® sauce to punch up the flavor.

Ingredients
- 1/4 cup plus 2 Tablespoons olive oil
- 1 large red onion, chopped
- 1/2 pound shredded carrots
- 6 cloves garlic, chopped
- 2 28 ounce cans of crushed Italian tomatoes (use the real deal)
- 1 Tablespoon dried basil
- 3 Tablespoons pesto sauce
- 3 Tablespoons Frank's RedHot® sauce (secret ingredient)
- 1 Tablespoon dried oregano
- 1/4 cup fresh parsley, chopped
- 3 Tablespoons butter

Method
- In a medium stock pot, heat oil.
- Add onions and garlic.
- Cook until soft.
- Add carrots and cook until all soft and lightly browned.
- Add herbs except pesto, and cook until just fragrant.
- Add tomatoes and salt.
- Bring the mixture to a boil, then reduce heat and simmer for 30 to 40 minutes.
- When ready to serve, stir in the pesto, hot sauce, and butter, and mix well through the sauce.

John's Clam Dip

This clam dip is so beloved that the one year it wasn't offered at John and Mike's Christmas party, there was an uprising! Luckily, John had the ingredients on hand and threw it together in a few minutes. And just like the little kid in the old Shake-n-Bake commercial, "I helped!" That's how I learned the recipe.

Ingredients

   2 cans of clams (size of tuna cans)
   1 stick (1/2 cup) of butter
   1 medium onion, chopped
   2-3 cloves garlic, chopped
   1 teaspoon parsley flakes
   1 teaspoon oregano
   1/2 teaspoon black pepper
   1 teaspoon basil
   1/2 cup Italian seasoned bread crumbs
   1 cup shredded cheddar cheese
   1/2 cup grated Parmesan cheese
   2 teaspoons lemon juice
   A dash of Tabasco® sauce

Method

- *In a saucepan, combine clams (with juice) and lemon juice. Simmer on low heat for 15 minutes.*
- *In other saucepan, melt butter, and sauté onions and garlic for 8 minutes.*
- *Add parsley flakes, oregano, pepper, basil, Tabasco®, and simmer on low for another 7 minutes.*
- *Combine ingredients of both saucepans into a deep baking dish.*

- *Stir in breadcrumbs, Parmesan, and 1/2 cup cheddar cheese until blended.*
- *Sprinkle top with the remaining 1/2 cup of cheddar cheese.*
- *Bake at 350 degrees for 15 minutes. Serve with buttery crackers.*

Chapter Thirty-Six: Colorful Living and Summer Dining—Summer Stock Theater, Local Dives, and a Talented Friend's Recipes

Here's a confession: I came to New York to be an actor. Now I'm just what is left of one. But I loved my time working in the theater. In the summers, I would often leave to do "stock". Summer stock is that time of year when many New York theater actors try to get out of the sweltering, sticky, and smelly city and go into the hinterlands of America to bring culture and art to the hearths and hamlets of the good ol' USA. At least, it used to be that twenty years ago or so when I was starting out. Back then, there were almost 150 regional and stock companies looking for actors every season. Now, years later, there are so few of these companies left. Many theaters that used to employ the young up-and-coming talent, filling their summer rosters with those hungry for experience and possessing the sheer desire to perform, have vanished. The companies just ran out of money or patrons. They are, in my opinion, a lost part of our American landscape.

Working at summer stock and in regional theaters over the years, I have come to see that there are many amazingly talented actors who work outside the shadow of the Broadway community. More importantly, from my involvement in theater, I have made a number of long-lasting friendships with individuals who changed my life. We learn different things from the people we call friends. Sometimes, our friends inspire us to strive harder and go further, and, sometimes, they help us realize that smelling the roses is as important as all the effort spent growing them. One such friend is Fred.

I met Fred in 2005 after returning to New York from performing in a three-year run of one of the national touring shows of Cameron Mackintosh's musical *Oliver!* I was referred to Fred because I wanted a vocal coach to help me work on some new music for auditions. Fred and I also hit it off socially, especially because of our shared sense of humor. Fred's wit and his ability to play off almost any common moment and find the humor in it is just hysterical. That afternoon after our first session, he suggested drinks, and over those drinks, we cemented a friendship that would later help me find balance between my very serious work life in the theater (and later, in catering) and my search for a sense of "real" life. You could say having been raised by two very hard-working, practical people that I often take on the role of the industrious ant in Aesop's Fable, The Ant and the Grasshopper. And although Fred is far from idle and impoverished, he could be cast as the grasshopper because he places value in taking time to enjoy life's artistry. Looking back on our relationship, I see now that Fred was determined to get this Ant to sing. Always leading by example, Fred wants his friends to stop and enjoy life.

Indeed, the one thing about Fred that I learned to appreciate is that he is one of those people who live for experiences. You know, in life, people value and collect all sorts of different things. Some people collect material objects. Some people collect friends just for the sake of having people around them. Some people collect money for a rainy day. Fred collects experiences. One of his favorite quotes is from the Broadway play *Auntie Mame* (adapted from Patrick Dennis's novel of the same name). "Life is a banquet and most poor sons of bitches are starving to death! Live!" It is a quote Fred lives by; you name it, he's done it. And if he hasn't done it yet, it is on his list of things to do.

The most enjoyable things on Fred's list have always been social gatherings: theater outings, bar crawls, dinners, and parties of every type. Fred is always the first one to come and the last one to leave any event. He often plays the role of cruise director for his friends, and he is great at it. Through Fred, I have been acquainted with a side of NYC few see. He has a particular love for old New York, and the spots he frequents (like Aaron Burr's carriage house, now a romantic and storied restaurant and bar) are special places indeed. Fred introduced me to many an old-school restaurant and tavern in NYC where we and a group of friends would spend the evenings—places where Frank Sinatra or Andy Warhol were rumored to have haunted in their prime. Wherever he is, Fred is always up for a good time, and sometimes you need a friend like that—someone who can call you out from your crappy day and present you with an amazing night. After all, if you are going to live in New York, you should take advantage of what it offers.

Fred and I connected about family and food as well. We share an appreciation and love of family recipes, especially ones passed down through generations.

Being a college professor with no classes in the summer, Fred heads to Holland, Michigan, in the summertime to satisfy his need for fun; he spends those months directing music for Hope Summer Repertory Theater. Hope is one of the theaters still around producing summer stock. The theater company members have what are called "Sunday suppers"—a Sunday-evening potluck. It's a long-standing tradition of the theater company and a very American one at that (the word *potluck* dates back to mid-nineteenth-century America).

With that said, I believe the real reason the potluck tradition has carried on is because I am sure Fred spearheads the weekly event. It satisfies two of his non-theatrical passions: social gatherings and cooking. Fred's chicken and mashed potatoes have always been sure-fire culinary delights for the theater troupe. But Fred can whip up more elaborate dishes as well. The magnificent meals he has created for his friends are examples of how he always lives his life to the fullest and has such joy including his friends along the way.

This mix of theatricality and culinary camaraderie at Hope is not uncommon in summer stock. In an earlier part of his career, Fred worked at plenty of other regional and summer theaters where Sunday evenings were a ritual of food, drink, and celebration.

Fred tells a story about working in Green Lake, Wisconsin, a wealthy resort area in the far north corner of the state that had a theater company during the summers. (Fred has so many great stories about the theater and theater folks it is hard to keep them straight, but this story I know well!) In town, the local place for actors and theater staff to congregate after the show was an old and dimly lit pub with a very Italian name, Stabadora's. Stabadora's had a cast of regulars, some of whom looked as if they had been there since the bar was built. Laverne, Stabadora's barkeep, looked like she was an original fixture as well. She donned blue eye shadow, had really big, dyed-blonde hair, and almost always had a cigarette hanging out of her mouth.

According to Fred, Stabadora's had some great greasy Italian and bar food, and the drinks were cheap. Beer sold for two dollars, and, for four dollars, you could order yourself a shot of premium liquor. There, by the glow of beer signs and Christmas lights, you could eat, drink, and talk shop until the early hours of the morning before crashing to rise again to rehearse and perform. I mean, tough life, right? Theater folk don't make a lot of money, but they know how to have a good time.

As Fred tells it, one night, hanging out at Stabadora's after the show, he noticed one of the regulars who had been drinking hard all night was having a hard time finding the door. The customer was falling-down blind-drunk, clearly listing to one side. Fred watched with concern as the fellow proceeded out the front door of the bar. Watching with horror from the bar's front window, Fred saw the guy get into his car, back up suddenly, and then almost drive his car into the river across the street. The car stopped right before it went over the embankment and into the water. Fred called Laverne over to the window. She watched with Fred as the guy slowly drove down the street, weaving from side to side.

Fred finally said to her, "Laverne, how could you let him leave?"

She answered in her heavy Wisconsin accent, "Oh yah, I know. It's too bad. Right?! Yah know, that's the reason I gave up driving? Oh, yah, it was. Well, after my second DUI, I said enough is enough! Never drove again."

Fred looked at her, not knowing what to say, and then changed the subject to something he was curious about. He asked her when the owners were ever going to get a new sign for the bar.

Laverne, looking perplexed, answered, "Fred, what are yah talking about?"

Fred explained, "Well, I've noticed that the sign out in front of the bar says Reilly's."

Laverne nodded, pouring another draft for a customer, "Yah, well what's wrong with that? The bar's name *is* Reilly's."

Fred looked puzzled then went on, "Okay, that may be, but everybody calls it Stabadora's, not Reilly's. Why is that? I thought the sign was just old or something. You know, part of the charm."

"Oh," she replied, her expression changing to a knowing look. "Yah, well, everybody calls it Stabadora's because years ago Dora got stabbed right here one night by her husband! Yah, that's the truth! And yah know, folks have called it Stabadora's ever since."

Fred is a master spinner of tales and has enjoyed telling this story many a time. It's just such a great story with the setting and the characters. As Fred explains, he would never know stories like this one if he hadn't done summer stock in some out-of-the-way places in this great nation of ours. And without a friend like Fred, I wouldn't know these stories either. Friends like Fred bring such richness and balance into our lives.

Sometimes, what friends provide is support, sometimes, it's inclusion, and, sometimes, it's just plain, old-fashioned fun. Certainly one way we find ourselves having fun with friends is sharing time around the dinner table. Good food and good friends is a combination that just makes the soul smile.

My friend Fred was also a wonderful cook and these are two of my favorite recipes from him.

Fred's Famous Roast Chicken with Lemon and Rosemary

Ingredients
    1 roasting chicken, 3 to 5 pounds
    1 large lemon or two small ones
    4 sprigs of rosemary
    5 cloves of garlic
    3 Tablespoons butter at room temperature
    Kosher salt and pepper
    1 Tablespoon lemon pepper
    2 teaspoons garlic powder
    2 Tablespoons flour
    1/4 cup Madeira wine
    1/2 cup light cream

Method
- Pre-heat oven to 425 degrees.
- Remove chicken from packaging and wash inside and out, pat dry.
- Generously season the outside and inside with salt and pepper.
- Let chicken sit uncovered for 3 to 4 hours in the fridge.
- Cut up the lemons and squeeze the juice into the chicken's cavity.
- Crush the garlic with the flat of a large knife.
- Stuff the chicken with the lemons and the rosemary sprigs and the crushed garlic cloves.
- Gently lift the skin under the breast from the back of the bird with your hand and rub butter, leaving some small bits of butter slathered under the breast skin. Slather butter over the rest of the bird gently, then season with salt, lemon pepper, and garlic powder.

- *With a piece of twine, truss the chicken's legs up to close the cavity.*
- *Place the chicken on the bottom of a well-oiled roasting pan (I use my large cast iron skillet because it makes the sauce prep so easy and it roasts things so well).*
- *Place the chicken into the oven and bake for 1 hour and 5 mins.*
- *Remove from the oven and allow to rest.*
- *Remove chicken from the pan. Then, over medium high heat, deglaze the pan with 1/4 cup Madeira wine, then add 2 Tablespoons flour and whisk vigorously to avoid lumps. Whisk in cream slowly until smooth. Season to taste. It may need very little.*
- *Slice chicken and serve with the pan sauce.*

Fred's Creamed Kale and Blue Cheese Potatoes Colcannon

Ingredients
 8 or 9 good sized Yukon Gold or Golden Yellow potatoes, scrubbed and diced into pieces (about 2 1/2 pounds)
 Handful of salt
 2 leeks, cleaned, light green and white parts only
 2 cups chopped kale, packed tightly
 4 scallions, thinly sliced on the bias, 1/2 cup reserved for garnish
 1 1/2 cups buttermilk
 1/2 stick butter, cut up
 6 ounces Maytag Blue Cheese (or other mild blue)
 1 Tablespoon minced garlic
 Salt and pepper to taste

Method
- Place potatoes in a heavy-bottomed pot with salt and bring to a boil.
- Cook until potatoes are easily pierced with a fork.
- Then remove from heat and hold warm.
- Meanwhile, bring another pot of water to a boil.
- Prepare an ice bath in a large bowl.
- Add kale and leeks, and blanche quickly until the kale turns bright green, then remove from the boiling water about 4 to 5 mins and place into an ice bath in a large bowl to stop the cooking.
- Drain on paper towels and set aside.
- Place greens into a blender with the scallions and blend with 3/4 cup buttermilk and 1/4 stick of room temperature butter.
- Blend until pureed and still a little chunky (i.e. not thin—think texture).
- Open potato pot lid and add the emulsion, mashing the potatoes until mashed. Add half the butter, blue cheese, salt and pepper to taste, and the garlic.

- *Mash and stir until well combined. If not loose enough, add the buttermilk a little bit at a time until you have the consistency of whipped mashed potatoes.*

To serve
- *Place the potatoes in a large serving bowl and garnish with the remaining butter and scallions or serve a dollop on a plate and place a knob of butter on each and garnish with the scallions.*

CHAPTER THIRTY-SEVEN: A NEW ORLEANS WEDDING, BUTTERFLY KISSES, AND JAMBALAYA

You know when a friend asks you for a favor—like moving them from one apartment to another, helping them paint or do some household chore, or lending them money—it can tax the limits of friendship. At the top of the list of friend asks has got to be being asked to be involved in a friend's wedding. Well, I have a story from my friend Bryan's wedding I would love to share. It's one of those experiences you only get when you say *Yes* to being a part of the day of The Dress.

So my friend Bryan, who I knew from work in Charleston, found himself a fabulous gal named Melissa to marry, and he called me up one day to tell me the good news. She was a young lady from New Orleans, from where he now lived, and they had set their wedding date for that summer. He said that his fiancée had heard a tape of me singing, loved my voice, and wanted me to sing at the wedding. He told me that he was willing to fly me down and put me up if I would agree to do it. Of course I said, "Yes!" Who could say no to a friend who asks you to be the musical guest star at their wedding? I certainly couldn't! Melissa was thrilled, apparently, and I was honored.

As the wedding date neared, Bryan advised that, due to a mistake on their part, there wasn't a room for me at the hotel. He asked if I would be okay staying at their home. I would have the run of the place, as they were staying at the hotel with everyone else. That was fine with me. So, on the appointed date, I packed my bags, boarded the plane, and arrived at the New Orleans airport.

Since I was being a bud and staying at the house instead of the hotel with the rest of the wedding party, to sweeten the pot, Bryan had his best man pick me up at the airport. He drove me to Bryan and Melissa's house which was across the big river bridge, the Crescent City Connection, in Algiers Point. Algiers Point had the distinction of being the first place settled across the river from the French Quarter back in the 1700s.

In late 1996, Bryan had purchased a home along the river in a part of town that was being regentrified. What that meant was that the two streets back from the water were beginning to be redeveloped by urban prospectors, but it was still a very underdeveloped part of town. As we drove through the area, we passed a fascinating array of houses in styles that spanned from the 1960s all the way back to the 1800s. It was an architectural history lesson of sorts. Every few streets, the houses' changing styles showed the era the houses were built, revealing the timeline of how the city had grown away from the water. Sadly, they also were mostly run-down and showing the effects of neglect.

Finally, we arrived at Bryan's house. The look on my face must have given away my surprise at what I saw, because the best man smiled and said, "Don't worry. It looks better on the inside." What I was facing was a grand old lady of an antebellum home that was in much need of a new paint job; she was spackled with bird droppings and mildew.

"It's called camouflage in this neighborhood," Bryan explained as he greeted me at the door and brought me into the house. "We've left her exterior a little worse for wear so people don't think there are things to steal in here."

Once inside, it was obvious that Bryan and Melissa had spent a great deal of time and money lovingly restoring the old house. It was stunning and well-decorated. Melissa embraced me in the entry hall and, taking my arm, told me how excited she was to have me singing in the wedding. Bryan handed me a welcome bourbon and offered me a tour of the house.

Moving from room to room, Bryan explained my stay there. As is typical of Southern hospitality befitting a friend, they had procured everything I could need during my stay—from milk, eggs, cereal, and pastries for my breakfast to towels, soaps, and even a medicine cabinet stocked with pain relievers to ease the wedding aftermath. In short, they thought of everything!

When he took me to my bedroom, however, I froze as I walked through the door. It was a beautiful room with a king-sized, dark mahogany bed and very tasteful appointments. But the thing that caught me off guard was the huge array of Mardi Gras dolls decorating the headboard of the bed. They ran from one nightstand to the other, like an arching totem pole. Each doll was nestled in the colorful costumes of the others, their little porcelain faces looking out from beneath their curly locks. Each peered at me with a blank stare and curling Kewpie-doll lips that ended in a slight smile. They were terrifying.

Now, I don't know about you, but some people fear clowns, the dark, or the boogieman. I fear dolls—ever since I was a child and my older cousin's boyfriend subjected me to *Trilogy of Terror*, a movie in which a rogue doll comes to life and kills Karen Black. It was the scariest thing I had ever seen—a doll cackling with the war cry of a zombie queen, chasing the protagonist all over the house, and stabbing her repeatedly with a knife—and it scarred me forever. And now I was to sleep in this bedroom with those dolls. "Oh no," I thought.

The terror continued as Bryan pulled a small pistol out of the nightstand. "We've been robbed four times, twice while we were home. If anyone comes in, just shoot 'em. This is Louisiana."

I stared at him, amazed at the duality of this Southern man. It was the duality I detest about the South: charming and truly warm, but detached and callous when dealing with "the other." And yet, he was my friend. Finally, I replied, "I'm not sure what scares me more: the fact that I might be robbed or the fact that you think I should shoot somebody." I left it at that, not knowing what else to say. And I left the pistol in the nightstand in the back of the drawer.

When I returned to the house later that night alone after the wedding rehearsal, I quickly went up to my room, turned on the lights and the television, and went to bed. I was too scared to sleep in the quiet or in the dark.

When I awoke the next morning, dark storm clouds ominously sat over the city. The weather was oppressive all day. It was the 100 degrees and 99 percent humidity that New Orleans is famous for.

As I was getting ready for the wedding, Bryan called in a slight panic. When he left the day before, he had forgotten in the house next door (which he also owned and was renovating) the butterflies that were to be released as part of the wedding ceremony. He asked that I bring the boxes of butterflies and explained where I would find them. He also explained that their three large dogs were in the other house as well. He assured me the dogs were securely barricaded in the kitchen. "I hope so," I replied. Large, angry dogs scare me about as much as dolls do.

As I hung up the phone, the power went out and the sky opened up. The pouring rain was coming down in sheets; I could barely see through the windows. Despite the rain, I ran next door, getting soaked.

Once on the porch, I slowly opened the door of the house. Thick, wet, humid air and the smell of mold and sawdust greeted my nose. And that's when I heard the dogs. Their thunderous barking overwhelmed me, and their thrashing movements sounded like they were the size of horses.

I carefully made my way through the front room, heading into the dining room, where I was to retrieve the butterflies from a closet. As I rounded the corner, I caught sight of the dogs: a huge German shepherd, a Doberman, and a Rottweiler! They were snapping and frothing, and ready to kill. They were huge and almost breaking down their barricade.

Frozen with fear and unable to take my eyes off the hounds of hell, I blindly reached out to open the closet. I pulled the knob and, to my shock, the entire door came off its hinges. Not knowing what to do, and the door hanging in my hand like a big piece of plywood, I simply turned around and backed into the dark closet, pulling the door backwards into place. I stood there for a moment in the dark, praying the precarious door would provide me some safety. With my heart racing, I fumbled around, feeling the shelves until I found the boxes Bryan wanted.

Now that I had located the butterflies, all I wanted to do was to get out of that house with them without incident. Continuing to hear the crazed dogs through the closet door, I panicked and gave the door a big kick, which sent it flying. The door landed with a thud, showering the room in a cloud of sawdust and dirt, and filling the shadowy house with haze. I dashed out of the closet and through the house, screaming like a crazy person. I threw open the front door and slammed it closed behind me. I stood on the porch with the butterfly boxes in hand, covered in sweat, panting, with the rain pouring down on me. Still hearing the muffled roar of the dogs, I thought to myself: "My God, what I'll do for friends in a time of need!"

When I climbed into the car that finally came to pick me up for the wedding, I was happy and relieved. I was heading to what promised to be a joyous occasion with friends and away from all my materialized nightmares. When I arrived at the old Custom House, the wedding venue, I handed off the butterflies and found my place next to the harpist. I had met her the previous evening at the rehearsal, and we had an instant connection. She was a salty old soul—bitter, caustic, and hilarious. I knew I was going to love her when she referred to an older, middle-aged woman dressed in an outfit for someone far younger as "mutton dressed as lamb."

The big change from the previous night's wedding rehearsal was that, because of the rain, the wedding had to be held under one of the monumental arched verandas of the venue instead of in the courtyard, now a lake from the deluge. The veranda was a gorgeous space, but it was very cramped. Long plastic rain curtains were draped over the open-air doorways, protecting us from the penetrating rain as well as prohibiting air from circulating within the space.

But a wedding must go on, and so it did. As the guests were entering, I sang the list of songs the bride had requested—so many songs that the harpist snarkily exclaimed with a wink that she hoped the guests were enjoying the "Forrest Show". Finally, the processional began. The bride appeared, looking beautiful. She came down the aisle to my singing of Schubert's *Ave Maria*.

The minister started the ceremony, and as the ceremony progressed, both the harpist and I noticed that everyone in the wedding party was starting to melt from the humidity and the heat. Finally, we got to the part involving the butterflies. On cue, everyone opened their boxes, releasing the butterflies as a symbol of the love being released into the world by the joining of the couple.

As the butterflies flew, I noticed that they weren't the colorful ones I had imagined but instead big, brown, moth-like ones. Suddenly, and much to my shock, the butterflies flew upward, crashed into the stone ceiling of the veranda, and then rained back down—either dead or stunned—upon the horrified attendees. People were shrieking in horror as the large, brown, and dying butterflies fell on them and twitched on the stone floor.

The old harpist, watching this, leaned over to me and said flatly, "Well, I hope their love does better than those fucking bugs did." I lowered my head and tried not to laugh, but I couldn't stop myself. I pretended I was coughing and walked quickly off the stage.

Then Melissa did the best thing she could have done: she just started laughing, as did everyone else. She told the minister to finish up, so we could get to the party. With the ceremony finished, everyone proceeded into the hall for a giant New Orleans-style reception with bottomless bourbons, bountiful buffets brimming with jambalaya and shrimp étouffée, and jazz and Zydeco music playing late into the night. I have to hand it to Melissa—humor was the best way to handle a disaster like that, just like a lot of things in life.

Experiences like this make me smile because friends often think you are doing them a favor when they invite you to be a part of their most dramatic and important personal moments. They might never know, however, that the hours of laughing at what you had experienced are worth a hundredfold the effort you expended to help them out. Every time I think about Bryan's wedding and what I endured that weekend, I laugh right out loud, even when I am by myself! Being their special guest brought me joy that day and many years thereafter. Bryan's ultimate "friend ask" turns out to have yielded a party favor that keeps on giving!

Tampa Jambalaya Casserole

Although jambalaya is a Cajun dish that is synonymous with New Orleans, my Grandma Irene got this recipe from her days in Tampa, Florida, where Cajun and Cuban foods mix with American standards.

Ingredients
- 4 lbs chicken thighs (skin on if possible)
- 1 Tablespoon kosher salt
- 1 Tablespoon black pepper
- 1 Tablespoon olive oil
- 3 cups chopped onions
- 2 cups chopped green bell pepper
- 2 cups sliced celery
- 1 bunch of scallions, chopped
- 6 cloves of minced garlic
- 1/3 cup chopped parsley
- 3 cups of short-grained white rice
- 28 ounce can of roasted tomatoes, drained
- 2 pounds andouille sausage, cut into pieces
- 1 Tablespoon salt
- 6 to 8 cups chicken stock

Method
- Preheat oven to 350 degrees.
- Season the chicken generously with salt and black pepper.
- Heat oil in a enamel braising pot.
- Cook chicken in batches until nicely browned on both sides.
- Remove when browned and hold to the side.
- Add the onions, peppers, and celery to the chicken fat in the pot and cook over low heat until they are softened.

- *Add the garlic, scallions, and half of the parsley.*
- *Raise the heat, then add the rice and cook a little, stirring.*
- *Add the tomatoes and the sausage to the pot.*
- *Return the chicken to the pot and add the chicken stock until the liquid covers the mixture by about an inch or so.*
- *Bring to a boil, then reduce the heat.*
- *Place the entire pot in the pre-heated oven and bake for about 50 minutes or until the rice is cooked and the liquid is absorbed.*
- *Just before serving, stir in 1 pound of tail-on uncooked shrimp.*
- *Cook until shrimp turns pink, about 8 minutes.*
- *Remove from the oven. Garnish top with remaining parsley and serve.*

CHAPTER THIRTY-EIGHT: BREAKING BREAD WITH FRIENDS ENSURES THE CIRCLE REMAINS UNBROKEN; OH YEAH, AND ENCHILADAS!

Life is about relationships. It's about making connections with others and making a difference in each other's lives. Food can play a significant role in that process. In fact, you never know how food might connect people to you and you to them. Or how, over a simple meal and drinks, you might find yourself connected to someone you never knew had a connection to you, your family, or your life. When we stumble over these small-world moments the question—*Shall the circle be unbroken?*—is answered. The reply: *No, it shan't!* The passing down of faith, knowledge, and love will indeed continue from one generation to the next. Often, that happens in the most obvious and direct ways, but sometimes (when we are lucky), it transpires in the most magical, mysterious manner.

In 1996, I met a fellow in New York City named Jerry. We met at a catering job through mutual friends and hung out one evening with a bunch of other waiters. As he and I talked, it became evident we had a lot in common. We were the same age. We had both lived in Jacksonville, Florida, at the same time as children. We then discovered that we had gone to the same school in kindergarten and first grade, and although we didn't have the same teacher, we realized we had been acquainted in those early school years long ago.

This small-world moment led to another. As Jerry and I became fast friends that summer, he introduced me to a couple he knew from Jacksonville. The couple, named Tim and Peg, were spending a year in New York exploring art, theater, food, and culture. They had taken a year-long sabbatical from their lives in Florida. Tim, who was about fifty years old (about eighteen years my senior), was a psychotherapist, and Peg was a dancer and artist. We met for brunch at a Mexican restaurant. It was one of those all-you-can-drink places that are popular in New York. (Just so you know, those restaurants only let you hang out for about an hour and a half and then give you the bill, sending you on your way.)

Well, over the course of that summer and the following fall, a varying group of friends would always meet every Sunday for brunch at that place. And more times than not, Tim and Peg would join us. As you can imagine, due to our restaurant loyalty, we got to know the manager and his wife really well; they were often the ones who waited on us. Needless to say, after about two months, we were part of the restaurant family and were no longer being asked to leave after an hour and a half. Instead, we had many a-roaring good time over huevos rancheros, breakfast enchiladas, Mexican migas, and bottomless margaritas for hours on end. The conversation was always intelligent, challenging, witty, and fun. And over the year that followed, we had some great times together.

One day, it came up in the course of conversation—probably because I was reminiscing about the first time my family cooked Mexican food at home—that I had lived in Hawaii as a child when my father's job took us there for a few years. I explained how much I loved family taco night out on the lanai. That was when Old El Paso™ and other Mexican food brands became so popular. Taco shells, refried beans right out of the can, red-tinted rice, a packet of Mexican seasonings mixed with ground beef, jarred salsa, and sour cream were enough to turn our patio table into a fiesta!

After hearing my dissertation on the rise of the taco dinner, Tim commented, "You lived in Hawaii, huh? That's funny because I lived there, too. When did you live there?"

I answered, "Well, it was during the end of the Vietnam War. My father was in the Navy."

"*I* was in the Navy during that time," said Tim. "Where was your father stationed?"

"At Camp Smith, up the hill from Pearl Harbor," I replied.

"*I* was at Camp Smith," said Tim curiously. "What did your father do?"

"He was Admiral McCain's intelligence officer."

Tim's face became serious and his eyes widened. "Oh my," he said. "I thought I recognized your name from somewhere. I was the communications officer on Admiral McCain's personal plane. Your father was my commanding officer's commanding officer! I knew your father!"

We both stared at each other for a moment. It was hard to believe, but as we spoke further, it became evident that Tim had actually known my father all those years ago. In fact, he had been at my father's promotion ceremony where, as a child, I had been present.

It was a great human moment of connectivity. However, what was even more astonishing was that, about eight months after Tim and Peg had left the city, Tim called me out of the blue to tell me he was sending me something. You see, Tim had just lost his mother. Apparently, she had not left her will in an obvious place. So, to find it, Tim and his sister had to rummage through every piece of paper in her house. This, of course, was not fun due to the sad circumstances, but also because his mother had been somewhat of a pack rat. He told me that he had found something in his search that he wanted me to have, and that he would mail it to me. I gave him my deep condolences, and hung up the phone a bit curious about what I was going to receive in the mail.

When Tim's letter arrived, I opened it. Inside was a yellowed, folded typewritten page that was covered by a folded note in Tim's handwriting. Tim's note read:

Dear Forrest,

Enclosed is a letter my mother had saved in her desk. It's addressed to her from the head of my command at Christmastime during the Vietnam War in 1971. She saved it along with all my letters to her during that time. I came across it while looking for her will, and I think you should have it.

All the best,
Tim

I then opened the worn, typewritten letter and read it to myself. It was a letter to his mother, thanking her for her son's service and wishing the family a Merry Christmas. There at the end of the letter was a signature I knew all too well. It was my father's. Tears came. I couldn't believe that somehow through time and space my father somehow found a way to speak to me again. As if to say, "I'm always here and a part of your life."

I was amazed. The circle of our family was unbroken. Through time and over a very simple meal with friends, I was reconnected to my father. All the parts of my past collided in one exchange over margaritas and Mexican food.

Everyone possesses this connectivity. Your life and times create a tapestry that is connected by events, family, friends, and foods that surround your memories. Whether you are a parent, grandparent, spouse, or single, by engaging with your personal food heritage and cooking food from your past, you share with others a part of yourself and your experiences with people whose memory you hold dear.

While writing this book, I shared parts of it with people in my life, and I was amazed at the responses. Their primary response was that they learned so much more about me and who I really am because of the stories I shared about these foods and the individuals who made them for me and my family. These readers have a deeper understanding of me and my history. They feel more strongly connected to me.

In our overly commercialized food culture, where every celebrity is writing a cookbook or popping up on food channels with a show about themselves, we are, perhaps, conditioned to overlook our own stories and our own heritage. However, more than ever, we should be sharing our stories. We don't need to write a book or star in a television show to do that. We can do this quietly and simply in our own homes with family and friends through cooking and keeping recipes alive that are held in our memories.

James's Midwest-Style Chicken Enchiladas

My friend James's mother gave me this recipe. I loved it when I was younger and had not yet explored real Mexican cooking. It's an all-American version of the Mexican classic. I know it looks a bit plain, but that's actually its charm. It is homey and rich and delicious. Serve it with lots of sour cream, fresh salsa, and refried beans or rice casserole, and you'll have an amazing meal.

Ingredients

1 1/2 large white onions, finely chopped
2 cups packed baby spinach leaves
8 ounce package cream cheese
2 small cans green chilies (mild or hot)
1 rotisserie chicken, taken off the bone and chopped
1 large 16 ounce can green enchilada sauce
14 flour tortillas
1/2 pound Monterey Jack cheese, grated
1/2 pound yellow cheddar cheese, grated
1/2 pint whipping cream
2 teaspoons garlic powder
2 teaspoons cumin
1/4 teaspoon salt
1 small can California black olives, sliced
4-5 scallions, chopped
Chopped cilantro or parsley

Method

- Sauté onion in butter.
- When onions are transparent, throw in spinach and let wilt. Add cream cheese, salt, garlic powder, and cumin. Add in the chilies.
- Stir in chicken and let cool down slightly.

- *Pour enchilada sauce into flat bowl or pie plate.*
- *Dip each tortilla into the enchilada sauce.*
- *Spoon mix into each tortilla and add a little Jack cheese.*
- *Roll and place seam side down into a greased casserole dish.*
- *Cover rolled enchiladas with remaining cheeses.*
- *Mix remaining enchilada sauce with whipping cream and pour over enchiladas, then top with olives and cover with aluminum foil.*
- *Bake at 350 degrees for 30 minutes.*
- *Garnish with chopped scallions and cilantro before serving. Serve with fresh salsa and sour cream.*

John Wayne's Mexican Chile and Cheesy Rice

This is a great side dish for any Mexican meal. Supposedly, it's rumored to have come from an article by John Wayne's wife.

Ingredients
- 2 cups white rice, cooked as directed on package
- 1 1/2 pints sour cream
- 1 8 ounce can of chopped green mild chilies
- 2 cups grated Jack cheese
- 1 Tablespoon cumin
- 1 Tablespoon garlic powder
- 2 Tablespoons chopped scallions

Method
- Mix all ingredients well. Place in casserole and bake in a 300 degree oven for about 20 minutes until warmed and melted. Garnish with scallions.

Velvet Patsy's Amazing Homemade Salsa

My friend Shawn (the proprietor of Velvet Catering in Burlington, Vermont) makes the most delicious salsa. This is his recipe. He named it after a character he created for the theater.

Ingredients
    1 28 ounce can whole tomatoes
    1/2 large red onion, coarsely chopped
    4 cloves garlic
    1/2 teaspoon salt
    1/4 teaspoon sugar
    1/2 teaspoon cumin
    Cilantro to taste (at least 1/4 cup)
    1 inch of a whole jalapeñ, diced
    Juice of one lime (add more if acid is needed)

Method
- *Drain the tomatoes and throw into food processor whole.*
- *Add everything else and pulse slowly until you reach the consistency you want.*
- *Taste and adjust seasoning and acid.*

CHAPTER THIRTY NINE: A SAVORY ENDING

Many people might describe me as a foodie.

I am not a foodie at all. I am a lover of food.

I love what food can do.

I love its power and ability to heal, uplift, comfort, and entertain—that power astounds me.

I love that emotion flows through a meal prepared for others.

I love that it can be edible art on the one hand, and fuel for life on the other. And not just the physical life, but the life force that connects, uplifts, and inspires. It fuels our bodies and our souls.

I believe food is a great conduit for connecting people, for teaching people about living and loving. People come alive around food, and memory is stirred by it. We can touch others profoundly through experiences surrounding its preparation and communal consumption.

When I was young and questioning everything, my father gave me a book. It wasn't the bible; it was a volume of the abridged writings of Ralph Waldo Emerson. From this book, I latched onto one of Emerson's most famous sayings: "The purpose of life is not to be happy. It is to be useful, to be honorable, to be compassionate, to have it make some difference that you have lived and lived well."

With that mindset, when we prepare comfort foods (or the recipes we love from our past), we honor not only ourselves, but also the people and times whose memories are connected to those recipes. We are keeping the recipes and the memories alive. And by sharing the dishes with others, we are making ourselves useful; we create community, an extended family, and happiness, all which help sustain and nourish both body and soul. That's why I love food. I love that it allows me to offer support, create pleasure, and foster contentment out of the simplest of ingredients.

My own understanding of this became painfully obvious in 2016. That May, I received a call from my sister-in-law Jennifer (who never calls me) in the middle of the workday. I knew before I picked up the phone that something was wrong, and it was, in fact, one of those calls you never want to receive. My stomach dropped and my heart broke when Jennifer told me through the phone that my brother Christopher had suffered a brain aneurysm and was in surgery fighting for his life. Within hours, I was on a plane to California and found myself sitting in an ICU unit waiting to hear if the operation had saved not only my brother's life, but also his brain's ability to function.

For three days, I sat with Jennifer, waiting for the MRI results to come back. Jennifer and I had never been alone together for such a long period. It's puzzling how someone who is part of your family can actually be somewhat of a stranger, but, given the distances our modern society puts on relationships, I suppose I shouldn't have been surprised by our unfamiliarity. So often today families are scattered all over the country, pursuing educations, careers, or lifestyle choices. And often, the time we get to see one another is limited to vacations, holidays, and special occasions.

But there Jennifer and I were, two people connected to my brother, one by blood and one by twenty-five years of loving commitment. We passed the time talking for hours in the hospital room. Over simple cafeteria meals, we exchanged our hopes, fears, and memories. We supported one another as best we could in the new reality we had been forced into.

Finally, word came that my brother was not brain dead, and he was expected to come out of his coma at some point. With this news, I returned to New York, and, weeks later, got word Christopher had woken up. I flew out to see him then and several times thereafter, and over the next weeks and months, he recovered enough to return home where he would continue to convalesce.

The stroke that occurred with the aneurysm had taken some of my brother's short-term memory, some of his vision, and most of his mobility. But the biggest loss was his ability to swallow. Who knew that this bodily function was a learned behavior and not a reflex? With therapy, we hoped this function would return to normal. Yes, he struggled with strength training and learning to move and use his limbs again, but his ability to swallow continued to be the main therapy focus.

When my brother arrived home, I visited him whenever I could—not just to support him, but also to give my sister-in-law a little break from the immense pressure of taking care of him. During my first visit, my presence seemed nothing more than a meager effort. Never in my life had I felt so completely incapable of affecting improvement in a situation. I was the outsider. Coming into a cocoon of tender care and intense togetherness, I witnessed my brother and his wife working out his recovery and their lives together.

On my fourth visit, however, my brother asked me to do something I found amazing and powerful. Before the accident, my brother had been the primary cook in the home. Now, unable to take care of himself or do anything to show his wife how much he loved her for what she was doing for him, he asked me to cook her a meal. It was not just any meal, but a dish he had made for them almost weekly during the fall football season. It was also a dish tied to our family's past.

You might remember me talking earlier about Louise Wilson, the young Italian woman married to my father's junior officer in Hawaii; she was the one who had introduced our family to new dimensions in Rhode Island-style Italian cookery. Well, for my brother's wedding, my mother made the young couple a cookbook that included all of her and Louise's favorite recipes and best entertaining tips. Of course, it contained recipes for fantastic pasta dishes and other Italian delights. But Louise also included a recipe for maybe the best chili my brother has ever had (I love this chili as well!). In fact, it's the very recipe Christopher would turn to weekly every football season when, on Sundays, he would make chili for Jennifer. And it is that recipe my brother told me to follow when he asked me to surprise Jennifer with a homemade dinner one evening when she had gone out for the afternoon. And that is what I did.

My brother looked on as I began prepping the meal. I sliced the onion and browned the beef, and I stirred in the tomatoes, the beer, and the can of refried beans (that's the secret ingredient). He directed me through it all. He told me how small he wanted the onions diced and to what degree of caramelization he wanted on the onions. He commented several times how delicious everything smelled. And, oh, how he wished he could be tasting the chili as well as smelling it. My heart broke realizing this gift he was giving his wife was being given truly selflessly, and it was being given through me. Suddenly, I realized that I was being useful, like Emerson championed. I was bringing compassion into the situation where I otherwise felt ineffectual. And, amazingly, I was able to do it through food.

When my sister-in-law came home, she was greeted by the smell and aroma of that all-too-familiar chili. And when we sat to eat dinner, she polished off two full bowls in no time, which my brother pointed out was unusual. He admitted that she never ate that much when he made it! Upon hearing that, Jennifer grinned. Her smile translated the cherished memory of past dinners with her husband, and it was a nod to better times and my brother's kitchen prowess. Dinner that night was indeed a good meal.

I have come to realize that my brother is probably the bravest person I know. To us, those who are living a normal life, trying to imagine what he is living through is impossible. I don't think he thinks of himself as brave. He's just trying to make it back to a place he's been before. Regardless, I think I know few people as brave as my brother or, for that matter, my sister-in-law. And showing love through food was one thing my brother could do to show his wife some comfort and a tiny amount of appreciation. Him asking me to make chili for Jennifer was brave and loving. And for me, being part of that moment was an honor.

You see, food really is love, and food is life.

Personal food heritage is your life's story. It is your story to share about the people who are a part of your history. The people who came before us and are dear to us ask only to be remembered. But that's not all. They also want us to be happy in the here and now and to keep on making new memories.

It is important to keep your personal food heritage alive; explore it and the people and memories around it. Then share it. Sharing adds positive energy into this ever-so-hungry world—a world hungry for food, love, and understanding.

I wish you joy in finding and sharing your story, keeping your recipes alive, and in living well.

Louise Wilson's Chili Recipe

No military wife worth her salt would be without a timesaving, budget-friendly recipe like a good chili. My brother swears by this chili recipe. And I agree with him. It is simple but good, and has a surprising ingredient—a can of refried beans.

Ingredients
    1 large white onion, chopped
    2 cloves garlic, minced
    1 pound beef, browned and drained
    1 can red kidney beans, drained and rinsed off
    2 cans diced tomatoes
    1 can of refried beans with lard
    1 jalapeño pepper, seeded and finely diced (optional)
    1 can lager beer
    2 teaspoons cumin
    1 package commercial chili seasoning
    Salt and pepper to taste
    2 teaspoons cornstarch mixed with about 1/4 cup of water
    Frank's RedHot® sauce for serving

Topping Options
    Shredded cheddar cheese
    Sliced California black olives
    Chopped red onion
    Chopped scallions
    Chopped cilantro
    Sour cream
    Frito's® Corn Chips
    Pickled jalapeños

Method

- *Brown the meat with onions and garlic, drain. Place all ingredients except cornstarch and water in a Dutch oven. Stir and cook on medium low to low heat for 1 to 3 hours. Before serving, stir in cornstarch mixture until well blended. Let mixture thicken, then serve.*

INDEX OF RECIPES

1970s' Ground Beef Casserole with Biscuits	93
1970s'-Style Shish Kebabs	70
A Charleston-Style Artichoke Dip	57
A Damn Good Pimento Cheese Recipe	177
A Tasty Southern Coleslaw	155
All American Deviled Eggs	55
Aunt Leoah's Asparagus Appetizers	48
Back-to-School Clam Chowder	33
Baked Brown Sugar Bacon Crackers	58
Best Newspaper Recipe Ever: Italian Chicken in Patty Shells	198
Best-Ever Greek Salad Dressing (Ingredients must be exact)	147
Big's Baked Creamed Corn (Almost)	157
Big's Depression Cornbread (comes out thin and crisp)	47
Big's Summer Squash Casserole	120
Big's Tomato Pie	116
Blender Hollandaise Sauce	258
Blender Mustard Béarnaise for Poached Eggs	313
Caesar Dressing with Fresh Herbs	305
California-Patio Mexican Salad with Creamy Avocado Dressing	19
Chatham Artillery Punch	63
Chinese Noodles with Pork and Peanut-Sesame Sauce	238
Cioppino: A San Francisco-Style Seafood Stew	303
Classic Roasted Asparagus	258
Company Strata	59
Cousin Martha's Tomato Salad	119
Cream Gravy with Sherry, Sausage, and Thyme	281
Creamed Oysters, a Low Country tradition	318
Cristin's Tomato Risotto	328

Daddy's Famous Hedden House Burgers	68
Daddy's Northern California-Style Scallops	39
Danish Layer Cake	141
Divine Chicken Divan	235
East-Coast Style Stuffed Flounder	267
Easy Huli-huli Chicken	233
Excuse me, but do you have Dijon Chicken	95
Family Meatloaf	24
Faux Lady Baltimore Cake (A Traditional Charleston Wedding Cake)	205
Fred's Creamed Kale and Blue Cheese Potatoes Colcannon	350
Fred's Famous Roast Chicken with Lemon and Rosemary	348
Fried Chicken and Cream Gravy	167
Grandma Irene's Curried-Chicken Main Course Salad	248
Grown-Up Bourbon Milkshakes	106
Hedden House Dressing	87
Homage to King Street Pharmacy: Colby Grilled Cheese Sandwiches with Dill Pickles and Milkshakes	80
Homemade 1970s' Beef Bourguignon Stew	214
Irene's Baked Cauliflower in Mustard and Horseradish Sauce	131
Irene's Beef Liver with Bacon and Onions in Brown Sauce	139
Irene's Beet Salad	136
Irene's Buttered Herbed Rice and Peas	135
Irene's Mashed Potatoes	170
Italian Meatballs in Tomato Sauce	336
James's Midwest-Style Chicken Enchiladas	368
Japanese Fruitcake	270
John Shells' Beef Tartare	61
John Wayne's Mexican Chile and Cheesy Rice	370
John's Clam Dip	338
Lammekjøtt, "Lamb sticks" in Norwegian, is a recipe for lamb shanks with a sour cream dill sauce	133

Lemon Butter Sauce	269
Louise Wilson's Chili Recipe	379
Louise Wilson's Magic Cake	96
Louise Wilson's Spaghetti Sauce (Italian Sunday Gravy)	89
Mama's Antipasto Salad	88
Mama's Shrimp Mousse	56
Mamie Eisenhower's Quiche	250
Martha's Baking Powder Biscuits with Ham	191
Maytag Blue Cheese Dressing	34
Mexican Cheddar-Jalapeño Crack Cornbread	49
Morrison's Cafeteria-Inspired Fried Shrimp	223
Morrison's-Style Macaroni and Cheese	227
My Heritage Thanksgiving Stuffing	9
Norwegian Meatballs: A Gabrielson Family Recipe	129
Norwegian Stuffed Cabbage Rolls with a Spicy Mustard Sauce	137
Oscar Benedict from Marianne's of Charleston	312
Oven-Baked Festive Fish Filets	91
Oven-Smoked Pork Butt BBQ	153
Pepper Jelly: A Spicy Southern Condiment	182
"Pineapple Pimento Mess" or Scalloped Pineapple Casserole	178
Restaurant-Style Double-Stuffed Jacket Potatoes	259
Roasted Steakhouse-Style Tomatoes	257
Saffron and Curry Rice Pilaf with Currants	72
Sauerkraut Tartar Sauce	92
Savannah Style-Crab Stew	295
Scalloped Tomato Casserole	118
Scarlet O'Hara Coffee Cantata Milkshakes	82
Seafood Stuffing	268
Southern Biscuits and Gravy	279
Spicy Tarragon and Dijon Shrimp with Bacon-Boursin Grits	288
Steak Hawaiian	256

"Sufferin Succotash Salad"	159
Super Meatball Sauce	337
Tampa Jambalaya Casserole	360
Tampa-Style Greek Salad à la Forrest	146
The Barnes Bourbon Brown Sugar Mustard Glazed Ham	107
The Best Hot Turkey Sandwich Ever!	31
Uncle Frank's Potato Salad	186
Veal Scaloppini and Musical Sauce	73
Velvet Patsy's Amazing Homemade Salsa	371
Walhalla Blueberry Peach Cobbler with Granola-Nut Crust	189
Walhalla Chess Cake	121

www.ingramcontent.com/pod-product-compliance
Lightning Source LLC
Chambersburg PA
CBHW081103080526
44587CB00021B/3431